Race Women Internationalists

Race Women Internationalists

Activist-Intellectuals and Global Freedom Struggles

Imaobong D. Umoren

UNIVERSITY OF CALIFORNIA PRESS

University of California Press, one of the most distinguished university presses in the United States, enriches lives around the world by advancing scholarship in the humanities, social sciences, and natural sciences. Its activities are supported by the UC Press Foundation and by philanthropic contributions from individuals and institutions. For more information, visit www.ucpress.edu.

University of California Press
Oakland, California

© 2018 by Imaobong Umoren

Library of Congress Cataloging-in-Publication Data

Names: Umoren, Imaobong Denis, 1990- author.
Title: Race women internationalists : activist-intellectuals and global freedom struggles / Imaobong D. Umoren.
Description: Oakland, California : University of California Press, [2018] | Includes bibliographical references and index. |
Identifiers: LCCN 2017055359 (print) | LCCN 2017058981 (ebook) | ISBN 9780520968431 (Ebook) | ISBN 9780520295803 (cloth : alk. paper) | ISBN 9780520295810 (pbk. : alk. paper)
Subjects: LCSH: African American women political activists—History—20th century. | Robeson, Eslanda Goode, 1896–1965. | Nardal, Paulette, 1896–1985. | Marson, Una 1905–1965. | Women political activists—United States—History—20th century. | Women political activists—Jamaica—History—20th century.
Classification: LCC HQ1236 (ebook) | LCC HQ1236 .U485 2017 (print) | DDC 920.72/08996073—dc23
LC record available at https://lccn.loc.gov/2017055359

Manufactured in the United States of America

27 26 25 24 23 22 21 20 19 18
10 9 8 7 6 5 4 3 2 1

To my parents
Denis Mbong Umoren (1949–2011) and
Eme Umoren (1958–2017)

CONTENTS

List of Illustrations ix
Acknowledgments xi
List of Abbreviations xiii
Preface xv

    Introduction   1

1. Black and Feminist Internationalism in Interwar Europe, 1920–1935   11

2. The Italian Invasion of Ethiopia, the Spanish Civil War, and Anti-fascist Internationalism, 1935–1939   37

3. Internationalisms during and after World War II, 1939–1949   67

4. Continuities and Changes, 1950–1966   92

    Conclusion   119

Notes 123
Bibliography 163
Index 183

ILLUSTRATIONS

Una Marson, *Tropic Reveries*. 59
Una Marson at the BBC. 60
Una Marson at the BBC, London, World War II. 60
Eslanda Robeson, London, 1920s. 61
Eslanda Robeson at the United Nations. 62
La Femme dans la cité, front cover. 63
"Paulette Nardal nous a quittés." 64
"Paulette Nardal est morte." 65
Place Paulette Nardal, Fort-de-France, Martinique. 66

ACKNOWLEDGMENTS

Throughout the process of researching and writing this book, I have been immensely grateful to a range of funding bodies for supporting my work. These include the Arts and Humanities Research Council; the Royal Historical Society; the UK/US Fulbright Commission; the Kluge Center at the Library of Congress; the British Association for American Studies; the Society for the Study of French History; the Beit Fund; St. Hugh's College; St. Cross College; Pembroke College at the University of Oxford; and the British Academy.

I appreciate the assistance of archivists and librarians in various locations for allowing me access and permission to reproduce source material. In particular, I would like to thank the National Library of Jamaica; the Moorland-Spingarn Research Center at Howard University; the BBC Written Archives; the Archives départementales de la Martinique; the Beinecke Rare Books and Manuscript Library at Yale University; the Bibliothèque nationale de France; the Centre des archives d'outre-mer; the United Nations Archives at Geneva; the Archives de la préfecture de police (APP), Paris; the National Archives at Kew; the Women's Library at the London School of Economics; the Bodleian Library, and the British Library.

Over many years, colleagues and friends have given much needed advice at crucial times. From the beginning of my project, while a student at King's College London, many of the ideas in this book were conceived of with the help of Richard Drayton, who has remained an important source of support. When I moved to Oxford, I was fortunate enough to work with Stephen Tuck and Mara Keire, who were excellent advisors. In 2013, Stephen Tuck, Elleke Boehmer, Justine McConnell, and Tamara Mollenberg and I cofounded the Race and Resistance program based at The Oxford Research Centre in the Humanities (TORCH). This program aided my work and career in more ways than I could have imagined. Audiences at Race and Resistance events offered constructive criticism and forced me to rethink my project. In particular, I would like to thank the cofounders as well as Tessa Roynon, Lloyd Pratt, and Michèle Mendelssohn.

The Women in the Humanities program at TORCH has been another pivotal source of support. I am grateful especially to the extremely generous donor who funded my Career Development Fellowship and Senia Paseta. The creation of TORCH has been instrumental in developing early career scholars' work and supporting the growth of interdisciplinary research. I would like to thank its business director, Victoria McGuinness, for her constant kindness and generosity. It has been a pleasure to work with her and the TORCH administrative team, including Hannah Penny, Sarah Bebb, Laura Miller, and Rabyah Khan.

Others I would like to thank include colleagues at Pembroke College and Master Dame Lynne Brindley, Kathryn Gleadle, Ruth Percy, Robert Gildea, Daniel Grey, Gareth Davies, Jane Garnett, Christina de Bellaigue, Anna Snaith, Mary Lou Reker, Sonia Song-Ha Lee, and Evelyn Brooks Higginbotham. Within the Society for the History of Women the Americas, I express gratitude to Jay Kleinberg, Rae Ritchie, Dawn-Marie Gibson, and Sinead McEneaney. I also wish to thank those who read and critiqued the manuscript at various stages: Patricia Clavin, Clare Corbould, Barbara Savage, Farah Jasmine-Griffin, Dawn-Marie Gibson, Kate Dossett, Gareth Davies, Tessa Roynon, and Stephen Tuck. My editors at the University of California Press, Bradley Depew and Niels Hooper, have been incredibly helpful. I would also like to thank the biographers of the three protagonists in this book whose foundational and important work inspired my interest, including Delia Jarrett-Macauley, T. Denean Sharpley-Whiting, Emily Musil-Church, and Barbara Ransby.

As always, I am most indebted to those closest to me, in particular Idongesit Umoren-Pitt and Angela Brown, for their encouragement and support. This book is dedicated to my father and mother. Their love and abiding presence has been a constant comfort without which this work would not have been completed.

. . .

Portions of chapters 1 and 2 were previously published as "This Is the Age of Woman: Black Feminism and Black Internationalism in the Works of Una Marson, 1928–1938," *History of Women in the Americas* 1, no. 1 (2013): pp. 50–72.

Portions of chapters 2 and 3 were previously published as "Anti-Fascism and the Development of Global Race Women 1928–1945," *Callaloo: A Journal of African Diaspora Arts and Letters* 39, no. 1 (Winter 2016): pp. 151–65.

Portions of chapter 4 will be published as "'We Americans Are Not Just American Citizens Anymore—We Are Also World Citizens': Eslanda Robeson, *New World Review*, and World Citizenship in the 1950s" in the *Journal of Women's History* (Winter 2018).

ABBREVIATIONS

AAWFM   All African Women's Freedom Movement
AFWIF   American Friends of the West Indies Federation
ALP   American Labor Party
ANC   African National Congress
ANP   Associated Negro Press
APP   Archives de la Préfecture de police, Paris
BBC   British Broadcasting Corporation
BCL   British Commonwealth League
CAA   Council on African Affairs
CAE   Comité d'Action Ethiopien
CAFRA   Caribbean Association for Feminist Research and Action
CAI   Centre des affaires indigènes
CAO   Committee of African Organisations
CARD   Campaign Against Racial Discrimination
CAW   Congress of American Women
CDIRN   Comité de défense des intérêts de la race noire
CDRN   Comité de défense de la race nègre
CPGB   Communist Party of Great Britain
CPUSA   Communist Party USA
IAFE   International African Friends of Ethiopia
IASB   International African Service Bureau
ICAA   International Committee on African Affairs
Jamsave Jamaican Save the Children
JLP   Jamaica Labour Party

LCP	League of Coloured Peoples
LDRN	Ligue de défense de la race nègre
LoN	League of Nations
LNU	League of Nations Union
LSE	London School of Economics
LUDRN	Ligue universelle pour la défense de la race noir
MCF	Movement for Colonial Freedom
NAACP	National Association for the Advancement of Colored People
NACW	National Association of Colored Women
PNP	People's National Party (Jamaica)
SLOTFOM	Service de liaison avec les originaires des territoires français d'outre-mer
STJ	Sojourners for Truth and Justice
TWWA	Third World Women's Alliance
UCL	University College London
UN	United Nations
UNIA	Universal Negro Improvement Association
UTN	Union des travailleurs négres
WASU	West African Students' Union
WIDF	Women's International Democratic Federation
WIF	West Indies Federation
WSSC	Women's Social Service Club (Jamaica)
YMCA	Young Men's Christian Association
YWCA	Young Women's Christian Association

PREFACE

Eslanda Robeson, Paulette Nardal, and Una Marson are the three protagonists of this book. Known by friends and family as Essie, Eslanda Goode Robeson (1895–1965) was an outspoken anthropologist and writer, and the wife of the artist-activist Paul Robeson. Born a year after Robeson was the Martiniquan journalist Paulette Nardal (1896–1985). Hailing from the island south of Cuba and east of Asia was the Jamaican poet, playwright, journalist, and broadcaster Una Marson (1905–1965). From the 1930s, all knew of each other, and Nardal and Robeson met, though they were not all in direct contact with each other throughout their lives.

None of these women were obscure figures in their day, but their careers and achievements were overshadowed by men. Marson, for instance, is known primarily in interwar London as assistant secretary of the League of Coloured Peoples (LCP), the Pan-African group established and led by Jamaican Harold Moody. In studies on 1920s and 1930s black activism in London focus has often centered on prolific male writers and activists like the close compatriots Trinidadians C. L. R. James and George Padmore.[1] Marson was well aware of male intellectual dominance and sexism, observing that "men in the past have never been overly partial to intellectual women."[2] Nardal's influential involvement in the Negritude movement was overshadowed by male leaders, namely Martiniquan Aimé Césaire, Senegalese Léopold Sédar Senghor, and French Guianan Léon-Gontran Damas. Reflecting back in 1963, Nardal remarked that they "took up the ideas tossed out by us and expressed them with more flash and brio. . . . We were but women, real pioneers—let's say that we blazed the trail for them."[3] For years, within academic scholarship, Paul Robeson cast a towering shadow over his wife.

Yet Una Marson, Paulette Nardal, and Eslanda Robeson formed part of an informal international network of travelling black women activist-intellectuals. Between the early and mid twentieth century, they traversed the world, built networks in feminist, student, black-led, anti-colonial, and anti-fascist organizations and made crucial alliances with key leaders. This enabled them to participate in global freedom struggles against multiple forms of oppression. Moreover, it enabled them to become what I have termed "race women internationalists."

Building on previous biographical studies of these women, this book is the first to unite them.[4] Placing the three figures alongside each other contributes to growing scholarship on black women's internationalism, black women's intellectual history, and more broadly, African diaspora studies. Adopting a comparative framework, the following pages illuminate Robeson, Nardal, and Marson's practices as race women internationalists.

Introduction

"Only the BLACK WOMAN can say 'when and where I enter, in the quiet, undisputed dignity of my womanhood, without violence and without suing or special patronage, then and there the whole *Negro race enters with me.*'"[1] With these forceful words, Anna Julia Cooper started a revolution. Born in Raleigh, North Carolina, the daughter of an enslaved black woman and her white master, Cooper rose to become an educator, orator, and author. Her prominent proclamation appeared in *A Voice from the South* (1892), a collection of essays and speeches that is recognized as one of the earliest expressions of a "race woman." Emerging after the Reconstruction period and coinciding with the Woman's Era, *race woman* was the term used to describe public women of African descent who aimed to "uplift the race."[2] Race women saw it as their duty to play a leading role in solving both the "race problem" and the "woman question." While the term could be pejorative, it also denoted a sense of high status and most race women claimed its positive overtones.[3] In her time and ours, Cooper was and is hailed as a leading race woman who understood the entangled relationship between race, gender, and class. As such, *A Voice from the South* is recognized as *the* black feminist bible.

But what is sometimes overlooked in Cooper's most quoted phrase is her audience. She spoke not only to black Americans but to the "whole *Negro race*" scattered in every corner of the globe.[4] She was speaking from experience. Through *A Voice from the South* and her involvement with the National Association of Colored Women (NACW) and Pan-African congresses, she challenged multiple forms of oppression across the Americas, Africa, Asia, and Europe by debating publicly and travelling frequently. Cooper was one of many such activist-intellectuals. Her contemporaries included clubwomen Ida B. Wells-Barnett, Mary Church Terrell, and

Mary McLeod Bethune; Pan-African black nationalists such as the Jamaicans Amy Ashwood Garvey and Amy Jacques Garvey and Panamanian-born but US-raised Maida Springer; leftists and communists Shirley Graham Du Bois, Thyra Edwards, Louise Thompson Patterson, and Trinidadian Claudia Jones; and African-born activists like Adelaide Casely Hayford, Constance Cummings-John, and Funmilayo Ransome-Kuti, to name just a few.[5]

When we listen carefully to Cooper, then, we hear not only the voice of an American race woman; we hear the voice of what I term a "race woman internationalist." Sharing a Pan-African sensibility, race women internationalists including Cooper and some of her contemporaries listed above were public figures who helped to solve racial, gendered, and other forms of inequality facing black people across the African diaspora. While the term is not uniform or static, many race women internationalists regularly travelled and were part of black diasporic networks and organizations in the United States, Africa, Europe, and the Caribbean that emerged in the wake of large-scale black migration from the late nineteenth century. The technological revolution in transportation following the opening of the Suez and Panama Canals in 1869 and 1914 facilitated the rise of travel and migration as shipping companies made voyages more accessible with new routes emerging and the cost of travel decreasing for the working and middle classes.[6]

Race women internationalists were part of the wider movements of Africans, Afro-Caribbeans from the British, French, and Spanish West Indies around the "circum-Caribbean migratory sphere," and African Americans during the Great Migration.[7] Their sojourns enabled them to create and participate in the transnational black public sphere and civil society, a figurative and physical global community beyond the imperial or nation state that engendered the growth of international organizations, associations, institutions, charities, and print culture.[8]

Race women internationalists self-identified as members of the "darker races of the world" and voiced what historian Nico Slate has called "colored cosmopolitanism."[9] According to Slate, the term describes men and women of color who forged "a united front against racism, imperialism, and other forms of oppression" and who "fought for the freedom of the 'colored world' even while calling into question the meaning of both color and freedom."[10] Becoming visible from the late nineteenth century, race women internationalists were part of New Negro womanhood, which scholar Treva B. Lindsey defines as "a mosaic, authorial, and constitutive individual and collective identity inhabited by African American women seeking to transform themselves and their communities through demanding autonomy and equality."[11] Yet New Negro womanhood was not confined just to black American women; it also included Afro-Caribbean and African women.

While none used the term *race women internationalist* to describe themselves, many black women activist-intellectuals practiced black, black feminist, Christian, liberal, conservative, radical, socialist, communist, and imperial internationalisms by establishing or contributing to internationalist organizations or newspapers; writing prose, poetry, short stories, plays, or songs; and forging friendships with white, black, and other people of color, who served as their allies. Race women internationalists came from different parts of the global and overlapping African diaspora, articulated varied political views, and practiced deeply connected internationalisms that enabled them to play key roles in what historian Michelle Mitchell has labelled "the politics of racial destiny," a concept based on the "wide-ranging yet singular notion that black people shared a common fate . . . [and that] enabled activists to propose a number of strategies—political, social, cultural, moral, physical, religious—to ensure the collective's basic human rights, progress, prosperity, health, and reproduction."[12]

Although the majority were middle class, working-class women, many of whom did not have access to domestic or international travel, could also practice race women's internationalism. They could do this in quotidian ways such as reading and writing responses to newspaper articles in the transnational black press. Alternatively, they could be involved in global black organizations, such as the Universal Negro Improvement Association (UNIA) cofounded by Jamaicans Amy Ashwood Garvey and Marcus Garvey. Race women's internationalism could further be practiced by working-class women through dancing to or creating the latest fusions of African American, African, and Afro-Caribbean music.[13]

Following in Cooper's footsteps and sometimes travelling and collaborating alongside the aforementioned women, this book centers attention on three individuals from the Anglophone and Francophone African diaspora—Eslanda Robeson, Paulette Nardal, and Una Marson—and forwards two arguments. First, the travels of Robeson, Nardal, and Marson usually, but certainly not always, enabled them to create and participate in the transnational black public sphere through their involvement in manifold political, cultural, and social networks. Second, their travels facilitated their practices as race women internationalists as they engaged with interconnected internationalisms—namely, black, feminist, Christian, anti-fascist, conservative, radical, and liberal—through their sojourns, writings, direct activism, and friendships, which enabled them to play a part in global freedom struggles against racism, sexism, fascism, and colonialism.

Raised in a middle-class family in 1895 in Washington, DC, Eslanda Robeson had mixed black and Spanish ancestry. The Goode family, including Eslanda, her mother (also called Eslanda), and her two older brothers, moved to Harlem after the death of Eslanda's alcoholic father in 1901. Neither a "slum or a fringe," wrote activist and writer James Weldon Johnson, Harlem is "located in the heart of Manhattan and occupies one of the most beautiful and healthful sections of the city."[14] Harlem's ideal geography and affordable brownstones attracted African Americans and Afro-Caribbeans. Black migration meant that the "city within a city" contained "more Negroes to the square mile than any other spot on earth."[15] Harlem was filled not just with blacks; it also enticed whites eager to slum as well as Chinese, Latinos, and Italian Americans.[16] Although racial mixing certainly took place, it existed alongside racial and ethnic antagonism. In the late 1910s, Robeson transferred from the University of Illinois to Columbia University to study chemistry. It was in Harlem where she first met the aspiring lawyer Paul Robeson.[17] Their relationship developed when they attended Columbia University's summer school in 1920, and they wed the following year.[18] As Paul Robeson's career as an actor and singer took off, Eslanda Robeson became his manager, securing him larger roles that propelled his fame.

Born in the Martiniquan town of Le François, Paulette Nardal was the eldest of seven sisters from an elite Catholic family. The Nardals were French subject-citizens who "elected their own deputies to the national assembly, lived under the National *code civil,* enjoyed the protection of French metropolitan laws, and largely ran their own municipal governments," but they also "lived in a racially organized colonial society with restrictive labor regulations and diminished social legislation under the authoritarian-administrative rule of non-elected French governors."[19] Paulette Nardal's father, Paul Nardal, was one of the first black Martiniquan men to receive a scholarship to study in France.[20] Later, he became one of the few black men to hold an engineering post at the Department of Public Works.[21] But his dark pigmentation stopped him from securing a senior position.[22] The color and racial prejudice that Paul Nardal faced proved that despite the lauded Republican rhetoric of *les droits de l'homme,* racism ruled the French empire. Paulette Nardal's mother, Louise Achille, worked as a schoolteacher and was a gifted musician.[23]

Nardal attended the prestigious Colonial College for Girls in Fort-de-France. Here she learned about the glories of the French Republic and its *mission de civilisatrice* in a capital city that attracted workers, traders, and tourists from Europe, the United States, and the French-speaking world, which made her curious about other parts of the Caribbean. In the late 1910s, after she had completed her secondary school education, she seized the opportunity to expand her horizons and learn English by moving to the capital of Jamaica. Nardal's time in Kingston enabled her to improve on her English-language skills and instilled a passion for English literature. After returning from Jamaica, she applied for and won a competitive scholarship to study for an advanced English literature degree known as the diplôme d'études supérieures at the Sorbonne and journeyed to Paris.

The youngest child of a middle-class Baptist pastor and mixed-raced mother, Una Marson grew up in the parish of St. Elizabeth in Jamaica. She attended Hampton High School modelled on British public schools, where she was one of a few dark-skinned girls.[24] Her complexion and scholarship status meant that she faced the prejudices of some of her white teachers and fellow peers. After leaving Hampton with a modest lower Cambridge certificate, Marson ventured to the capital in the early 1920s, following the death of her father and the family's relocation, which was undergoing rapid modernization.[25] A burgeoning civic culture existed in Kingston and within a few months of her arrival in the city, Marson immersed herself in it. She served as a volunteer in the Salvation Army; it appealed to Afro-Jamaicans, some of whom felt excluded by Anglican, Presbyterian, Baptist, and Wesleyan churches because of their class and color.[26] She also gained employment as assistant editor of the *Jamaica Critic* a "socio-political monthly journal" and later took up a position as a stenographer.[27]

In 1928, Marson made history when she became Jamaica's first woman editor-publisher of the magazine *The Cosmopolitan* (1928–1931).[28] She aimed to make *The Cosmopolitan* "an indispensable publication, and one that will be read by every man and woman truly interested in their own and the welfare of Jamaica at large," but it also included stories about the United States, such as the growing popularity of Jamaican-born writer Claude McKay, the UNIA, and black intellectuals.[29] An aspiring writer, Marson used *The Cosmopolitan* to showcase her poetry and short stories. In 1932, Marson migrated again, this time to Britain, where she lived for the next four years.

The lives of Robeson, Nardal, and Marson shed insight into how respectability, travel, politics, and faith differently shaped black womanhood. All three figures adhered to but also challenged the politics of respectability.[30] As high school and college-educated women, they were seen to typify intelligence, refinement, and modernity. But the single status for the majority of Nardal and Marson's lives (the latter married briefly in her fifties) reflected their choice not to follow the path of matrimony expected of women from their backgrounds. In particular, Marson was skeptical of marriage. In her debut 1932 play *At What a Price?*, staged at the Ward Theatre in Kingston, she subtly critiqued the pressure placed on young women to marry and penned satirical poems in *The Cosmopolitan* such as "To Wed or Not to Wed" that poked fun at the miseries of marriage. Yet as she aged, her views on marriage changed, and by the 1950s she argued that married women should give up work and fully immerse themselves as mothers in the home, leaving employment open only for single women.[31] That neither Marson nor Nardal had children undermined the imperative of motherhood for black women. But it was a topic they rarely spoke about either in public or private, which indicates that it was perhaps not a deliberate choice. Although married, Eslanda Robeson and Paul Robeson shared an open marriage from the 1930s onward that allowed both of them the chance to engage in extramarital affairs.[32] In order to pursue her career, Eslanda Robeson had her mother take responsibility for her son when he was a child.[33]

In their attitude towards working- and lower-class women, Nardal and Marson both held up middle-class behaviors and morals as the norm that should be aspired to. However, Robeson was far less concerned with working-class women's behavior. At times, all of the women tried to help less privileged women by raising awareness of the challenges they faced. But at other times they harbored paternalistic attitudes towards the poor.

The relative autonomy the women held in their personal lives provided them with opportunities to explore the world. When asked why she pulled up "roots every five years or so and (went) after a new experience of life," Marson confessed, "I am an odd one."[34] But she was far from exceptional. The deep desire for adventure, career advancement, search for self, or an expensive European education explains the hours, days, and weeks that Marson, Nardal, and Robeson spent on steamships and, later, planes. They journeyed for professional, political, and personal purposes and did so using their own financial savings and organizational funds. Yet although they could all afford to travel, economic insecurities plagued Marson in particular; her many volunteering roles meant that she did not always have a regular salary.[35]

In the 1920s and 1930s, Europe was the continent that Nardal, Robeson, and Marson gravitated to. In later years they ventured further to the United States and countries in the Caribbean, Africa, and Asia. At times, their voyages to known and unknown destinations were considered dangerous. For instance, colonial authorities, police, and intelligence services monitored Robeson's and Nardal's travels and were especially wary of any potential dissent they could spread among colonial subjects.[36] At other times, they enjoyed the comfort of travel.

As the women sojourned across the seas, their movements chime with literary scholar Carole Boyce Davies's concept of "migratory subjectivity," which she identifies as being part of black women's literature and lived experiences.[37] According to Davies, "it is the convergence of multiple places and cultures that re-negotiates the terms of Black women's experience that in turn negotiates and re-negotiates their identities."[38] In many ways, travelling illuminated Nardal's, Marson's, and Robeson's multiple identities based on their national, regional, racial, colonial, class, color, and gendered identifications, enabling them to live "between races, cultures, languages, and nations."[39] Yet these interactions were shaped by conflict and hierarchy, especially visible when the women lived in the contact zones of global cities defined by Mary Louise Pratt as "the space of imperial encounters, the space in which peoples geographically and historically separated come into contact with each other and establish ongoing relations, usually involving conditions of coercion, radical inequality, and intractable conflict."[40] The trio's travels also embodied Gloria Anzaldua's idea of borderlands where "two or more cultures edge each other, where people of different races, sexualities, classes, genders occupy the same territory."[41] The politics of the locations they lived in support arguments made by historical geographer Katherine McKittrick, who states that "the category of black woman is intimately connected with past and present spatial organization."[42]

Most importantly, crossing multiple national borders influenced the politics of Nardal, Marson, and Robeson. In the early 1920s, Robeson was not overtly political but she had been "brought up in a household wide awake to every phase of the Negro problem in America."[43] When she moved to Europe, she became more involved in the "Negro problem" beyond America's shores through her work with leftist black diasporic political groups that fuelled her radicalism. Nardal's initial conservatism had been shaped by her privileged position within French colonial hierarchies. Yet in the 1930s she came to collaborate with a range of figures whose political views she did not fully support. In her twenties and thirties, Marson had been a progressive, but as she aged, her politics changed and by the late 1950s, reactionary rhetoric replaced some of her left-leaning views. The varied political views expressed by the women reveal that labels like radical, conservative, progressive, and reactionary are too limiting when describing them. Such terms fail to take into account the flexible nature of the women's political thought. This fluidity serves as a reminder of arguments made by historian Kate Dossett that black women tended to share overlapping ideological positions, not oppositional ones.[44]

Of the three women, only Marson self-identified as a feminist. First-wave feminism in Jamaica emerged from late nineteenth-century middle-class nationalism and was influenced by British and American women's movements, which resulted in it reproducing colonial class and race hierarchies.[45] *The Cosmopolitan* specifically targeted upwardly mobile and aspirational single, middle-class black and brown working women and became a space for Marson to write about feminism. Its feminist focus was displayed in the bold editorial statement "this is the age of woman: what man has done, women may do."[46] Scholar Rhoda Reddock defines this as a type of liberal feminism "which sought integration of black women (and men) into the established system rather than a more radical politics" such as calling for the extension of the franchise for all.[47]

While Robeson certainly held what today would be described as feminist politics, she eschewed this term mainly because of its associations with middle-class white women.[48] Yet from the 1940s onwards, Robeson would come to voice what historian Erik S. McDuffie calls "black left feminism."[49] Nardal understood the importance of women's involvement in the public and political sphere and belonged to feminist-affiliated organizations but did not use the moniker. Although Marson, Robeson, and Nardal did not label themselves as black feminists, they were aware of the matrix of race, gender, class, and other intersectional identities facing black women and belonged to its long tradition.[50] To disqualify them because they did not use the term fails to take into account the complexity and the changing nature of black feminism as an intellectual and activist project.[51]

Alongside impacting their identities and politics, sojourning also influenced the religious views of Marson and Nardal in particular. Marson's Christian faith increased when she struggled to adjust to living in Britain in the 1930s and in the United States in the 1950s. A committed Catholic, Nardal's faith drove her anti-fascist and pacifist activism in the interwar years and post–World War II

Martinique. Robeson was neither an atheist nor regular churchgoer, but she recognized the important power of black churches in civil rights protest in the 1950s and 1960s.

Numerous biographical works by scholars including Delia Jarrett-Macauley, Alison Donnell, Emily Musil Church, T. Denean Sharpley-Whiting, and Barbara Ransby have greatly helped to reveal the three figures' importance to struggles against racism, fascism, sexism, and colonialism; this book is significantly indebted to all those scholars.[52] It builds on these previous studies but focuses on particular periods in Robeson's, Nardal's, and Marson's lives, looking at them in light of each other to highlight comparisons and connections that shine new perspectives on their identities, politics, and travel.

By examining the differences and similarities between the three women, this book contributes to the burgeoning scholarship on black women's internationalism.[53] Existing and forthcoming work attest to the vibrancy of the field. Scholars such as Sharpley-Whiting, Carole Boyce Davies, Cheryl Higashida, Erik S. McDuffie, Dayo Gore, Tanisha Ford, Keisha N. Blain, Tiffany Gill, and Nicholas Grant and journals such as *Palimpsest: A Journal of Women, Gender, and the Black International*, established in 2012, evidence the rise in research.[54] This scholarship demonstrates how middle- and working-class black women from a variety of geographical locations and ideological positions expressed internationalisms through fashion, activism, literature, leisure, music, and travel. Within this research, there remains a tendency to center attention on groups of women united by their country of origin, political affiliation, or organizational membership—namely, in club, black nationalist, Harlem Renaissance, communist, or radical leftist groups. This focus is important but it can sometimes overlook women who were not explicitly part of these networks or who moved in and out of different networks. It can also obscure the links between black women of different political ideologies and from varied parts of the African diaspora. By focusing on Nardal, Marson, and Robeson in unison, this study adopts a comparative approach to elucidate the breadth of race women internationalists.

Furthermore, by considering the trio beyond the interwar years, this book interrogates the impact of the Cold War, international organizations like the United Nations, departmentalization, and decolonization. This broader chronological perspective, from the 1920s to the 1960s, also allows for a closer look at the continuities and changes that occurred in the women's activism and thought and adds to increasing scholarship of black women's intellectual traditions.

In 2007, scholars Carol B. Conaway and Kristin Waters observed that "when black women speak, if they are heard at all, their thoughtful assertions often are viewed as issuing from nowhere, lacking theoretical substance, disconnected from long-standing systems of classic Western thought."[55] In recent years, many scholars have redressed this trend, especially those mentioned above. In 2015, another edited collection delved deeper into black women's intellectual history with its editors identifying what they call "intellectual history 'black woman–style'" as "an approach that understands ideas as necessarily produced in dialogue with lived experience and always inflected by the social facts of race, class, and gender."[56] Black women's ideas are found in an array of arenas "from political podiums, church pulpits, and the streets into intimate sites of writing: the letter, the short story, the poem, and the novel."[57]

This study reveals how as organic intellectuals, Robeson's, Nardal's, and Marson's ideas and actions regarding feminism, fascism, race, colonialism, Pan-Africanism, and civil rights derived from their everyday experiences. It focuses on how they were practiced through writings in newspapers, plays, poetry, short stories, speeches, anthropology, and interviews.[58] They were also practiced through travelling. By centering their sojourns, this research demonstrates how travel was critical to developing the women's intellectual thought and challenges travel scholarship that privileges the travelogue because their experiences were not always found in travel texts.[59] Alongside writing and travelling, the women were able to develop affective bonds of friendship that also facilitated their practices as race women internationalists.[60]

In order to tell the story of Nardal, Marson, and Robeson, this book explores a broad range of sources including published and unpublished newspaper articles, poems, short stories, and plays written in English and French. Despite these sources, tracing these women's lives has proved difficult. Robeson's, Nardal's, and Marson's mobility has meant that records of their lives are scattered across sundry locations, while other records have vanished or are classified as missing. Only Robeson and Marson have named archives in Washington, DC, and Jamaica respectively, while records of Nardal's life are located in Paris, Aix-en-Provence, and Fort-de-France. But the majority of her personal papers were destroyed, first at sea in 1939 and then in the 1950s following a fire at her home, meaning that questions continue to remain unanswered, especially regarding her personal life.[61] From the existing sources, it is clear that all the women did not want their activism or ideas to be forgotten. Marson and Robeson in particular, kept records of their speeches and published their own writings when publishers refused, sometimes at considerable expense.

While this book aims to explore both the political and personal elements of the women's lives, the fragmented nature of their archives and Nardal's and Marson's choice not to publicly discuss aspects of their personal lives means that this goal is limited. Yet by paying attention to the interiority of the women's lives, this book shows the ways in which the women challenged the "culture of dissemblance." According to historian Darlene Clark Hine, "because of the interplay of racial animosity, class tensions, gender role differentiation, and regional economic variations, Black women, as a rule, developed and adhered to a cult of secrecy, a culture of dissemblance, to protect the sanctity of inner aspects of their lives."[62] Robeson, Nardal, and Marson sometimes followed, but sometimes disrupted dissemblance by making explicit references to the way in which their emotions and feelings, especially loneliness, shame, and optimism, shaped their activism and thought.

This book takes a thematic and chronological approach. Each chapter opens by setting the different contextual scenes before moving on to discuss the women. The first two chapters center on Nardal's, Marson's, and Robeson's experiences in London, Paris, Geneva, Madrid, and their travels farther afield to show how the differing contexts laid the groundwork for their practices as race women internationalists through their engagement in overlapping networks that enabled them to engage in black, feminist, and Christian internationalism. The third chapter explores how the Second World War and departmentalization in Martinique posed challenges and opportunities for the women to expand their involvement in black, feminist, imperial, and liberal internationalism. The final chapter considers the impact of the Cold War and decolonization in shaping Robeson's and Marson's investment in black, radical, and feminist internationalism. The sparse nature of some sources and the group biographical approach explains the uneven coverage in some of the chapters, where one or two women take priority. For instance, in the latter part of Nardal's life, she retreated from the activist terrain, so the final chapter focuses on Robeson and Marson. Ultimately, *Race Women Internationalists* is a piece of recovery history that simultaneously reinterprets our understanding of the role that black women activist-intellectuals played in global freedom struggles.

A Voice from the South spoke to the immediate historical moment of the Woman's Era and appeared just before *Plessy v. Ferguson* (1896) enshrined Jim Crow as law of the land in the United States. But it had roots in one century and consequences in the next. In a later passage, Cooper urged all women to take up leadership positions. Why? Because "woman's strongest vindication for speaking [is] that *the world needs to hear her voice.*"[63] *A Voice from the South* acted as a call to arms for a generation of black women activist-intellectuals. Robeson, Nardal, and Marson took up Cooper's call. The following pages trace their trajectories.

1

Black and Feminist Internationalism in Interwar Europe, 1920–1935

In 1919, as world leaders descended on the historic town of Versailles to decide the fate of Germany, promote world peace, and forge new international organizations like the League of Nations (LoN), prominent black politicians, activists and intellectuals convened the second Pan-African Congress in Paris on February 22. W. E. B. Du Bois and Senegalese Blaise Diagne, the first black African to be elected deputy to the French National Assembly, arranged the meeting of figures from the United States, Africa, and the Caribbean to debate what they hoped would be the greater expansion of rights for people of African descent in the aftermath of the First World War. Members and attendees of the congress called on the nascent LoN "to ensure that all Africans received education, adequate medical care and protection of the rights to traditional lands."[1] While both the Treaty of Versailles and the Pan-African Congress failed to deliver on their aims, the events marked the beginning of a decade that would see black women actively participate in global politics. One of those women, Paulette Nardal, moved to Paris in the early 1920s, a city she called home until the dawn of the next world war.

The twenty-five-year-old journeyed at the height of African, African American, Antillean, Asian, and Latin American migration to France. Population figures for African and Antillean colonials rose, ranging from 10,000 to 15,000, and continued to climb throughout the following decades.[2] Many gravitated to the "City of Light." Historian Michael Goebel reports that "with a population of roughly 100,000 non-Europeans by 1930, the French capital accommodated more people from the Global South than any other contemporary city worldwide, except perhaps New York."[3] Like Nardal, many black colonial migrants came as students looking to further their education at some of France's leading universities, while others came seeking employment.

In the wake of the devastation wrought by World War I, a renewed interest emerged among white French colonial officials and the general public about Africa and black culture. The continent's people and history came to represent "a lush, naïve sensuality and spirituality that cold, rational Europeans had lost."[4]

The increased fascination with Africa and blackness reached its height during the so-called Jazz Age. Advertisements flaunting the 1931 Colonial Exhibition, which included replica African villages transported from parts of Francophone Africa, offered white French men, women, and children an up-close view of the civilizing mission. Alongside these representations, St. Louis–born Josephine Baker's exoticized topless, banana-skirt performances in *Danse de sauvage* skyrocketed her to fame.

The *vogue noire* that captivated the city increased the working opportunities for blacks, and more artists and dancers popular in Harlem made the voyage. Joining Baker on stages across Paris and other parts of France were dancers Florence Mills, Ethel Waters, and Adelaide Hall and musician Duke Ellington, all of whom played in hip bars and clubs that drew large crowds of blacks, whites, and Asians. Black American veterans who had served in France were another sizeable group who chose after 1918 to take refuge from the horrors of Jim Crow America by staying in Paris. Other blacks in Paris occupied positions as sailors, domestic servants, clerks, professionals, and hotel and catering staff, and some were vagabonds.[5] Alongside the growth of nonwhites, the interwar era also saw thousands of European immigrants flock to France from Germany, Italy, and Russia.[6]

Although France offered those of African and Asian descent a chance to earn an income and escape racial violence, it was far from a racial utopia. The racism that underpinned French colonialism also operated throughout the country. Scholar Gary Wilder has argued that blacks in France "confronted the emancipatory and oppressive aspects of both the universalizing and particularizing dimensions of French colonial politics."[7] In response to and in order to challenge some of the unequal treatment they faced in France, many blacks "created a dense network of voluntary associations, including political groups, student organizations, mutual aid societies, workers' cooperatives, trade unions, sports clubs and literary groups."[8] They wrote fictional and nonfictional works that engaged with race, colonialism, gender, music, and dance and expressed a range of political views including communism, republicanism, liberalism, and black nationalism.[9]

At the Sorbonne, Nardal interacted with other black students. She studied her degree at the same time that Anna Julia Cooper was preparing her PhD thesis there, and it is likely that Paulette and her younger sister Jane, who was reading classics at the Sorbonne, attended Cooper's successful dissertation defense in 1925. Another black American female student that the Nardals may have met was Jessie

Fauset, writer and editor of *The Crisis*, the magazine of the National Association for the Advancement of Colored People (NAACP).[10] Nardal also developed an important friendship with Léopold Sédar Senghor, the future president of Senegal. As a student, Nardal delved into American and African American literature, history, and culture, writing her thesis on Harriet Beecher Stowe's novel *Uncle Tom's Cabin*. On completion of her studies, she went back to Martinique, where she taught English. But a few years later, she returned to Paris, serving as parliamentary secretary for Joseph Lagrosillière, deputy of Martinique, and embarking on a career in journalism.

In the decade that Nardal arrived in Paris, Eslanda Robeson was living in Harlem but would soon make London her new home. In August 1925, she undertook her maiden voyage across the Atlantic, when she followed Paul Robeson for the London performance of the popular play *Emperor Jones*.[11] London, like Paris, was awash with black Africans and West Indians as well as Indian colonials.[12] Although the black presence in Britain dated back to Roman times, the late nineteenth century saw increasing numbers of black men arrive as part of imperial trade.[13] During the First World War, black seamen and other colonials took advantage of job shortages to work in Britain.[14] With more colonials in Britain, the metropole became an important space for discussions about race and empire, such as, in 1911, the Universal Races Congress, held to form "friendly feeling and co-operation among all races and nations."[15] In the aftermath of that meeting, activist Dusé Mohammed Ali started the Pan-African newspaper *African Times and Orient Review*, to strengthen links between blacks across the British empire.[16]

Yet the greater black presence in Britain also sparked racial violence. Between January and August 1919, race riots erupted in London, Liverpool, Newport, Bristol, Cardiff, Barry, Hull, Glasgow, South Shields, and Salford, with white crowds attacking blacks and mixed communities.[17] Competition for jobs and housing among blacks and whites underpinned the riots.[18] Sexual and gendered tensions relating to interracial relationships and marriages between black men and white women also contributed to the violence. In total, five died and two hundred and fifty were arrested.[19] Bearing similarity to France, the racism that governed the British empire operated in Britain through both overt and covert color bars.

By the 1920s, the black British population was around 20,000.[20] The following decade saw larger numbers of African American, West Indian, and West African students, entertainers, seamen, activists, writers, businessmen, petitioners, and colonial civil servants sojourn in the imperial metropolis.[21] Eslanda Robeson was immediately struck by the presence of blacks and African culture in Britain. Unlike the United States, where Robeson "heard little or nothing about Africa," in London she found "news of Africa everywhere: in the press, in the schools, in the films, in conversation."[22] The Robesons arrived at a time when millions of Britons were celebrating the "greatest of all the imperial exhibitions," the British Empire Exhibition held at Wembley Stadium in 1924 and 1925.[23] The exhibit was pro-imperial and racist, forcing protests by West African student groups like the Union of Students of African Descent (USAD) about racist coverage in newspapers.[24] As in Paris, the black presence impacted popular and political culture, leading to a rise of student-led, Pan-African, and radical black organizations and newspapers.

Emperor Jones propelled Paul Robeson's fame, enabling the couple to enter the trendy West End and Soho, which Ellington and Mills regularly frequented.[25] These cosmopolitan spaces saw the blurring of racial, gendered, and class hierarchies. As the Robesons tapped into this scene, their friendship circle widened to include figures such as Rebecca West and Emma Goldman.[26] After the play closed, Eslanda and Paul Robeson explored Europe further, spending their vacation in Villefranche-sur-Mer on the Riviera in France, where they befriended writers Claude McKay, Sylvia Beach, James Joyce, Ernest Hemingway, Gertrude Stein, and Max Eastman.[27] They soon returned to the United States, but in 1928, a year after the birth of their son, Paul Robeson Jr. (nicknamed Pauli), London became the Robesons' permanent residence.

Seven years after Robeson first came to London, Una Marson arrived. With the meager profits from "At What a Price?" Marson purchased a £30 return ticket from Kingston to Plymouth on SS *Jamaica Settler* in June 1932 and arrived the following month.[28] While curiosity took Marson to Britain, so too did a healthy dose of romanticism for her "mother country." She weighed the choices of going to Britain or the United States, but chose the former due to her "passionate longing for the land of Shakespeare, Milton, Tennyson, Keats, Shelly, Byron, [and] Wordsworth."[29] By this point in her life, Marson was a relatively successful literary figure, having founded a magazine, produced a play, and published two volumes of poetry: *Tropic Reveries* (1930) and *Heights and Depths* (1931). Yet most of her work circulated only within Jamaica, and she longed to attract a larger audience.

Nardal's, Robeson's, and Marson's journeys to Europe laid the foundations for their practices as race women internationalists. Britain and France—in particular, London and Paris—were critical contact zones for what Marc Matera describes as "African diasporic formation, intellectual production, and political organization where the larger context of empire represented the generative common ground for African and Afro-Caribbean intellectuals' and artists' imaginings of a global black community."[30] Black internationalism sat at the center of these imaginings. Scholars Michael O. West, William G. Martin, and Fanon Che Wilkins note that "at the core of black internationalism is the ideal of universal emancipation, unbounded by national, imperial, continental, or oceanic boundaries—or even by racial ones."[31] As a political philosophy, black internationalism functioned to promote black self-determination and sought to understand the links and differences between black populations around the world.[32] Rather than assuming a common sense of unity and solidarity, black internationalism was shaped by both similarity and difference.³³ From the late 1920s, the three women contributed to the creation of the transnational black public sphere through the networks they built with Pan-African, black student-led, and feminist organizations; their writings in newspapers and their poems; their interactions at elite academic institutions; and their travels throughout the continent that enabled them to practice black and feminist internationalism.

LA DÉPÊCHE AFRICAINE, LA REVUE DU MONDE NOIR/THE REVIEW OF THE BLACK WORLD AND THE CLAMART SALON

The Belgium-based, French-language *Le Soir colonial* and the Antillean monthly anticommunist and liberal *La Dépêche africaine* were two publications that sparked Paulette Nardal's career in journalism.³⁴ She was introduced to the latter publication through her sister Jane, who had been involved with *La Dépêche africaine* since its inception in February 1928.³⁵ Edited by Guadeloupean politician Maurice Satineau and organ of the moderate black organization Comité de défense des intérêts de la race noire (CDIRN), the Republican *La Dépêche africaine* focused its attention on French West and Equatorial Africa and espoused a reformist position.³⁶ Yet the Paris-based newspaper did not just cover stories relating to Africa. The black, white, French, Antillean, male and female journalists featured in the publication wrote articles about colonialism, women's rights, and European politics.³⁷ With this diverse array of contributors, *La Dépêche africaine* appealed to a broad audience of colonial administrators, activists, and intellectuals.³⁸ Compared to other Antillean newspapers in Paris such as *Le Cri des nègres* or *La Race nègre*, *La Dépêche africaine* had a large circulation of around 12,000 to 15,000.³⁹ Unlike Jane Nardal, who wrote political pieces in *La Dépêche africaine* like "Black Internationalism," Paulette's contributions to the journal focused more on culture, with the majority of her writings appearing between 1928 and 1932 in the section "La Dépêche littéraire/The Literary Dispatch."⁴⁰ Although Nardal shared Satineau's politics, her writings centered on tracing the experiences of Martiniquans in Paris and showcasing the vibrancy of the black diasporic cultural presence in shaping the cosmopolitan colonial metropolis, a space where historian Jennifer Anne Boittin says, the "center and the periphery of empire coincided."⁴¹

In the pages of *La Dépêche africaine* Nardal informed readers about African American artists such as the talented sculptor Augusta Savage. The two met at the salon of famed Martiniquan writer René Maran, author of the novel *Batouala*, which won the coveted Prix Goncourt. In the article "A Black Woman Sculptor," Nardal recounted Savage's childhood in Florida, praised her role in nurturing young black artists in New York, and detailed the overt racism she experienced as a black woman in a field dominated by white artists and European aesthetics.⁴²

In another article, "The Negro and Drama," Nardal waxed lyrical about the powerful performances of Afro-Algerian dancer Habib Benglia and Paul Robeson in *Emperor Jones*.[43] In other pieces, she traced the similarities and differences between Antillean and African American music and noted the new dance halls that were becoming more popular with colonials.[44] Historian Rachel Gillet states that Nardal emphasized the respectability of the Antillean Beguine dance over that of African American jazz due to her belief that the latter promoted primitive representations of blacks.[45] Nardal's concern with racial representation in dance and music demonstrates how she upheld the politics of respectability in order to challenge racist stereotypes. The value she placed on Antillean dance can also be seen as part of her elevating Antillean culture over American culture. This was a frequent debate among blacks in France.

Documenting the everyday experiences of being a black Martiniquan woman in Paris was another important feature of Nardal's writings in *La Dépêche africaine*. In 1929, she published the short story "In Exile," which tells the tale of an elderly Martiniquan woman named Elisa, who has been living in France for the last five years. At the story's opening, Elisa expresses her marginalization in the metropole, stating, "This land does not truly suit an old Negress."[46] Her life offers "no room for contented idling, for happy and animated conversations in the evening with her roommate and her other friends, exiled like her—just seemed too painful."[47] Due to her unhappiness, Elisa tries to "get herself repatriated as soon as possible."[48] However, she soon receives a letter from her son, who lives in South America, telling her that he will come to Paris to take her back home, which lifts her spirits. "In Exile" was a way for Nardal to give voice to the experiences of loneliness that black women faced in France, which were not only fictional. Paris was an "instrumental modernist crossroads," argues Jennifer M. Wilks, "where, through geographic and cultural dislocation, black women writers such as Nardal . . . negotiated intersecting categories of identity in their own lives as well as those of their characters."[49]

In the interwar years, black men outnumbered black women in France, due in part to men's greater mobility and the reluctance of some parents to send their daughters from Africa or the Antilles to be educated or live alone in Europe. Yet, despite their smaller number, some notable black women did live in France in the 1920s and 1930s. From the Caribbean, the Nardal sisters; Suzanne Césaire (née Roussi), who studied philosophy at the University of Toulouse and married Aimé Césaire in the late 1930s; Guadeloupean writer Suzanne Lacascade; and Martiniquan Gisèle Dubouillé all spent time in different parts of France.[50] Black American women who lived in France included Josephine Baker; the writers Anna Julia Cooper, Jessie Fauset, Dorothy West, Nella Larsen, and Gwendolyn Bennett; student Shirley Graham (later Shirley Graham Du Bois); Anita Thompson Dickinson; Tuskegee Institute educator Clara Shepard; artists Augusta Savage and Loïs Mailou Jones; and Ada Bricktop Smith, entertainer and owner of the popular nightclub

Chez Bricktop in Montmartre.⁵¹ In order to challenge the marginalization and isolation black women experienced and to help blacks from different parts of the world interact with each other and members of other communities, Nardal created the Clamart salon.

On Sunday afternoons Paulette Nardal and her sisters Jane, Alice, and Andrée opened the apartment they shared in the Parisian suburb of Clamart to men and women, whites and blacks, and Arabs, Muslims, Christians, Jews, and agnostics from around the world for the salon, or *cercle d'amis*, as Paulette preferred to describe it.⁵² The salon became a pivotal space for interracial, intraracial, and international interaction. The list of African Americans who attended the salon included some of the most popular figures of the day, such as writers Alain Locke and Countee Cullen, singers Roland Hayes and Marian Anderson, activist Mercer Cook, educator Shepard (who lived with the Nardals), and doctoral student Ralph Bunche. Hailing from Africa and the Caribbean were the likes of Léopold Senghor, Aimé Césaire, Léon-Gontran Damas, Claude McKay, René Maran, Nicolás Guillén, Étienne Léro, René Ménil, Jules Monnerot, and Nardal's cousin, the Martiniquan scholar Louis Achille.⁵³

In the 1990s, reflecting on his experience at the salon, Achille remembered that oftentimes the group debated "Parisian or world-wide current affairs.... We reflected on colonial and interracial problems; the growing influence of men and women of color in France; and we warned one another of any expressions of racism in order to fight against them elsewhere, through appropriate means."⁵⁴ Wilder argues that the "Nardals promoted an internationalist black humanism that placed a particularizing interest in cultural difference, a universalizing commitment to rational public discourse, and a cosmopolitan ethic of Panafrican connection in the service of one another."⁵⁵ These different aspects of the salon were also tied to its distinct gendered ethos. For Achille, there existed at the Clamart salon "a feminine dominance that determined the tone and the rites of these convivial afternoons quite unlike a corporate circle or a masculine club."⁵⁶ Within this feminine space, new ideas about race, colonialism, and identity would come to be understood as Negritude.

As a political and literary movement among black French colonials in the interwar years, the term *Negritude* first appeared in the third edition of the black student newspaper *L'Étudiant noir*, established in 1935 by Césaire, Senghor, and Damas as the literary arm of the Association des étudiants martiniquais en France, which Nardal also belonged to.⁵⁷ It was later popularized by Césaire in his 1939 poem "Notebook of a Return to My Native Land/Cahier d'un retour au pays natal." As a black internationalist expression, *Negritude* stood for racial essentialism, the celebration of blackness and African culture.⁵⁸ Negritudian thinkers rejected notions of assimilation, preferring instead to advocate cultural *métissage*.⁵⁹ "Negritude represented nothing less than a global assertion of black emancipatory modernity," writes historian Kevin Gaines.[60] Although later male figures gave literary weight and nuance to Negritude, its origins are located in the Nardals' home.

The Clamart salon also spawned an influential black publication that fostered the spread of Negritude. Although *La Dépêche africaine* was a relatively successful and popular newspaper, it suffered from internal challenges and external interference.[61] Divisions among editors and writers about the newspaper's content and financial instability caused problems for the publication.[62] While it was not anti-colonial or radical, the newspaper still worried colonial authorities, who tried to ban its distribution in Africa, fearing that it would incite potential dissension in the colonies. Police surveillance of CDIRN members also stymied the newspaper. In 1923, the Ministry of Colonies streamlined its surveillance of colonial migrants under the Center for Native Affairs/Centre des affaires indigènes (CAI), later known by the acronym SLOTFOM (Service de liaison avec les originaires des territoires français d'outre-mer).[63] The CAI employed a number of police informants in colonial communities to infiltrate civil and political organizations, which black colonials were aware of.[64] Informants fostered tensions within groups but were sometimes mistaken for criminals by the police and arrested.[65] The Paris police force aggressively monitored the activities of radical and anti-colonial activists such as members of the Comité de défense de la race nègre (CDRN) and the Ligue de défense de la race nègre (LDRN). In response to the challenges facing *La Dépêche africaine,* Nardal joined forces with Haitian dentist Dr. Léo Sajous to cofound the bilingual journal *La Revue du monde noir/The Review of the Black World* (1931–1932).[66]

Promoting black internationalism, race consciousness, solidarity, and pride lay at the heart of *La Revue du monde noir/The Review of the Black World.* The editors were Paulette and Jane Nardal, Sajous, Shepard, and white Frenchman Louis-Jean Finot.[67] Contributors included people who attended the Clamart salon as well as notable figures like the French Guiana–born Félix Éboué, who would become the first black governor of Guadeloupe in 1936 and then Chad in 1939, and later a Free French leader during the Second World War. *La Revue du monde noir/The Review of the Black World* aimed to "create among the Negroes of the entire world, regardless of nationality, an intellectual, and moral tie . . . to defend more effectively their collective interests and to glorify their race."[68] To fulfil the journal's global goals, articles in its pages touched on a diverse array of issues such as African art, the Antillean beguine, the Scottsboro trial, Booker T. Washington's Tuskegee Institute, and printed poetry by Langston Hughes and Claude McKay.[69] Its first six issues included news about the United States, the United Kingdom, France, Haiti, Cuba, Ethiopia, and Liberia.

Paulette Nardal wanted *La Revue du monde noir* to not only cover global issues but to reach a wide audience, especially in the United States. She sent copies of the journal to Locke in Washington, DC, and in turn he provided her with a copy of his 1925 anthology *The New Negro,* which Jane Nardal intended to translate into

French but did not complete.⁷⁰ Avid readers of black American literature, the Nardal sisters built connections with other editorial activists like Nellie Bright, an African American teacher, who sent Jane Nardal the National Urban League's publication, *Opportunity*.⁷¹

Alongside editing and translating, Paulette Nardal published an influential article titled "Awakening of Race Consciousness," where she makes the significant claim that black female students in Paris were the first to develop race consciousness and set about creating a global black community. Nardal's argument chimed with another article she had written two years earlier in *Le Soir colonial*, where she argues that "women of color, up until now considered inferior, have begun to play an active role in major social movements."⁷² In "Awakening of Race Consciousness" Nardal states that one of the consequences of migration to Europe was that it increased Antilleans' race pride and interest in Africa.⁷³ According to Nardal, racial attitudes among Antilleans changed because the "ensuing estrangement they felt in the metropolis, where Negroes have not always been so favourably received as they seem to be since the Colonial Exhibition, had given them a real Negro soul, in spite of their Latin education."⁷⁴

Held at the lavish Bois des Vincennes, the 1931 Colonial Exhibition drew nearly thirty-three million visitors and lasted for three months.⁷⁵ The exposition "promoted a unified identity for *la plus grande France*, imparting to the French a sense of belonging to a greater global community with a common purpose."⁷⁶ Unlike black radicals who loudly protested the exhibition for its racist depiction of Asian and African colonials, Nardal saw it in a positive light as helping the white French population understand black French subjects. Yet she was not naïve about racism in France and knew that it played a part in explaining why blacks in France were not "favourably received."⁷⁷

But Nardal was aware that a gendered explanation was needed to take account of the different experiences facing black men and women. In her words, "The coloured women living alone in the metropolis, until the Colonial Exhibition, have certainly been less favoured than coloured men who are content with a certain easy success. Long before the latter, they have felt the need of a racial solidarity. . . . They were thus aroused to race consciousness. The feeling of uprooting . . . was the starting point of their evolution."⁷⁸

Nardal understood that the "easy success" with which black men assimilated into Parisian life was aided, in part, by their relationships with white women. Interracial relationships between black men and white women in France were common. They had an impact on black women, which was a topic delicately discussed when Nardal and Eslanda Robeson first encountered each other in the summer of 1932. Nardal accepted Robeson's request for an interview, and when the two met, they instantly warmed to each other. Robeson described Nardal in glowing terms, remarking that "her lovely clear dark-brown skin has bronze lights in it; her face is full of intelligence and repose; her voice is low and soft, cultured and controlled, and her diction faultless."[79] The two women sat for hours talking about French colonialism, Antilleans in Paris, and interracial relationships. Nardal informed Robeson that "the Negro boys often have great success, and are sometimes lionized by the French girls; the mulatto is often successful, too. But the Negro girls of the better class, often proud and sensitive, have a difficult time; their own boys are much more interested in making conquests in the new field, and leave them sadly alone; and French boys are not interested in them, except as friends."[80]

The reference to black men "making conquests in the new field" was Nardal's way of expressing black men's sexual interest in white women and vice versa. For many black women, interracial relationships or marriages between black men and white women remained a sensitive issue because it had the effect of reinforcing racist and sexist notions of white women as attractive and sought after, and black women as unattractive, unchaste, and unwanted.[81] Nardal was consciously aware of how class determined interracial relationships, adding that "Negro boys who mingle with white people in France usually marry beneath them."[82] Interestingly enough, Nardal did not discuss interracial relationships between black Martiniquan women and white men. These relationships were less prevalent or perhaps too taboo to address. Yet there were many interracial relationships among African American women like Bricktop and Baker with white French men. Although there were lesbian relationships among African American women, this was not a topic they addressed.

Due to the double marginalization black women faced due to their race and gender, Nardal argued that this led some, like herself, to conduct academic research on black history and literature, such as her work on Stowe, and to form groups like the Clamart salon. This led many to try to combat their ostracism and develop race consciousness.[83] According to Wilks, Nardal's article reflects how "the construct of gender is as important as geography and nation in the articulation of racial identities."[84] It further served as a critical way in which Nardal articulated the gendered dimensions of black internationalism.

At the end of her seminal article, Nardal poses the intriguing question "Should one see in the tendencies here expressed a sort of implicit declaration of war upon Latin culture and the white world in general?"[85] The answer is no. In Nardal's opinion, "We are fully conscious of our debts to the Latin culture and we have no intention of discarding it."[86] But Nardal wanted to "go beyond this culture, in order to give to our brethren, with the help of the white scientists and friends of the Negroes, the pride of being the members of a race which is perhaps the oldest in the world."[87] Nardal's comments reveal that she fused her notion of race consciousness with both European and African culture, an idea also expressed by Jane Nardal in her 1928 article "Black Internationalism."[88] Paulette Nardal grounded her ideas on racial identity and acceptance of French assimilation to a middle path between conservatives who invalidated African culture and people on the left who called for an Afrocentric black nationalism.

The Clamart salon and *La Revue du monde noir/The Review of the Black World* were important spaces of unity and division. In 1932, a breakout group inspired by Marxism, including Léro, Ménil, and Monnerot, left the journal and salon to create the short-lived *Légitime défense*. According to Damas, who also left *La Revue du monde noir/The Review of the Black World*, believing that it was not radical enough, it had "many problems; financial, political, police."[89] The tensions that existed within *La Revue du monde noir/The Review of the Black World* reflected the larger divisions among blacks in Paris based on differences relating to citizenship status, language, and religion.[90] The most frequent division affected upper-middle-class Antillean citizens and proletarian Africans.[91]

Despite the moderate tone of the articles and partial funding from the Ministry of Colonies, *La Revue du monde noir/The Review of the Black World* did not escape surveillance.[92] The Ministry of Colonies viewed the journal suspiciously, stating that it aired views "that are clearly hostile to our influence in Africa, although in its mission statement it only declares philanthropic goals."[93] The ministry soon withdrew its funding, which explains why *La Revue du monde noir/The Review of the Black World* lasted for less than two years.

Yet, regardless of the many challenges they faced, Nardal and other blacks in Paris did not give up on the importance of racial cooperation and solidarity. After the demise of *La Revue du monde noir/The Review of the Black World*, Nardal continued to give voice to the gendered dimensions of black internationalism in print. In March 1935, she was the only woman featured in the first edition of *L'Étudiant noir*, contributing a short story translated into English as "The Wolof Puppet." It describes the reaction of a westernized black Caribbean woman to a black Senegalese man dressed in a ridiculous outfit, selling peanuts to whites in a café in the Latin Quarter. Despite her initial embarrassment at the man's caricature and their obvious class differences, the female protagonist admits that their blackness connects them regardless of their economic and colonial differences.[94] This encounter mirrors the development of Nardal's race consciousness, which according to literary scholar Brent Hayes Edwards was not based on a predetermined sense of solidarity but rather was created and "practised across difference."[95]

Alongside their black internationalism, Nardal and her sister Jane were also active within women's organizations—namely, the Women's Civic and Social Union/Union féminine civique et sociale, which had been created in 1925 as a religious alternative to secular feminist groups and was committed to working with Catholic women "in the defense of women's civil rights."[96] Although there are few sources about their involvement with the group, both sisters were involved in its Commission for Understanding among Races, and between 1935 and 1939 Paulette Nardal contributed to the organization's journal, *Le Cerf*.[97] Their participation in the organization highlights how they brought an intersectional lens to the group, providing the perspectives of black women to other Catholic women.

Nardal's involvement in *La Dépêche africaine*, *La Revue du monde noir*, and the Clamart salon reflected a commitment to combatting the racial and gendered isolation that she and other black women in France faced by practicing a gendered black internationalism through literary, social, and political networks and print that compared and contrasted with the activities of Una Marson across the Channel.

THE MOTH AND THE STAR, THE LEAGUE OF COLOURED PEOPLES, AND *THE KEYS*

When Una Marson first arrived in London in 1932, she reached out to prominent members of the West Indian community and was soon introduced to fellow Jamaican Harold Moody. Born in Kingston in 1882, Moody came from the middle class.[98] He first moved to Britain in 1904 to study medicine at King's College London. Upon completion, the color bar prevented him from gaining employment. In response, he set up a private practice near his home in Peckham, which many colonials frequented.[99] In London, Moody participated in Christian circles including the Congregational Church, the Congregation Union, Christian Endeavour, the Christian Brotherhood, the Anglicans, the Quakers, and the London Missionary Society, and he served as a lay preacher.[100]

Moody and Marson shared many similarities that served as the basis of their friendship. The two came from the same class background and held onto a strong British imperial identity that consisted of patriotism and pride in the monarchy, English history, and the empire. Moody's home became an important space that housed many blacks when they first arrived in Britain. While settling into her new life in the capital, Marson lived with Moody, his white English wife, nurse Olive Moody, and their three children in their home at 164 Queen's Road in Peckham.[101] After securing accommodation, Marson attempted to find work in London that would help to sustain her literary career. But within a few weeks, she quickly realized that finding employment would prove more difficult than she had expected. The "young coloured woman has to face many problems," she admitted.[102] "In London, most avenues of work except that of entertaining in the dance or music halls, are closed to coloured people."[103] When Marson looked for work as a stenographer, one agent informed her that "she didn't register black women because they would have to work in offices with white women." Another agent told her that in spite of her excellent references, "firms did not want to employ a black stenographer."[104]

The racism and sexism Marson encountered in seeking employment influenced her sense of isolation, depicted in her poem "Little Brown Girl," which appeared in her third poetry collection, *The Moth and the Star* (1937). The poem sees Marson bombarded by questions from a white interrogator who wonders why she speaks English so well and voices ignorance about the location of the West Indies, which the interrogator assumes to be somewhere near India. The white person probes into Marson's racial identity, asking, "Would you like to be white / Little brown girl?"[105] This question reinforces the underlying connotations of white supremacy. The Londoner answers the question by noticing that Marson tosses her head as if she is "proud / To be brown."[106] When the voice of the brown girl emerges in the poem, she says,

> ... the folks are all white—
> White, white, white
> And they all seem the same
> As they say that Negroes seem.[107]

Here, Marson reverses the trope that colonists and travel writers used in their inability to distinguish between blacks.

"Little Brown Girl" stands as an eloquent exposition of how Marson became more aware of herself as a woman of color in a predominantly white Britain. This awareness shaped changes in her identity. Within months of her arrival in London, Marson made a symbolic political statement: she stopped straightening her hair.[108] Marson's critique of the dominance of white beauty standards for black women was long-standing. Following the 1931 all-white Miss Jamaica beauty contest held in Kingston, she had written in *New Cosmopolitan* that "there is a growing feeling in many quarters that 'Miss Jamaica' should be a type of girl who is more truly representative of the majority of Jamaicans."[109]

In the poem "Kinky Hair Blues" from *The Moth and the Star*, Marson gives further voice to the physical and psychological consequences of black women's idealization of European beauty aesthetics through the mixture of Jamaican patois and African American rhythms. "Kinky Hair Blues" stands in contrast to her poem "Black Is Fancy," in which the protagonist expresses confidence in her identity as a black woman; Marson's poem predates by several decades the Black Power movement's slogan "Black is beautiful." Collectively, these poems and others, including "Cinema Eyes" and "Black Burden," explore emotions of black pride, pleasure, and pain that Marson encountered in London, which contributed to her more explicit definition of herself as a racialized woman. Marson's experiences in London mirrored that of black women in Paris. Like Nardal, the sexism and racism that Marson faced instilled within her a desire to forge networks among other blacks living in Britain, which she did through the League of Coloured Peoples (LCP).

The LCP was one among a host of West African and Afro-Caribbean student- and activist-led black internationalist organizations that challenged racism and colonialism in Britain, the Caribbean, the United States, and Africa and stressed the urgency of racial unity. Some of the most influential groups included the nonpolitical African Students' Union, the African Progress Union (APU), the Union of Students of African Descent (USAD), the Society of Peoples of African Origin (SPAO), and its newspaper entitled *African Telegraph*, edited by Felix E. M. Hercules. Another was the influential West African Students' Union (WASU), established in 1925 by Nigerian University College London law student Ladipo Solanke, Sierra Leonean Dr. Herbert Bankole-Bright, and Joseph Boakye Danquah from the Gold Coast.[110] WASU grew out of the short-lived Nigerian Progress Union that Solanke had formed with Ashwood Garvey in 1924. It became a leading African student organization with its popular journal *Wasu*, established in 1926. There also existed the African Races Association of Glasgow, which included students and workers and later affiliated with WASU.[111] Alongside the growth of black organizations in the 1920s and 1930s, white Quakers, members of the Liberal and Labour Parties, and feminists concerned with the color bar and keen to foster interracial cooperation united in 1931 to form the Joint Council to Promote Understanding between White and Coloured People in Great Britain.[112]

The LCP quickly became a leading black internationalist organization committed to tackling racial discrimination and supporting black colonials in Britain and other parts of the world. The LCP's ideology had firm foundations in "equality, justice, and fair play."[113] Its key objectives were outlined in the first issue of its flagship journal, *The Keys*, whose title referred to Gold Coast educator Dr. James E. Kwegyir Aggrey's analogy of racial harmony: the pianist uniting black and white keys. The LCP sought to "promote and protect the social, educational, economic and political interests of its members; to interest members in the welfare of coloured peoples in all parts of the world; to improve relations between the races; and to co-operate and affiliate with organisations sympathetic to coloured people."[114] The LCP headquarters were in London, but the group had branches in other areas of Britain, including in Liverpool and Cardiff, and further afield in British Guiana, Jamaica, Panama, and Sierra Leone.

Despite its socially conservative politics, the LCP collaborated with a range of other groups in London including radicals, black nationalists, Pan-Africanists, Labour Party politicians, white liberals, white conservatives, and the Colonial Office. Its diverse membership included figures such as C. L. R. James; Saint Lucian W. Arthur Lewis, later an economist and Nobel Prize winner; Trinidadian cricketer Learie Constantine; anthropologist Bronislaw Malinowski; and Margery Perham, an expert on colonial rule in West Africa.[115]

While tensions existed between the LCP and WASU, they shared members and similar aims.[116] Both groups also created spaces in London for blacks. In the 1930s, WASU opened a hostel on Camden Road in London that became an important social and living space for blacks.[117] In October 1934, with funds from colonial governments in West Africa and the Caribbean, the LCP helped to establish Aggrey House, a social and residential space for blacks.[118]

Although a middle-class-dominated organization that promoted Christian ethics and middle-class respectability, the LCP did concern itself with the problems of the black working class and colonial seamen.[119] While there were more black men involved in the group, based on their larger numbers in London, black women such as the Trinidadian activist Audrey Jeffers, the Nigerian law student Stella Thomas (the first African woman called to the Bar), and Marson played important roles in the organization.

Between 1932 and 1935, Marson served as secretary of the LCP, enabling her to practice black internationalism. In this role, she organized the LCP's annual conferences, which brought together blacks from different parts of the world. It was here where she met African American, Afro-Caribbean, and African figures such as James, Paul and Eslanda Robeson, Jomo Kenyatta, Ladipo Solanke, Louis Mbanefo, Desmond Buckle, and Ofori Atta, a king from the Gold Coast. Together they discussed changes in colonial policy in the Caribbean and West Africa and debated how to support anti-racist campaigns in the United States.[120] For instance, in 1931, the LCP expressed racial solidarity when its members raised money for the Scottsboro trial. It also invited Ada Wright, the mother of two of the defendants, to address the LCP on her European tour in June 1932.[121] Marson's interaction with Atta was meaningful as it sparked her increasing interest in Africa. Rumors persist that their relationship went beyond friendship and that the two had a brief affair.[122] Like the Clamart salon, the LCP was not just a political but also a social space. Marson helped organize the groups' social events, which usually revolved around cricket matches, tennis, and garden parties.

In January 1933, Marson organized an important social event that brought West Indians and West Africans together on the London theatre stage. She cast members of the LCP in the London-based version of her play *At What a Price?* The play told of the coming-of-age of country girl Ruth Maitland who follows thousands of young men and women, like Marson, to Kingston, where she finds work as a secretary for the light-skinned Gerald Fitzroy.[123] In the city, Ruth makes friends with other working women and revels in her newfound freedom, far from the prying eyes of her parents. Although she is warned about the dangers of city life, especially the all-too-eager young and married men, she begins a romantic affair with Fitzroy, who is already engaged to a brown woman. Their brief romance leads to pregnancy and although Fitzroy proposes marriage, Ruth declines due to their class and color differences. Refusing to live her life as a fallen woman in the city, Ruth returns home to her understanding parents and resolves to marry her childhood sweetheart, Robert, who promises to accept the child as his own. The production was first shown at the Young Men's Christian Association (YMCA) and then at the Scala Theatre, making it the first black play shown in the West End.[124]

The inclusion of upper- and middle-class West Africans in a play about Jamaica staged in London presented a powerful message of self-determination. This was echoed in Moody's opinion that the success of the production would "bring home to the British public the fact that we can manage our own affairs effectively and therefore need not to be forever under tutelage. It will also bring our own people together and help us to have more confidence in ourselves . . . and assist us to find a basis of fuller co-operation."[125] The play served as evidence of the importance of the creative arts in black internationalist expressions for Marson, a belief she shared with other colonial students. In 1933, Marson organized a musical event at the Indian Students Hostel, which reveals her investment in forging Afro-Asian alliances in London.[126]

In addition to her role as assistant secretary, Marson served as editor of the LCP's quarterly journal, *The Keys*, an appointment she held on and off from 1933 to 1935. While *The Keys* was principally devoted to issues facing "our brothers and sisters within the British Empire," including racial discrimination in Cardiff, Liverpool, and London, it refused to ignore "the claims of other peoples of colour who owe allegiance to a flag other than our own. . . . Never was there a greater need for unity within our ranks."[127] Indeed, the international scope of *The Keys* was evident through its circulation: over two thousand copies were distributed in "East Africa, West Africa, South Africa, India, West Indies, Bermuda, America, and Great Britain."[128] In the pages of *The Keys*, Marson played a role in giving voice to global black politics. For instance, stories in the journal documented the conditions of gold-mining workers in Kenya, black African laborers in South Africa, and Aborigines in Australia; and the persecution of Jews in Germany. As editor, Marson also penned pieces that contributed to debates about racism and racial unity.

Marson's poem "Nigger" appeared in the first issue. It recounts the incident of a group of white children shouting the racist moniker to her as she strolls along the streets of London. In the closing stanzas Marson prays, asking,

> God keep my soul from hating such mean souls, . . .
> God save their souls from this great sin
> Of hurting human hearts that live
> And think and feel in unison
> With all humanity.[129]

The poem's ending reflects one of Marson's responses to racism: to turn to religion. She was to do this in different periods of her life.

Marson struggled to speak candidly about the racism she encountered. In 1934, she confessed that "In America they tell you frankly where you are not wanted by means of big signs, and they don't try to hide their feelings. But in England, though the people will never say what they feel about us, you come up against incidents which hurt so much that you cannot talk about them."[130] Marson's inference that the subtlety of British racism was more damaging than the overtness of Jim Crow indicates the severity of the daily racism she encountered. Yet rather than being silenced by racism, Marson used creative fiction to explore further her and other blacks' experiences.

In 1934 she wrote her second play, *London Calling*, about a group of black colonial students in London, which was performed in Jamaica three years later. The plot concerns a sister and brother, Rita and Sydney, students from Novoka, an imaginary non-African British colony, presumably in the Caribbean. After invitations from aristocrat Lady Burton requesting their company at her home in Kent, they, along with fellow colonials Alton and Frank, ask their friend Alota, an African law student, to dress them as Africans because they "have only English customs in Novoka."[131] In act 1, Marson refers to Pan-Africanism when Prince Alota pities the Novokans saying, "It is very sad that you have no language ... and no customs ... but I will help you," and Alton replies, "That's kind, and after all we are cousins," thereby echoing their common African ancestry.[132] In act 2, when Alton, Rita, and Sydney arrive at the Burtons' residence, Lord and Lady Burton and their staunch Tory son, Douglas, exhibit a plethora of racist stereotypes regarding their guests. The Burtons, for example, are worried that they will leave black marks on the sheets.[133] Douglas fears that they will "bring their idols and make funny noises and burn things in their rooms."[134] Furthermore, according to Lady Burton, the fact that her guests have eaten before arriving at her home exemplifies their "uncivilized" nature.[135] Themes of interracial relationships, bigotry, and prejudice pervade the play. But it ends on a romantic note with Rita agreeing to marry Alton.

According to critic Elaine Campbell, the play is "basically a romantic comedy."[136] Campbell's analysis downplays its significance. If we unite Marson's life and those of her characters, we can see that she used *London Calling* as a mirror to reflect to her Afro-Jamaican audience the racist attitudes of British colonials and conservatives, who viewed African and Afro-Caribbean subjects as little more than backward children. This mirror image would have discomforted many members of Marson's middle-class audience, who idolized the "motherland." The play would have also served as a warning to Afro-Jamaicans planning on visiting London that the racism the characters face may be addressed to them too. Moreover, the play serves as another example of the ways in which Marson challenged racism by stressing the significance of bonds of racial unity among blacks from different parts of the diaspora, an issue she detailed in *The Keys*.

One of Marson's most lengthy editorials came in the 1935 New Year edition, where she wrote a rousing message urging racial cooperation. Although blacks lived in "a world that has freed the Negro," Marson argued that the white majority "still looks upon his land as spoil and himself as chattel—and Negroes are trying to make money for themselves, quarrelling among themselves or passing their leisure away in amusements of one kind or another."[137] Here, she identified the failures of emancipation and the strategy of divide and rule that affected intraracial relations.

Marson remarked that, due to differences in European colonialism and geography, "Negroes in some parts of the British Empire do not suffer from segregation and so they are content."[138] But with advancements in technology, "the whole world is coming closer together; it is inevitable with the development of modern science—and the Negro world must come together," she stated.[139] She stressed that "if the matter of nationality makes it more difficult for American Negroes to join Negroes in the British Empire, under the British flag, we must unite to contribute our quota to the markets of the world as a race." She encouraged better-off blacks to help the working class, demanding that "what one Negro has done, thousands of Negroes can do, but those who have 'got there' must help others to 'get there' also."[140]

Marson promoted the importance of self-determination, dispelling myths about blacks' dependency on whites and asking, "And who is going to do these things for us? We have got to do it ourselves—if we can co-operate." She argued against blaming governments, commenting, "We are under a democratic government and that government is acting as trustees for us until we can stand on our feet in this hard, cruel and materialistic world, or in other words under the strenuous conditions of modern times." Marson had little interest for communism, saying it "won't help us" and urging, "If every educated Negro will feel the burden of his brother too great for him and help him to carry it—then things will be done. Then, and only then will the Negro race be a race contributing richly to the world."[141]

Although this editorial captures Marson's passion for the importance of racial unity, later in the year she undermined her own argument when she wrote an article in *News Chronicle* criticizing Paul Robeson's call to create a club for black dramatists. According to Marson, "The cry for Negro culture is putting the cart before the horse and the first task of the negro who has achieved is to teach his people the value of unity." She stated that "the negro worries too much about what the white man thinks of him and too little about what he is himself in the eyes of people of his own race."[142] What Marson deemed necessary for blacks to achieve was "sound, wise leadership by men and women able and willing to sacrifice for the good of their own people."[143] Marson's article was full of contradictions, as there was no correlation between the creation of a black drama group and a lack of racial unity. Her critique of Paul Robeson may have been based on his communist sympathies and her fear of being upstaged.[144] The article stirred up debate within black organizations, and WASU responded by defending Paul Robeson.[145] Marson's disagreement with Robeson demonstrates that while she and groups like the LCP understood the necessity of racial unity, in practice personality politics and differences in political opinions oftentimes undermined their messages.

Notwithstanding discussions about African women that occurred at a few LCP conferences, the organization and *The Keys* maintained a masculine mission, aiming to state "the cause of the Black Man."[146] There was little room for Marson to write about women's issues as she had done in *The Cosmopolitan*, so she turned to the British Commonwealth League (BCL) for feminist succor. The growth of organizations such as the BCL, the International Council of Women, the International Alliance of Women, and the Women's International League for Peace and Freedom facilitated the spread of feminist internationalism in the first half of the twentieth century.[147] Although dominated by middle-class white women, these organizations attempted to have a global reach. Historian Marie Sandell writes that "integral to all their activities was the belief . . . that women could, and should, organise across national borders and racial and language differences since women in all societies were subordinated to men and being denied their rights."[148]

Formed in 1925, the BCL's motto was "to secure equality of liberties, status, and opportunities between men and women in the British Commonwealth of Nations."[149] It promoted the growth of women's groups within the empire and aimed to "raise the status of women of the less forward races."[150] The implied meaning behind its aim troubled Marson, who struggled to forge bonds with other women because of their paternalistic attitude toward non-Western and nonwhite women.[151]

Yet Marson was an active member, and her involvement saw her practice black and feminist internationalism in varied ways. For instance, she addressed the ninth annual conference in 1933, based on the topic "the mother of today within the British Commonwealth," delivering a speech called "The Rights of the Native Mother," alongside Audrey Jeffers from Trinidad, Miss Caley from Africa, and Ruby Rich from Australia.[152] She attended meetings alongside her African friends, including Kenyan student and later leader Jomo Kenyatta.[153] She also forged friendships with white feminists who were interested in Africa and race relations such as Winifred Holtby, who became her close friend and mentor.

Holtby and Marson were first introduced when they spoke together on the topic "bars to careers" at a BCL meeting in 1934.[154] Holtby was an important figure within interracial circles in London through the LCP and the Joint Council to Promote Understanding between White and Coloured People, and she shared a passionate concern about the struggles of black South Africans.[155] One evening they spoke late into the night at Holtby's Chelsea flat about interracial relations, colonialism, and women's rights.[156] Unfortunately, however, Holtby and Marson did not have much time to develop their relationship because of Holtby's premature death in 1935. In a poem dedicated to Holtby, Marson described her as a "valiant woman . . . with sympathies as wide as they were true."[157]

As Marson was able to bring discussions of race into her feminist involvement, she also began to express anti-colonial views. At the 1934 BCL conference, she made a brief speech criticizing colonial education. A report of her remarks noted that she argued that "the child using books which upheld the glory of Empire grew to manhood and womanhood knowing nothing and caring less, for the land of his forefathers—Africa—and the race to which he belonged." She went on to argue that "duty to one's country and people should be taught before duty to an Empire that took little interest in these children." If not, children would continue to grow up with "an inferiority complex." She disliked the practice whereby "books which were out of date in British schools were shipped to the colonies, and special books, not used in England, were sent to colonial schools—history books extolling the glories of the British Empire." "The aim of Colonial Education," Marson argued, should be to "produce useful citizens of their own countries and not merely flag-waving Britishers."[158]

These sentiments came within two years of Marson living in Britain and reflect how far her thinking on colonialism had changed. Once an admirer of all things British, her experience in London forced her to rethink her relationship to an empire that treated her as a second-class citizen. Although she was not a radical anti-colonialist and she sought colonial reform, her remarks shed light on how her experiences in London developed her Jamaican nationalism. It is interesting that Marson had more space to critique colonialism within feminist international groups than in the LCP. She seems to have faced restrictions against speaking freely in the LCP, and while the BCL was no radical group advocating anti-colonialism, it still provided a platform for Marson to express her views on colonialism to perhaps a more receptive and less hostile audience. Indeed, Marson revelled in the involvement with feminist international groups, exclaiming that "England is a wonderful country for its women's organisations."[159]

As news of her reputation as a bold activist in these groups travelled back to Jamaica in 1935, the white-led Women's Social Service Club (WSSC) wrote asking her to represent it at the twelfth annual congress of the International Alliance of Women for Suffrage and Equal Citizenship (IAWSEC), a European-led organization established first as the International Alliance of Women in 1904 and then renamed in 1926.[160] Although Marson never joined the WSSC, she accepted the invitation and travelled with the English delegation to Istanbul alongside veteran feminist Margery Corbett Ashby, who was president of the IAWSEC from 1923 to 1946, and Margaret Ingledew.[161] Representatives from over thirty nations attended, with delegates coming from Brazil, India, Syria, Persia, Palestine, and Australasia.[162] As the only black woman delegate, Marson's presence at the congress was historic.

In her speech, Marson claimed to "talk on behalf of all the Negroes of the world, not only Jamaicans" and confessed, "Although I don't know much about Africa, I consider it a part of my being because my forefathers came from there."[163] Her remarks touched upon lynching in the United States, the work of the NAACP, and African women's rights. She called on participants to "defend and help my race."[164] Marson's speech is an example of how her work with feminist international organizations enabled her to express both black and feminist internationalism. Reflecting on the conference, later, Marson focused her remarks less on any divisions that may have existed among the women and focused instead on the positive unity among delegates, remarking that "we all came together as though we were one big family and it was wonderful to see how everyone was eager to learn something of other countries."[165]

Her speech garnered positive press, with the liberal *Manchester Guardian* commenting that the "negro woman of African origin from the former slave world of Jamaica brought a new note into the assembly and astonished them by the vigour of her intellect and by her feminist optimism."[166] Marson relished her time in the limelight and after the conference enjoyed a meeting with Turkish president Kemal Atatürk, whom she spoke highly of but whose role in limiting women's rights she overlooked.[167] She then spent a holiday in Capri living with an Italian woman sculptor whom she had met at the conference.[168]

During her time in Istanbul, Marson met Lithuanian Princess Gabrielle Radziwill, who was a member of the League of Nations (LoN) secretariat and liaison officer with women's organizations.[169] Marson asked Radziwill if she could be considered for an invitation to attend the LoN Assembly meetings as temporary collaborator of the Information Section.[170] There were three main reasons why Marson wanted to spend time at the LoN. First, she wanted, in her words, to "not only to enrich my rather meagre knowledge of the League's work, but I consider it of tremendous importance and value for me to have personal insight into its work so that I shall better be able to advocate its usefulness and importance." Second, working at the LoN would help her write a "booklet setting out the work of the League for use in Elementary and Secondary schools" in the Caribbean. Lastly, she intended to "contribute various articles to the Press and through this means, will bring to the notice of all sections of the people in those parts of the British Empire, the great work of the League in the worthy cause of universal peace and goodwill."[171]

Marson's reasons reflect her keen interest in international relations and gaining a fuller understanding of the intricacies of the LoN. Her plans to spread more information about the LoN to children indicate her commitment to challenging the limited education in the Caribbean, which focused on British colonialism. She wanted instead to develop students' interest in the world beyond the British empire, which she saw the LoN as representing. Her plans to share more information about the LoN within the press reveals that she recognized newspapers as critical avenues through which she could share information about the organization and in turn practice liberal internationalism.

In June 1935, the secretary of the LoN, Joseph Avenol, invited her to be one of thirty participants to travel to Geneva and study the work of the organization.[172] Excited by this new opportunity, Marson told her friend British American heiress Nancy Cunard, "I was one of 30 people invited from 28 countries to do collaboration work. A negro had never been there before."[173] She spent three weeks working at the LoN as a *collaborateur* within the Information Section.[174] Her work at the LoN indicates how through her involvement in black and feminist internationalism, Marson also got the chance to engage in liberal internationalism. Although she was not at the LoN for a long time and there a few sources that tell of her experiences or any of her planned writings or activities, her presence there indicates the merging of overlapping internationalisms.

EUROPEAN SOJOURNS, WASU, AND THE LONDON SCHOOL OF ECONOMICS

At the same time that Marson was in London, Eslanda Robeson was practicing black internationalism through her continental travels, involvement with WASU, and academic studies at the London School of Economics (LSE). Initially Robeson had a positive view of London, proudly gushing in the biography she penned in 1930 of her husband's privileged experience that in London "he did not have to live in a segregated district; he leased a charming flat in Chelsea near his friends; he dined at the Ivy."[175] However, the two did encounter racism. A year earlier, for instance, Paul Robeson had gotten a taste of the color bar when the Savoy Grill in London refused to serve him. He challenged the establishment, and the incident gained press coverage in *The Daily Mirror*, but Eslanda Robeson omitted this incident from his biography.[176] Perhaps she felt that it was not important to include. But its absence also shows how she at first tried to stress the differences between the Jim Crow United States and England.

While serving as her husband's manager, she travelled with him and his musical partner, Larry Brown, on concert tours throughout Europe and Britain. During these trips, they met African and West Indian students, many of whom voiced their experiences of racism and exclusion in the metropole.[177] In her anthropological travel narrative *African Journey* published in 1945, Robeson reflected on her early years in London. She writes that "Paul and I began to seek out all the Africans we could find . . . in England, Scotland, Ireland, France; in the universities, on the docks, in the slums." She stresses the similarities she found between herself and the Africans, noting that "the more we talked with them, the more we came to know them, the more convinced we were that we are the same people: They know us, we know them; we understand their spoken and unspoken word, we have the same kind of ideas, the same ambitions, the same kind of humor, many of the same values."[178]

These sentiments reveal how Robeson's black internationalism was centered on the bonds of unity and sameness between, in particular, Africans and African Americans, most of whom would have shared similar class and educational backgrounds, even though she did reach out to working-class blacks. With this romanticization, Robeson was undermining arguments made by some academic anthropology scholars and students that Africans shared no connections to people of African descent in the West, an issue that she would later tackle as a student.

The new friendships the Robesons were making with Africans and Afro-Caribbeans in Britain and their own encounters with racism led to their increasing involvement in black organizations. In the 1930s, the couple began to regularly attend LCP events, but Eslanda Robeson in particular warmed to the WASU, due in part to its more radical stance reflected in the links it shared with groups such as League Against Imperialism (LAI), the Communist Party of Great Britain (CPGB), and the Negro Welfare Association.[179] In a letter to Harold Moody, Robeson accused the LCP of "trying hard to fit into a white world and a white future."[180] Robeson's remarks reveal a simplified view of the LCP's politics, perhaps conflating their insistence on interracial understanding and cooperation with anti-black sentiment. That she preferred WASU over the LCP demonstrates the development of her left wing and anti-colonial sympathies. Through their involvement with WASU, the Robesons stressed the need for race pride and unity not only in the sphere of politics but also in culture. Members of WASU warmed quickly to the famous couple and granted them honorary membership.

The Robesons' links with WASU saw them gain more connections with other colonials and influential writers and activists living in Britain. Notably, they developed friendships with George Padmore, C. L. R. James, British writer Leonard Barnes, American Quaker and world traveller Anna Melissa Graves, law student Rajni Patel, filmmaker D. G. Tendulkar, and future first prime minister of India Jawaharlal Nehru.[181] The relationships Eslanda Robeson forged with these figures widened her understanding about the different forms of colonialism in Africa, the Caribbean, and Asia. As she began to discover more about the British empire, she became curious about knowing more about other black networks in Europe, especially in France.

Robeson had first visited France in August 1925; while she was residing in London, she and her friend Bert McGhee spent five days on holiday there.[182] On their way to the South of France later in 1925, the Robesons saw two performances starring Josephine Baker in Paris.[183] Eslanda read them as unfavorably reinforcing racist exotic stereotypes of blacks.[184] Although she was aware of the popularity of African Americans in Paris, she yearned to know more about their experiences as well as those of black Antilleans and Africans.

In the summer of 1932, Robeson ventured to Paris with Prince Kojo Touvalou Houénou, a leading figure in France's black community.[185] The two had first met in 1924 at the Harlem home of NAACP leader Walter White and instantly became friends.[186] In the 1910s, Houénou had enrolled at the University of Bordeaux to read law and later became a committed Garveyite, holding a senior position within the Universal Negro Improvement Association (UNIA). Alongside René Maran, he cofounded the journal *Les Continents* and launched the radical Universal League for the Defense of the Black Race/Ligue universelle pour la défense de la race noire (LUDRN).[187] Houénou played a crucial role as go-between and translator for African American visitors in Paris, introducing them to other prominent black members of the city. With Houénou's help, Robeson met and interviewed a range of figures including Houénou himself, Paulette Nardal, Habib Benglia, Maran, Bricktop, Baker, under-secretary of state for the colonies Gratien Candace, his secretary Issac Beton, musician Clarence Cameron White, Cecelia Kennedy Yerby (the African American wife of doctor William James Yerby), artist Aaron Douglas, and lawyer Kobina Sekyi.[188] These interviews formed a two-part article under the title "Black Paris," which "captured the transnational, multi-lingual, and creative cosmopolitan ethos of the African diaspora in Paris."[189] They appeared in Dorothy West's magazine *Challenge*, which aimed to "bring out the prose and poetry of newer Negroes" in the United States and other parts of the African diaspora.[190]

In the articles, Robeson informed her American audience about the varied roles blacks played in Paris. She observed that "Negroes form a definite part of Parisian life, and play an important and recognized role in the political, educational, intellectual, literary, and theatrical life of Paris, in the ordinary every-day life and in the night life."[191] Yet she was well aware that there was not a homogeneous united black community in Paris, commenting that "Negroes from the French West Indies (Antillean) dislike African Negroes because they have an older civilization; cultured Antilleans are often sent to Africa as civil servants by the French Government."[192] She also informed readers that before coming to Paris, Francophone Africans and Antilleans knew little about African Americans: "The average French Negro has no idea that there are important men and important work in Negro art in America. In Martinique, the Negroes think all American Negroes are prize-fighters, because a prize-fighter once visited the Antilles; they know nothing of Negro art and Negro music in America."[193] But in Paris, Robeson observed, African Americans, black Africans, and Antilleans began to learn more about their cultural differences and similarities, thanks in part to the role of figures like Nardal and others whom Robeson interviewed. Like the writings of Nardal and Marson, Robeson's "Black Paris" shows how print culture was a space for black women to give voice to black internationalism in Europe.

Getting an in-depth insight into black politics and culture was not the only reason why Robeson ventured to Paris. In the early 1930s, the Robesons' marriage faced difficulty. Paul Robeson conducted numerous affairs and intended to divorce Eslanda Robeson in order to marry white British actress Yolande Jackson. Eslanda went to Paris to gain evidence of Paul Robeson's extramarital affairs to help in the divorce proceedings the couple planned to file. During their separation, Eslanda began having relationships with other men but by 1933 the two reconciled and decided to practice an open marriage. Above all, the encounters Robeson had with blacks in Paris deepened her interest in learning more about Francophone and Anglophone African culture and history, which prompted her in 1933 to read anthropology at the LSE.[194]

Studying anthropology expanded the networks and friendships through which Robeson practiced black internationalism.[195] Like the Sorbonne, the LSE was a cosmopolitan academic institution that welcomed a large cohort of students from the Americas, Asia, and Africa. Anthropology was a prominent and popular course to study at the LSE given the renowned expertise of academics like Polish-born professor Bronisław Malinowski and New Zealand economic anthropologist Raymond Firth.[196] Many black colonials gravitated to anthropology in their attempts to learn more about European colonialism and contribute to overturning racist myths and stereotypes about people of African descent.[197]

Robeson befriended a host of African students, including Jomo Kenyatta, the Nigerian Nathaniel Akinremi Fadipe, Ugandan student Akiki Nyabongo, South African Z. K. Matthews, later a leader in the African National Congress (ANC), and African American Allison Davis.[198] Robeson enjoyed her time at the LSE, regularly attending seminars, and wrote a letter to her friend and fellow anthropologist Zora Neale Hurston about some of her experiences. In response, Hurston wrote, "What you tell me about your studies is thrilling. I feel so keenly that you have at last set your feet on the right road."[199] At the LSE, Robeson formed a particularly close bond with Kenyatta, who she described as a "brilliant, informed, gentle, tolerant, courageous human being."[200] Kenyatta helped Robeson break out of the academic restrictions she faced when studying anthropology. She explained that "before I met Kenyatta . . . I was studying anthropology (and Africa) in theory. Kenyatta brought it to life for me. . . . I was fascinated by his stories, and he . . . gave me much interesting and useful information about his tribe, the Kikuyu."[201] This comment shows that Robeson was more interested in understanding African lives in Africa than in abstract theories within the discipline, an inclination that would later inform her fieldwork and travels to sub-Saharan Africa.

A year after she enrolled at the LSE, Robeson travelled again, this time to the Soviet Union. The country was seen as an ally in struggles against racism due to its claim to practice nondiscrimination towards women and its religious and ethnic minorities, and its capital served as an important contact zone for black internationalist activity.[202] The 1930s marked the zenith of African American interest in the Soviet Union.[203] Numerous left-wing activists, artists, intellectuals, and workers ventured there, including W. E. B. Du Bois, Langston Hughes, Marian Anderson, William Patterson, Louise Thompson Patterson, Thyra Edwards, Williana Burroughs, Hermina Dumont Huiswoud, and Maude White.[204] In 1934, the Robesons embarked on their own "magic pilgrimage" to the communist nation.[205] They went to Moscow so that Paul Robeson could start working on a film with Soviet director Sergei Eisenstein about famed Haitian revolutionary leader Toussaint L'Ouverture.[206] During their stay, Eslanda and Paul Robeson interacted with a host of famous blacks such as Marian Anderson and William Patterson.[207] The trip also turned into an unplanned Goode family reunion, as Eslanda Robeson's brother, Frank, had recently moved to the country, where he eventually settled.[208]

In the Soviet Union, the Robesons' celebrity status ensured that they received special treatment. The couple were escorted around the most modern hospitals and schools.²⁰⁹ Their heavily supervised trip meant that they saw only positive aspects of a contradictory country.²¹⁰ While the Soviet Union passionately proclaimed the absence of state-sanctioned racism, persecution of its religious and ethnic minorities raged. Like its western neighbors, the Soviet Union's imperial reach controlled millions of non-Europeans.²¹¹ As the 1930s progressed, ex-communists such as George Padmore criticized the hypocrisy of the Soviet empire. The Robesons, however, remained unaware of Stalin's purges of dissidents and were enthusiastic about the country, sending Pauli to spend part of his school years there. The fact that Eslanda Robeson was interested in communism and the Soviet Union is related to her interest in radical left-wing politics, which, unlike Nardal and Marson, she developed during her time in Europe and which would strengthen in the following decades.

. . .

Nardal, Marson, and Robeson challenged the racist and sexist experiences that they faced in 1920s and 1930s Europe by playing an active role in the creation of and participation in the transnational black public sphere, which enabled them to practice varied internationalisms. For Nardal, this was evident in her writings in black newspapers and in the Clamart salon. Although these spaces were short-lived, they were significant due to the ways in which Nardal brought a gendered lens to black internationalism.

Marson's involvement with the LCP was an avenue through which she emphasized the need for racial unity within the political and creative spheres. Her writings also exemplified divisions among blacks about how racial unity should be cultivated. Yet the LCP offered no room for Marson to express feminism. In turning to feminist international groups, Marson was able to speak both about issues relating to gender and race beyond London in other parts of Europe. Through her involvement with the BCL she was able to give voice to her increasing anti-colonialism, which she could not express in the LCP. Her brief spell working at the LoN demonstrates how she also contributed to liberal internationalism.

Like Marson, Robeson practiced black internationalism in London. For Robeson, it was through her work with WASU, her writings in black newspapers, and her academic studies at the LSE. Unlike the other two women, Robeson's travels to Paris and Moscow show how she linked together different parts of black Europe. In further contrast to the two other women, Robeson's experiences led to the early development of her radical politics.

The years 1920–1935 were pivotal in laying the foundations of the women's practices as race women internationalists. When war was declared in an East African country in 1935 and a European nation in 1936, all three women would expand their networks within the public sphere and practice other types of internationalisms.

2

The Italian Invasion of Ethiopia, the Spanish Civil War, and Anti-fascist Internationalism, 1935–1939

In late October 1935, 400,000 Italian soldiers marched across the Mareb River and spread the disease of war from Europe to the Horn of Africa, four years before war infected the world.[1] Italian dictator Benito Mussolini invaded Ethiopia (also known as Abyssinia) to avenge Italy's defeat by the Ethiopian army at the 1896 Battle of Adowa. Like his European enemies and allies, Mussolini had his sights set on strengthening the Italian empire and sought Africa as his new backyard. By invoking humanitarian sympathy, Mussolini emphasized the benign, almost benevolent nature of the invasion, arguing that the Italians would liberate Ethiopians from slavery, which was mapped along religious, ethnic, and color lines. Slavery played a role in weakening the already weak Ethiopian emperor, Haile Selassie, who was struggling to unify competing ethnic groups.[2]

Existing tensions between Italy and Ethiopia concerning the Walwal border began in November 1934 and precipitated the October invasion.[3] The League of Nations (LoN), Britain, France, and the Soviet Union aided Italy's egregious encroachment by imposing meek sanctions, which failed to include an embargo on oil, Italy's most essential import.[4] The LoN's policy not to sell arms to countries at war meant that, in contrast to the militarily strong Italy, assisted by its fascist friend Nazi Germany, Ethiopia remained an unequipped underdog.[5]

The Italian invasion of Ethiopia sent shock waves throughout the African continent and its diaspora. In South Africa, black workers protested and refused to load ships bound for Italy. Two thousand black South Africans tried to enlist in the Ethiopian army, as did around five hundred British Guianese, but their governments refused to allow this.[6] Strikes erupted in British Guiana and on the island of St. Lucia. In Trinidad, numerous "Hands Off Abyssinia" rallies occurred.[7] In

London, the crisis politicized the League of Coloured Peoples (LCP), and the group raised money for refugees fleeing the conflict and petitioned the crown to intervene.[8] In Harlem, riots broke out, with skirmishes between blacks and Italian Americans, worsening long-standing tensions. In New York and Washington, DC, scores of aid organizations were formed, including the Committee for Ethiopia, the Ethiopian Research Council, the Provisional Committee for the Defense of Ethiopia, the American Committee for the Defense of Ethiopia, and the Friends of Ethiopia, to name a few.[9] African Americans founded and led the majority of these groups, apart from the interracial American Committee on the Ethiopian Crisis/American Aid for Ethiopia and the Committee for Ethiopia.[10] Even well-established organizations like the NAACP tried to lobby the US government on behalf of Ethiopia, but to no avail.

Ethiopia's special significance spurred the rapid reaction to the war among people of African descent. Despite Selassie's reluctance to be identified as "black" or "Negro," Ethiopia remained the "jewel in the crown of an imagined black world" due to its 7,000-year independence.[11] Its Christian history ensured its critical contribution to ancient civilization. In scripture, Psalm 68:31 prophesied that "princes shall come out of Egypt; Ethiopia shall soon stretch out her hands unto God," which was understood as God's promise to bring those of African descent out of suppression.[12] The invasion appeared to map onto a seemingly obvious black-versus-white racial divide, with black nationalists seeing it as a race war, while communists read it as the start of a fascist war.[13] It triggered the beginning of the Popular Front, a period when the Communist Party of the United States of America (CPUSA) forged left-liberal links to halt the tide of fascism.[14]

The Italian-Ethiopian crisis changed the attitude that descendant Africans in the diaspora had towards Africa. Acclaimed African American journalist Roi Ottley knew of "no event in recent times that has stirred the rank-and-file of Negroes more than the Italo-Ethiopian War."[15] For many black Americans, it altered the dominant narrative of "uplift" promoted through missionary, emigration, and repatriation schemes in the nineteenth century to one of collaboration and compassion, which was echoed in Langston Hughes's poem "The Ballad of Ethiopia," where he implored,[16]

> All you colored peoples
> No matter where you be
> Take for your slogan
> Africa be free.[17]

With mass rallies, telegrams, and delegations, African Americans played important roles in Ethiopian politics.[18] Communists helped establish the Provisional Committee for the Defense of Ethiopia, which united Harlem-based Communists and nationalists to forge community activism on behalf of Ethiopia.[19]

In the Caribbean, the war dovetailed with the rise of Pan-Africanism and working-class political consciousness. In Trinidad, it also infiltrated popular culture. The 1936 calypso "The Gold in Africa" by artist Growling Tiger attacked Mussolini's invasion of Ethiopia with lyrical wit and humor.[20] The calypso begins with Growling Tiger disputing Mussolini's public statements and arguing that the reason behind the invasion was that Mussolini wants gold in Africa. Growling Tiger called Mussolini a criminal and offers a few alternative suggestions of countries Italy could invade if it wants imperial power, citing Japan, England, and France. With these lyrics, it was no surprise that the colonial government labelled the song seditious and banned it.

A year after the Italian invasion, the war between General Francisco Franco's fascist forces and Republican Loyalists erupted in Spain. The roots of the Spanish Civil War originated from deep-seated political, social, and economic divisions among figures on the right and left and in the church.[21] The crisis that began on July 17, 1936, the day Franco launched the insurrection, galvanized African diasporic mobilization. Although many African Americans could not fight for Ethiopia, they resolved to play a part in the anti-fascist struggle by fighting for Republican Spain.

In a short story about the war entitled "700 Calendar Days" one African American, Oscar Hunton, who wanted to go to Ethiopia explained his decision to fight for the Republican cause, quipping that Spain "ain't Ethiopia, but it'll do."[22] Hunton was one of the 80–100 African American soldiers who enlisted in the Abraham Lincoln Battalion, an international brigade that rallied against Franco.[23] These men saw links between events in Ethiopia and Spain, which was captured in the communist slogan "Ethiopia's fate is at stake on the battle fields of Spain."[24] So too did Nardal, Marson, and Robeson.

The Italian invasion of Ethiopia and the Spanish Civil War prompted Nardal, Marson, and Robeson to work under the broad banner of anti-fascist internationalism that was also linked to other internationalisms. Nardal and Marson were both emotionally affected by the attack on Ethiopia and became important activists in Paris and London, providing humanitarian relief, raising funds, and informing the public on the war. Their versatile activism saw them move in and out of republican, colonial, communist, women's, Pan-African, academic, and Catholic networks. Rather than attaching themselves to one particular organization, they bridged political, gender, class, and religious divides, which enabled them to create overlapping, connected networks that expanded their anti-fascist, black, and Christian internationalism. In contrast, through travelling to various countries in Africa, Robeson contributed to the defense of not only Ethiopia but Africa as a whole, which strengthened her anti-colonial politics and black internationalism. Similarly, her sojourn to war-torn Spain in 1938 led to her standing in coalition with Republican Spain and playing a role in anti-fascist internationalism.

"RISE OF THE RACES": NARDAL'S AND MARSON'S RESPONSES TO THE ITALIAN INVASION OF ETHIOPIA

In the same month that Italian soldiers invaded Ethiopia, an article entitled "Rise of the Races/Levée des races," which had appeared in the French *Métromer*, was reprinted in the Senegalese newspaper *Le Périscope africain*.[25] Its author, Paulette Nardal, makes three important points. The first disputes the suggestion of some commentators that just because blacks were defending Ethiopia and Japan was supporting them, this alliance represented the coming of a "race war." She explains that the Ethiopian crisis had captured the "attention of the entire world" and reminds readers that during the First World War, ten thousand Somalis had volunteered to fight for France.[26] These facts proved that rather than a race war, those who supported the Ethiopians were fighting a war for democracy.[27]

The second argument she emphasizes is that the Ethiopian crisis elicited an emotional, racial, and rational response. It stirred among "black populations disseminated around the world—who still yesterday were so indifferent to one another . . . [a] common soul again in the common defense of Ethiopia." This common soul exists because they remain connected to their racial identity despite being "so loyal, so assimilated, so conformist" to European colonialism. According to Nardal, "the reasoned element of this awareness of racial solidarity is on one hand a reaction against the feeling of inferiority that one sought to inculcate in the *Noir*, and on the other hand his original sense of justice."[28] In other words, Nardal understood the Ethiopian crisis through the lens of race and equality.

Her third point is that the black diasporic response to the war represents a humanistic reaction because both whites and blacks want a type of colonialism geared "toward more humane ends."[29] Rather than challenging colonialism, Nardal wants it to be reformed to improve the rights of all its subjects. The article offers a snapshot into why the normally moderate Nardal found herself at the center of radical anti-fascist networks.

In the spring of 1935, Paris served as the home of several left-wing organizations and activists committed to defending Ethiopia. The initial gathering of the International Committee for the Defense of the Ethiopian People/Comité international pour la défense du peuple éthiopien, held in September, brought together around eighty blacks, whites, and Arabs.[30] Feminist and women-led groups active in the struggle included the Egyptian Feminist Union/Union féministe egyptienne, the International League of Women, and Women Educators for Peace/Ligue internationale des méres et éducatrices pour la paix, and the World Committee of Women against War and Fascism/Comité mondial des femmes contre la guerre et le fascisme.[31] Nardal supported these groups but chose to participate in black, male-dominated communist organizations, which offered her a chance to continue to practice black internationalism.

Unlike Marson or Robeson, Nardal was most active in creating new anti-fascist and humanitarian organizations that collaborated with a range of other political groups. Her first foray into activism began when she cofounded the organization Ethiopian Action Committee/Comité d'action éthiopienne (CAE) on May 18 alongside a group of communist-affiliated Antillean and African men. These included the Martiniquan René Maran, the Sudanese Tiémoko Garan Kouyaté, the Dahomean Augustin Azango, the Malagasy Albert Raakoto Ratisimamango, and the Martiniquan R. Cenac Thaly.[32] Their activities aroused the attention of the Paris police force. In 1935, the police opened a file about activists involved in the Ethiopian struggle, noting the dates and times of meetings and information about members' birthplaces, educational statuses, addresses, and sometimes their personal lives.

According to a Parisian police report dated in August, the CAE "has a clear goal, that of defending specifically the policy of the Emperor of Ethiopia. The group is trained in the delicate game of current global politics." The report further notes that the CAE sent a telegram outlining its aims to the LoN. The CAE had also printed thousands of copies of a thirty-page bulletin to recruit members, and "several people of color from different nations have joined the group." The report lists the key figures involved in the organization and notes Nardal's new address in Paris at 50 rue Falguière, where she lived after leaving Clamart in April.[33] Furthermore, it states that Nardal is the mistress of Joseph Lagrosillière, deputy of Martinique.[34] There is no evidence to support this claim but it is significant. Privacy was certainly Nardal's preference and she rarely publicly wrote or spoke about her personal life. Given her committed Catholic faith, the claim made in the report seems inaccurate, but it reflects how far the police went in infiltrating the personal lives of the individuals they monitored. By accusing Nardal of having an affair with Lagrosillière, the police tried to discredit their professional credibility.

The CAE was a sprawling organization that collaborated with suffragists, the Comité international pour la défense du peuple éthiopien, and the French Communist League against Imperialism and Colonial Oppression/Ligue française contre l'impérialisme et l'oppression coloniale.[35] The CAE's links with other radical organizations further raised police suspicion. Another police report states that the CAE held an event on June 29 with the communist Negro Workers Union/Union des travailleurs nègres (UTN) at the Hotel des Sociétés Savantes, which attracted over 120 delegates. The CAE established a sister organization named Friends of the Ethiopian People/Les amis du peuple éthiopien that collected economic policy information documenting the social and political problems facing Ethiopia.[36]

While committed to the CAE, Nardal also worked with other groups. She participated in the Ethiopian Defense Committee/Comité de défense d'Éthiopie. The group aimed to "centralize, harmonize and stimulate their efforts towards a solidarity acting in favor of Ethiopia."[37] The Ethiopian Defense Committee shared transnational links with the London-based International African Friends of

Abyssinia, which later changed its name to the International African Friends of Ethiopia (IAFE).[38] Established in 1935 by C. L. R. James; Amy Ashwood Garvey; her partner, the Trinidadian musician Sam Manning; Barbadian radical Chris Jones; Peter Milliard from British Guiana; Theophilus Albert Marryshow from Grenada; Mohammed Said from Somaliland; I. T. A. Wallace from Sierra Leone; and Jomo Kenyatta, the IAFE was an influential black group advocating support and raising money for Ethiopia.[39]

As a leader within the IAFE, Ashwood Garvey campaigned on behalf of Ethiopia throughout Britain. On August 25, 1935, she spoke at Hyde Park, sharing the platform with the Ethiopian ambassador, Dr. Charles Martin, also known as Workeneh Eshete. Here, Ashwood Garvey declared that "no race has been so noble in forgiving" as blacks have and "the hour . . . [has come] for our complete emancipation."[40] Other speakers that day included Chris Jones, Arnold Ward, and Prince Ras Monolulu (born Peter McKay in St. Croix). Monolulu famously waved the Ethiopian flag in the background. Ashwood Garvey also spoke at Labour Party and League Against Imperialism meetings in London.[41] Under the auspices of the IAFE, she planned, but ultimately did not take, a fundraising trip to New York to buy medical supplies for Ethiopia with George Padmore, who had been recently expelled from the Communist Party because of his criticism of its imperial policy and who joined the IAFE when he moved to London. However, this plan did not materialize.[42]

The IAFE also worked with other groups including the Abyssinian Association, and British feminist Sylvia Pankhurst's weekly radical Pan-African newspaper *New Times and Ethiopia News*.[43] By 1937, the IAFE morphed into the radical International African Service Bureau (IASB). James and Padmore took the helm of this organization and its publications *International African Opinion, Africa and the World,* and *African Sentinel*. Ashwood Garvey waned into the background, and within a few years she left London and returned to the United States.[44]

Nardal also served as secretary to the pacifist World Committee against War and Fascism/Comité mondial contre la guerre et le fascisme and worked alongside members of the UTN to post its newspaper *Le Cri des nègres,* which condemned the invasion in its April-May issue.[45] It rarely included women's views, but Nardal became one of the first women to have her voice printed in the newspaper.[46] As secretary of the World Committee against War and Fascism, Nardal authored a memo reprinted in *Le Cri des nègres* that detailed information about the organization.[47] In it, Nardal explains that the group was "constituted outside of any political party" and invites "people moving in the spirit of justice to enlighten French public opinion on the need to prevent the Italo-Ethiopian conflict whose consequences pose a danger to world peace." Nardal's comment illustrates how she foretold the global ramifications of the Ethiopian crisis. The World Committee against War and Fascism comprised black women and men from Somalia, Algeria, the United

States, Cuba, Guadeloupe, Madagascar, Morocco, Martinique, Guyana, Tunisia, West Africa, Syria, China, Indochina, Japan, and South and Central America. The memo also includes the telegram that the organization sent to the LoN calling on it to honor Ethiopian independence because of its membership in the League.[48]

However, Nardal's role at the UTN provoked tensions. In a meeting of the UTN general assembly in October 1935, some members accused Kouyaté and Nardal of dividing blacks in Paris along class lines.[49] While her gender and class may have contributed to the tensions, Nardal did not comment on the nature of the problem. She managed to negotiate class and gender boundaries within the organization and administered funding raised in support of Ethiopia from the Gold Coast, Nigeria, and Sierra Leone through the International Committee for the Defense of Ethiopian People/Comité international pour la défense du peuple éthiopien, which had links to the UTN.[50] Two months after the UTN incident, the Nardal family suffered the loss of Paulette's sister Andrée, who died soon after her wedding. Throughout the coming months, Nardal grieved her sister's death while remaining engaged in the Ethiopian struggle.

Nardal's Ethiopian activism did not spring simply from her anti-fascist and pacifist political beliefs. It closely chimed with her Catholicism. She understood her involvement as linked to her belief in helping the oppressed. Catholics in France responded quickly to the invasion. In October 1935, eighty Catholic writers signed a manifesto in the Parisian daily newspaper *Le Journal* (1892–1944) and denounced "the inequality of the races."[51] Their views contrasted with that of the pope, who blessed the war.[52] Nevertheless, in April 1936, the Catholic University Association of Secular Missionaries/Association universitaire catholique des laïques missionnaires, a group Nardal belonged to, asked her and another black Martiniquan, the communist Anita Véry, to chair a series of conferences in Belgium, advocating international aid for Ethiopia.[53]

The spring of 1936 was a decisive period in the war, and the Italians had conquered most of the country. As Ethiopia looked set to fall, public opinion turned from sympathizing with the Ethiopians and moved towards blaming them for their inadequate military arsenal and criticizing Selassie's leadership. Nardal and Véry passionately appealed for an end to the Italo-Ethiopian war in Louvain, Ghent, Liège, Anvers, and Brussels.[54] While in Belgium, Nardal wrote a series of articles about the twists and turns of the war, "The Italo-Ethiopian Conflict and Colonization/Le conflit italo-éthiopien et la colonisation," in the Belgian journal *Revue de l'Aucam*.[55]

In all, Nardal's activism within the CAE and her travel to Belgium reveal the breadth of her anti-fascist and black internationalism. Although her political beliefs were conservative, the Ethiopian invasion forced her to expand her networks and work alongside groups whose politics decidedly differed from hers but who were united in defending the African country. As an elite black woman working in male- and working-class-dominated organizations, Nardal's actions demonstrate how committed she was to challenging gendered and class boundaries. Her faith guided her activism, and the fact that she worked with Catholic missionary groups demonstrates that she was willing to stand in opposition to the pontiff.

In London, Una Marson's response to the Ethiopian war differed from Nardal's in that she did not establish anti-fascist groups or collaborate with communists or radicals. Nor did religion play a part in her activism. But she was at the center of efforts to raise relief and increase British awareness about events in Ethiopia, thereby contributing to anti-fascist internationalism. Marson first heard news of Mussolini's intentions while working at the LoN headquarters in Geneva. Immediately, she contacted the head of the Ethiopian delegation, General Teele Hawariate, and expressed her wish to help what she saw as "another coloured country unfairly attacked." Unlike those who blamed the Ethiopians for the invasion, Marson confessed that she could not excuse herself "on the ground that the Abyssinians were backward and also divided among themselves. When people are in trouble we do not dwell on their faults."[56] Despite her belief in Ethiopia's backwardness, Marson desperately wanted to visit the country, but she was warned about potential dangers, so she accepted a position to assist at the Ethiopian legation in London as Charles Martin's English-speaking secretary, alongside Ethiopian student Emmanuel Abraham.[57]

At the legation, Marson began an intense study of Ethiopian culture, history, geography, and politics and corresponded with various agencies.[58] "The entire correspondence of the Legation passed through the Minister's hands to me," she recalled. "He made pencil notes on the letters and sent them to me. I dealt with thousands of thousands of letters."[59] Marson's involvement with the Ethiopian struggle occurred against a backdrop of the rise of fascism in Britain; Oswald Mosley had established the popular British Union of Fascists in 1932.[60] Her role at the legation challenged fascism in Britain and Italy and caught the attention of outside observers, who frequently called on her to give speeches about the invasion.[61]

In April 1936, the League of Nations Union (LNU) invited Marson to discuss Ethiopian politics at a West Ealing church. Formed in October 1918 in Britain, the LNU promoted the ideals of the LoN. According to historian Helen McCarthy, it "became one of Britain's largest voluntary associations and a powerful advocate of democratic accountability and popular engagement in the making of foreign policy."[62] In her speech, Marson disputed the centrality of slavery in Ethiopia, arguing that "slaves were merely a part of the establishment under a very mild form of serfdom. Many slaves now become free under certain conditions and all children born to slaves are also free."[63] She identified problems in Ethiopia not with internal divisions, but with external intervention. According to Marson, if the Ethiopians developed at their own pace, "not immediately opening up the resources of the country for the benefit of outsiders, their ultimate attainments would have been an advance on Western Civilization."⁶⁴ Marson's speech rehabilitated Ethiopia and by extension Africa's reputation by drawing on its history, an approach used by many other black intellectuals.⁶⁵

One month after Marson's speech on May 2, the Italian army conquered Ethiopia.⁶⁶ Selassie succumbed to defeat and travelled to England to arrange a negotiation. On June 3, he arrived at London's Waterloo station, receiving a warm welcome by the LCP, the IAFE, the Negro Welfare Association, the Pan-African Federation, the British Guiana Association, the Gold Coast Students Association, and the Kikuyu Association of Kenya, among others.⁶⁷ Although these groups welcomed Selassie with open arms, the British government did not emulate the gesture. Westminster and Whitehall rebuffed Selassie's requests for intervention, so he took his case directly to Geneva. Marson followed Selassie to Geneva, serving as his secretary. In this role, she saw firsthand the toll the war took on the leader. On June 30, she watched from the diplomatic gallery as Italian journalists heckled Selassie while he pleaded with the LoN in Amharic.⁶⁸ Marson also got to see the real challenges that Ethiopia faced in brokering peace. Despite Selassie's request for aid, the LoN remained staunch in its refusal to intervene.

After returning from Geneva, Marson resumed her work at the legation and was sought out by the Association for Ethiopia to join their organization.⁶⁹ But she suffered a nervous breakdown caused by her hectic work schedule. As her health deteriorated, she decided that it was time to return home, and she booked a two-week passage back to Jamaica. On September 24, 1936, the SS *Cavina* docked in Kingston Harbour, and newspaper journalists swarmed around Marson. Posing for photographers, she offered a sanguine sound bite affirming the strength of Selassie, a man who continued to retain "great faith in the British people, the League and his God." She candidly confessed her fears, saying, "The Italians are just waiting for the rains to be over and when they are, nothing will prevent them from going to the Western portion of Abyssinia and taking it over. Abyssinians cannot fight poison gas and they have not got ammunition. I do not know what will happen, nobody knows."⁷⁰ Marson's distress could be heard in her uncertainty, but in 1937 it turned into grief when she learned that the Italians had executed two of Charles Martin's sons, Benyan and Yosef. In response, Marson penned the poignant poem "To Joe and Ben," in which she admitted,

> I wept for you
> As you two gallant sons
> Went forth
> From the brightness
> Of an English summer
> To die
> On the mountain heights
> Of Ethiopia.⁷¹

Due to the success of the Italian army, Selassie remained in London until 1942, when a coalition consisting of the Ethiopian army and Free French, Belgian, and British forces successfully ended the Italian occupation of Ethiopia.[72]

Although differences existed between Nardal's and Marson's activism, they both behaved like "sociopolitical chameleons," to borrow Jennifer Boittin's term, attaching themselves to various political and religious networks that widened their anti-fascist and black internationalism and enabled them to travel to other parts of Europe.[73] Eslanda Robeson did not adopt this practice. For her, the events in Ethiopia overlapped with her anthropological studies, furthering her desire to travel to sub-Saharan Africa, which deepened her anti-colonialism and served as another way for her to practice black internationalism.

A VOYAGE TO THE CONTINENT: ESLANDA ROBESON IN SUB-SAHARAN AFRICA

In May 1936, Eslanda Robeson undertook a three-month journey visiting South Africa, Basutoland, Uganda, Kenya, Sudan, the Congo, Tanzania, and Egypt alongside her eager eight-year-old son Pauli. In her diary, she scribbled notes, the names of people she met, and the places she visited, extracts of which appeared in her landmark 1945 text *African Journey*, which differed from standard anthropological texts produced by scholars like Bronislaw Malinowski, Franz Boas, and Melville Herskovits. Although *African Journey* included historical facts, economic statistics, and ethnographic photographs, it also relied heavily on the tradition of racial vindication literature.[74] African American anthropologists who engaged in vindicationist scholarship, argue anthropologists Faye V. Harrison and Ira E. Harrison, "emerged in reaction to racist assertions that Africans are degraded savages, that Africans and African Americans have no culture."[75] *African Journey* shared traits with Zora Neale Hurston's 1938 quasi-anthropological text *Tell My Horse: Voodoo and Life in Haiti and Jamaica*. Robeson and Hurston practiced on the margins of the discipline. In the words of cultural anthropologist Maureen Mahon, Robeson "constructed a text that reached beyond an academic audience while making an argument about the integrity of black culture." Robeson placed herself and Pauli in the narrative, writing in a lively style, allowing the reader a window into her personality and politics.[76]

The reasons behind Robeson's voyage were personal and political. In the opening paragraph of *African Journey*, she divulges, "I wanted to go to Africa. It began when I was quite small. Africa was the place we Negroes came from originally. Lots of Americans, when they could afford it, went back to see their 'old country.'"[77] Her identification of Africa as a "country," not a continent, indicates Robeson's early romanticization of an imagined black Africa. Pauli joined his mother so he too could learn about his "old country." Having spent the majority of his life in Europe, Pauli was "astonished and delighted to see all the Africans" on the set of his father's 1935 film *Sanders of the River*.[78] In the film, Paul Robeson played an African chief, and Jomo Kenyatta had a small role too.[79] *Sanders of the River* portrayed negative stereotypes of Africans that offended many blacks. The film embarrassed the Robesons and is known as one of the last pro-colonial film roles Paul Robeson played.[80] On the film set, Pauli remarked, "Why, there are lots of brown people . . . lots of black people too; we're not the only ones." His parents were "profoundly disturbed by the realization that he had been living in an entirely white world." They decided to open up Pauli's worldview; their hope was that "he will see millions of other brown and black people, he will see a black world."[81]

The fruitful but often frustrating encounters Robeson had with her peers and professors at the London School of Economics (LSE) were another motivation for her African visit. Even though she boldly declared, "I *am* Negro, I *know* what we think, how we feel. I know this means that, and that means so-and-so," staff and students consistently called her European.[82] Robeson protested, declaring, "What do you mean I'm European? I'm *Negro*. I'm African myself . . . How dare you call me European!" She informed her classmates that "going to school and having money doesn't make me a European. Having no schools and no money doesn't make the African primitive." Yet, her lack of fieldwork experience left her vulnerable to accusations such as "'You've never been out there, you've never seen them and talked with them on their home ground; you can't possibly know.'"[83] She made up her mind "to go out to Africa and see and meet and study and talk with my people on their home ground. Then I [will] be able to say truly: I have been there too, and I *know*."[84]

With the help of African friends in London, Robeson planned what she described as an "ambitious" travel itinerary.[85] It consisted of travelling by sea from "England to Cape Town and Port Elizabeth" before meeting her African friend Rosebery Bokwe, "who had finished medicine at Edinburgh University . . . and his sister Frieda and her husband, Zach Matthews, whom we had known in London." Next, mother and son "would go to Johannesburg and maybe see the mines; and perhaps work in a trip to Swaziland; and maybe . . . run up to see Tshekedi Khama, the African regent."[86] After this they planned to visit Mozambique and Mombasa, then meet Akiki Nyabongo in Kampala and follow him to his home in Toro, where Robeson planned to do fieldwork on herdspeople before flying home from Entebbe.[87] Robeson's itinerary was costly but aided by Paul Robeson's financial assistance.

Before Eslanda Robeson could begin her intrepid voyage, however, she needed to secure various visas. This proved far more challenging than she had expected and made her realize that "if you are Negro, you can't make up your mind to go to Africa, and just go."[88] Fearful of the spread of anti-colonial dissent, the British and French colonial officials were particularly wary of high-profile African Americans visiting Africa. Robeson came to understand their anxiety, writing:

> The white people in Africa do not want educated Negroes traveling around seeing how their brothers live; nor do they want those brothers seeing Negroes from other parts of the world, hearing how they live. It would upset them, make them restless and dissatisfied; it would make them examine and re-examine the conditions under which they, as "natives," live; and that would never do at all.... In fact it would be extremely dangerous.[89]

The potentially subversive nature of Robeson's trip as a lone African American woman piqued concern at the Colonial Office. But after she presented her academic credentials from the LSE, she assuaged their worries and they helped arrange her visas.[90] The one visa Robeson did not receive was from South Africa. After numerous visits to South Africa House, Robeson understood that officials viewed her intention to travel there as suspicious. Rather than feeling discouraged, she decided that "Pauli and I will just get on that ship, with or without visas. When we get there, all they can do is to refuse to let us land. If they do that, I'll set up a howl there," and she told Paul to "set up a real howl" in London "and then maybe they'll do something." Paul Robeson thought the idea sounded "just crazy enough to work."[91] But it never came to fruition. On May 30, 1936, Eslanda and Pauli Robeson commenced their African journey, climbing on board the SS *Winchester Castle* at Southampton harbor. When they arrived in South Africa, they managed to enter the country without any "howls" because the connections they had made with prominent South Africans eased their passage.

As soon as she set sail, Robeson's anti-colonialism was evident through the copious comparisons she made between the ways in which racism operated in South Africa and in the American South. On board the ship, Robeson noticed that her fellow passengers were "mostly South Africans, whose attitude toward the Negro I find very familiar, very like that of our 'Deep South' Southern white folks in America, only more so."[92] Throughout the country, Eslanda Robeson found herself "recognizing the tone of voice, the inflection of these South Africans. 'Native' is their word for our 'nigger'; 'non-European' for our Negro; 'European' means white; and 'South African' surprisingly enough does not mean the millions of original black people there, but the white residents born there, as distinguished from the white residents born in Europe who are called 'colonials' or 'settlers.'"[93]

She compared the covert modes of travelling in South Africa and in the Jim Crow South, noting, "You are passed from friend to friend, from car to car, from home to home, often covering thousands of miles without enduring the inconveniences and humiliations of the incredibly bad Jim Crow train accommodations and lack of hotel facilities for Negroes."[94] Robeson noticed how class structured racism when she drew parallels between African Americans and poor white South Africans. Of poor whites, she remarked, "It is said they are lazy, shiftless, and ignorant.... The same things are said about Negroes."[95] Throughout her travels, Robeson felt sympathy and empathy towards poor Africans, black and white, often giving money to the poor she passed on the road. When she and Pauli gave a "charming Basuto family two half-crowns," she remarked that they thanked them with "such dignity I could have cried."[96] But when Pauli gave a couple of coppers to poor white children, they received "no thanks of any kind. An unpleasant sight."[97]

The many comments Robeson made about the similarities of racism in South Africa and the United States demonstrate how her trip deepened her knowledge about the links between colonial and racial oppression in South Africa and the Jim Crow South that was linked to her Pan-Africanism. The emphasis Robeson placed on similarity was also linked to what Mahon has described as Robeson's articulation of "diasporic politics of identification" based on a "self-conscious construction of connections among people of African descent that views their history and fates as linked and considers that link to be politically, culturally and emotionally meaningful."[98]

During the trip, Robeson forged new friendships with activists that enabled her to gain more insight into local and global politics. For instance, she met North Carolina–born Max Yergan, a community activist working for the YMCA, with whom she would collaborate closely in the coming years. Through Matthews and Yergan, Robeson befriended Alfred Xuma, another important ANC leader. Her meetings with these figures led to fervent political discussion about the Italo-Ethiopian war, political unrest in India, the education of African and black American children, the role of Japan in Manchuria, the Spanish Civil War, and former German African colonies. The "big talk, challenging ideas, [and] enthralling discussion" that Robeson had with her friends in South Africa had a lasting legacy. She acknowledged that "the walls of our world moved outward, and we caught a glimpse of things in the large."[99] During her stay in South Africa, Robeson also attended the historic All-African National Convention held in Bloemfontein. There, Robeson met with female leaders and discussed health, child policy, and women's organizations across the world.[100] An emphasis on the political role and agency of African women features heavily in *African Journey*, and Robeson repeatedly disproves the notion that African women were uninterested in politics.

After their stay in South Africa, the Robesons ventured to Uganda. There, Eslanda Robeson benefitted from the "young, intelligent, friendly, and efficient" expertise of Nyabongo.[101] He knew the history and background of the Toro people and helped Eslanda Robeson conduct research. While closely watching the Toro's herding practices, Robeson took the opportunity to reflect on the anthropological discipline she hoped to master and asked a group of Ugandans "what they thought of visiting anthropologists, and how they liked being 'investigated.'" They responded by taking "the searching and impertinent questions as a game, giving the most teasing, joking, and fantastic answers they could think of, so that the interpreter would have a most difficult time trying to translate the answers into something that would sound 'serious and respectful.' (Shades of scientific anthropological data!)"[102] The fact that Robeson sought out the answer to this question illustrates her unease with the comments that LSE students had made to her in the past. It suggests her complicated relationship to anthropology and her awareness of the limits of academic research that would later lead her to focus more on journalism.

In Uganda, Eslanda Robeson formed close bonds with the "delightful, intelligent, companionable" Toro women. While some of the women spoke English, Robeson also tried to learn their Rotoro language.[103] Despite communication challenges, the women "often went off into gales of laughter over misunderstandings, and we all agreed after the second day that one of the most important words in any language is 'why?'"[104] These women nursed Robeson and Pauli back to health when they suffered from indigestion, a reminder that illness was a common consequence of travelling in Africa. These interactions provide another example of how Robeson actively engendered connections with African women. Through her interactions with women, Robeson also became aware of class divisions. She remarked that she found it "very hard to accept this division of Africans here in Uganda into upper and lower classes, yet everywhere it exists. There is a definite aristocracy usually connected with cattle, and a definite common man usually connected with agriculture."[105] These class divisions mapped onto gender inequalities.

Eslanda and Pauli also briefly ventured to Central Africa. In the Congo they confronted the fact that neither class, nor wealth, nor fame, nor education, nor being a *distinguée* (a distinguished elite) could bleach one's complexion. While trying to secure accommodation for the evening, a white hotel manager refused to accommodate Eslanda, Pauli, and the two black African men who travelled with them. The white district commissioner intervened on their behalf but managed only to get one room for Eslanda and Pauli. The two men were forced to sleep in the cars. When the Robesons opened the door to their room, they found a space "scarcely fit for animals."[106] In this instance, the Congolese racial hierarchy placed Eslanda and Pauli with the Africans, strengthening their solidarity.

A trip to Entebbe, a large town in Uganda, which Robeson described as a "European world in the very heart of Africa," and a visit to the British governor of Uganda were the last visits on the Robesons' itinerary.[107] On their penultimate day in Uganda, Eslanda and Pauli attended a dinner at the governor's house. Robeson described him as a "friendly, intelligent man, interested in and anxious to get on with his job of administration," but she was "firmly against patriarchal administration." He asked her for suggestions about improvements the colonial government could make in Uganda, which proved to be a "quandary" because she felt she couldn't tell him she believed "his office should be held by an African."[108] Nonetheless, she offered three recommendations: that there should be improvements in higher education for Africans; that the governor should query the reports by district commissioners, who are disliked by the community; and that the colonials should try to learn the local languages. The governor kindly received Robeson's suggestions.[109] Yet later that night she asked herself a set of testing questions, "Should I have said more to the Governor? Should I have posed some of the problems? Was this the time and place? Had I muffed an opportunity?"[110] She concluded, "I had gone as far as I could with His Excellency." Robeson consoled herself with the news that at least discussions about improving African education circulated.[111]

The following day, exhausted but excited, Eslanda and Pauli arrived at Entebbe Airport to take their first plane flight together. On the plane, the Robesons encountered a stereotypical English colonial from South Africa. He was "on the elderly side, red faced, choleric, and given to asserting himself" and had "the utmost contempt for 'the blacks.'"[112] Of Pauli, he uttered, "Pity he's black. Pity. Could go far." Robeson, rising to her son's defense, replied, "He'll go far *because* he's black. . . . His color, his background, his rich history are part of his wealth. We consider it an asset, not a handicap." She felt sorry for the "typical Colonial," who seemed "weak, uncomfortably self-conscious, lonely, pathetic, and frightened."[113] As for her black kin all over the world, she claimed, "We have not built any walls to limit our world. Walls have been built against us, but we are always fighting to tear them down, and in the fighting, we grow, we find new strength, new scope." She summarized her thoughts by declaring, "I am glad and proud I am Negro."[114]

Robeson's pride did not stem from her trip, but the ups and downs of her time in Africa strengthened her racial consciousness and her views against fascism and colonialism and her support for women's equality. This change was evident in her stressing throughout *African Journey* the promising future of Africa and Africans. The text is evidence of how Robeson strove to give voice to the modernity of Africa as a continent "involved in international politics and populated by intelligent citizens who maintained cultural traditions in spite of colonialism and were capable of self-governance."[115] The strengthening of Robeson's anti-colonialism and widened black internationalism was evidenced when she returned to London and the following year helped to establish, alongside Paul Robeson, the International Committee on African Affairs (ICAA).

The ICAA sought to educate the public on conditions in Africa. High-profile European, African, Caribbean, African American, and Indian intellectuals, liberals, Christians, and corporate philanthropists were part of the group. Members included Ralph Bunche, Max Yergan, René Maran, Alfred Xuma, Mordecai Johnson, D. D. T. Jabavu (a professor at Fort Hare), Hubert T. Delany, Fred and Edith Field, Channing Tobias, Frieda Nuegebauer, Mary Van Kleek, and Raymond Buell.[116] That Robeson was the first contributor to the ICAA, generously donating $300, shows her firm belief in the importance of the organization.[117] Her role, albeit initially small, grew when the ICAA transformed into the Council on African Affairs (CAA) in 1942 in the United States.

The CAA promoted links between the struggle for African American rights and colonized people globally. Paul Robeson served as chair of the CAA, stating, "Our fight for Negro rights here is linked inseparably . . . with the liberation movements of the peoples of the Caribbean and Africa and of the colonial world in general."[118] A number of leading activists, journalists, and scholars influenced the CAA, including Yergan, Mary McLeod Bethune, W. E. B. Du Bois, E. Franklin Frazier, Alphaeus Hunton, and Charlotta Bass.[119] Through their involvement with the CAA, the Robesons got to know the future Ghanaian leader Kwame Nkrumah, whom they had first met in London.[120]

In the same year that the ICAA was established, Marson's health was restored and she resumed practicing anti-fascist and black internationalism through her role as a writer, reflecting on her Ethiopian activism, promoting Jamaican nationalism, and celebrating the African aspects of its culture.

JAMAICA'S AFRICAN CULTURE 1937-1938

By the end of 1936, Una Marson had recovered, and the following year her career received a boost when she joined the editorial team of a new weekly progressive publication, *Public Opinion*.[121] Created at a time of nationalist political fervor, *Public Opinion* sought to give Jamaica a "voice in her own destinies."[122] It paralleled the growth of political parties, specifically the Peoples National Party (PNP), led by former Rhodes scholar Norman Manley, and was the organ for the party. A member of Jamaica's brown and near-white upper-middle class, Manley was a leading lawyer who was married to white Jamaican artist Edna Manley. His cousin Alexander Bustamante was an important figure in the labor movement, and in 1943 he founded the conservative Jamaican Labour Party (JLP), the political wing of Bustamante's Industrial Trade Union established in 1938, which stood in opposition to the PNP.[123] The PNP had been established in the midst of labor riots that swept across the Anglophone Caribbean between 1934 and 1938. In Jamaica, riots broke out at the Frome Sugar Factory in Westmoreland as workers demanded better wages and working conditions and an end to racial discrimination. The disturbances were quelled by military action. They soon triggered riots elsewhere in the region and led to a government inquiry, known as the Moyne Commission.[124]

Public Opinion emerged out of the growth of literary writing throughout the Anglophone Caribbean and shared similarities to *Beacon* and *Kyk-Over-Al*, both based in Trinidad.[125] Unlike Jamaica's largest newspaper, the *Daily Gleaner*, it mixed culture with left-wing politics and was part of the transnational black press.[126] The editors included Jamaican writers and political activists like O. T. Fairclough, Frank Hill, H. P. Jacobs, and Edna Manley. Women's voices appeared frequently—namely, those of Marson, Manley, teacher and activist Amy Bailey, Aimee Webster, and Eulalie Domingo, the pianist and wife of nationalist W. A.

Domingo, who was active in New York. Sarcastic, sage, and sometimes controversial, Marson's columns focused on religion, feminism, civil society, crime, tourism, and the plight of children. The latter issue was of particular concern to Marson and in June 1938 she established the Jamaican branch of Save the Children, known as Jamsave.

Marson also used the pages of *Public Opinion* to reflect on her Ethiopian activism. In July 1937, she wrote an article entitled "Racial Feelings?," where she unleashed an attack on Jamaicans for their apparent lack of racial consciousness and compassion towards Ethiopia. She explains how her work at the delegation had exposed her to the "reaction of peoples in all parts of the world to the Abyssinian crisis," and she "watched with greatest interest the mail that came in from coloured peoples—letters of sympathy, cuttings from newspapers, [and] donations." But, she notes, "as lists of donations from various sources were frequently made public, I commit no breach when I say that Jamaica showed the smallest part of sympathy, practical or otherwise as compared with all other coloured countries of the world."[127] The reason why Jamaicans showed so little support to Ethiopia was, in Marson's opinion, that they lacked "racial feelings."

According to Marson, if Jamaicans "regarded themselves as being bound by blood ties to coloured peoples throughout the world, there would have been some such spontaneous evidence of sympathy when the fortunes of the last great Black Empire were at stake." She denounces Jamaicans who refuse to see themselves as descendant Africans, recounting conversations with Jamaicans who told her "'I regret the coloured blood in me' or 'I refuse to be called a Negro.'" Marson stresses that "some of the finest and bravest men that ever lived came out of Africa and the coloured people of America are the most progressive in the world because they have now accepted themselves." By emphasizing the strengths that derive from racial acceptance, Marson uses the example of African Americans to challenge Jamaicans who lack racial solidarity.[128] Her positive statements about African Americans resonate with the beginning of a correspondence she began with James Weldon Johnson in 1937.[129] She started writing to Johnson after her friend the Jamaican writer Rupert Meikle sent him a copy of *The Moth and the Star*. Over the next eight months, she and Johnson discussed her poetry and Marson sought his advice on how she could publish her work in the United States.

In "Racial Feelings?" Marson comments that her conversations with "people from Ceylon, India, [and] Africa on such matters, and even with other West Indians ... make one hang the head in shame at the disloyalty of coloured Jamaicans to their island and to one another." Rather than invoke shame as a strategy to reinforce the dominance of brownness and whiteness, Marson uses it as a weapon to chastise Jamaicans for persistent divisions. At the end of the article, Marson appeals to Jamaicans to "not be ashamed to be a link in the great chain of dark-skinned peoples. History has shown us, and is showing us today that there is as much barbarity among white races as among black races."[130] By invoking the barbarity of white races, she challenged the myth of black savagery.

But Marson's critique was misguided. She overlooked the work of Universal Negro Improvement Association leaders who organized Ethiopian Allied Defence fraternities in 1935.[131] The Ethiopian crisis also influenced riots in Jamaica in the late 1930s.[132] Furthermore, Marson failed to take into account that the crisis in Ethiopia spurred the growth of the Rastafarian movement in the slums of Kingston. In other words, she oversimplified the response to the Ethiopian crisis.

While the Italian invasion of Ethiopia galvanized many people of African descent, it also divided opinion. Some African Americans, for instance, argued that donating money to Ethiopia diverted attention from the pressing problems they faced.[133] In 1935, the *Pittsburgh Courier* made the following statement in an editorial: "Much as we all sympathize with Ethiopia, it is evident that our burdens here are sufficiently heavy without assuming those of Negroes 7000 miles away. It is noteworthy that, while our disabilities have been fairly well publicized throughout the world since Emancipation, no aid has ever come from our brethren across the seas."[134] Many shared this viewpoint. Some also criticized Ethiopia for its lack of civilization and the continuance of slavery.[135]

Marson's ideas can be understood within the context of Jamaican racial politics. She directed her comments at the predominantly brown and black middle-class people who tried to rid themselves of all associations with blackness and Africa. In order to counter degrading myths about Africa, Marson used her playwriting pen to remind Jamaicans of the importance of their African past and heritage. This was central to her third and most successful play, *Pocomania,* produced in 1938, the year that marked the centenary of emancipation in the Anglophone Caribbean.

Marson based *Pocomania* on the Afro-Jamaican religion Pukkumina. In it she challenged the idea of African backwardness and promoted a celebration of African culture. In Jamaica, over centuries of colonial rule, Christianity had dominated, but enslaved Africans brought across the Atlantic their Islamic and animistic religions.[136] These religions did not disappear. According to Cuban sociologist Fernando Ortiz, they underwent the process of transculturation and merged with Christianity.[137] Pukkumina fused the Afro-folk spiritual elements of Myal with the Christian aspects of the Great Revival in 1860s Jamaica.[138] Other Caribbean creolized religions most famously include Vodun or Vodou in Haiti and the Shouters in Trinidad.[139] Pukkumina emphasized spirit possession, leading to some Christian missions condemning it.

The plot of *Pocomania,* briefly stated, concerns the relationship between Pukkumina and the middle-class, Afro-Jamaican protagonist Stella Manners. From childhood to adulthood, Stella has been fascinated by the religion, but her father, the local Baptist parson, opposes it. Throughout the play, Manners builds a relationship with the revivalist leader, Sister Kate, and secretly attends Pukkumina meetings. In the final scene, Manners goes to the Nine Night wake for the now deceased Kate. Hiding in the bushes, she watches as the evening ends in a brawl. The play finishes with Manners swapping her interest in Pukkumina for love of her fiancé, David.

In the play, Marson counters negative connotations of Pukkumina and celebrates the religion as evidence of the continuing relevance of African culture in Jamaica. The fact that Stella has held on to her passion for Pukkumina from youth to adulthood symbolizes the abiding spiritual call to Africa within her mind, body, and soul. In act 2, scene 2, David voices the fascination of Pukkumina for Afro-Jamaicans, claiming that "our people are full of emotion, vitality, rhythm—that's why Pocomania appeals to them."[140] That David bases his apt assessment about the appeal of Pukkumina on emotion illustrates the importance of African forms of bodily expression to Jamaica that persisted despite the horrors of the Middle Passage. Although Manners renounces the religion, preferring to live the life of a married middle-class woman, Marson's *Pocomania*, like *African Journey*, tried to vindicate and rewrite Africa not as a backward land but as a continent with a rich and relevant history. Reminding her audience of their African past was also a way to spread black internationalist notions of race consciousness and racial unity.

An increasing interest in Africa yoked Marson, Robeson, and Nardal together after Ethiopia's defeat and the subsequent Italian occupation. In 1936, Nardal was appointed as secretary to Deputy of Senegal Galandou Diouf, who was committed to extending the rights of Africans.[141] He published and edited a range of newspapers, including *Le Périscope africaine*, and contributed to *Le Soir colonial, Démocratie*, and *Le Sénégal*.[142] It is believed that Nardal travelled to Senegal, but there is sparse information about her experiences.[143] Nonetheless, her closer interest in French African politics was also apparent in a report she wrote, entitled "The Family and Social Evolution of Black Women," for the Second International Congress of the Mother At Home, held in Paris in June 1937.

In her report, reprinted in *Univers, bulletin catholique international*, Nardal argues that motherhood united black women from the Caribbean, Africa, and the United States. The "spirit of sacrifice" Nardal saw in lower-class women also appeared in their middle- and upper-class counterparts who would "strip all their savings to give their children a profession or trade which will also be their wealth." Regarding poor African and Malagasy women, Nardal voices class and race respectability politics, bemoaning their "ancestral ignorance," believing that "their principal concern is to adorn themselves in jewelry, fragrances, and silky fabrics." Children of these women, she states, suffer confusion, torn between two different conceptions of life based on their indigenous and French cultures due to their lack of assimilation. Later in the report she congratulates the Women's Civic and Social Union /Union féminine civique et sociale for its work in linking white women with black women in Madagascar, to whom they provided assistance; she stresses that this collaboration should stretch throughout the whole of French Africa. Nardal ends the report with strategies she thought would improve black women's development, including an end to racism, interracial collaboration, and social workers providing support for men and women.[144]

The report shows that through the women's and religious networks in Paris Nardal collaborated with, she, like Marson, was able to speak about gender and race but through a much more conservative and colonial framework. It also shows that she was committed to seeing groups of interracial women working together to spread the benefits of assimilation, which she thought would improve the lives of all women. Nardal's interest in African politics also appeared in two further articles she wrote in 1939, which featured in the journal *La femme dans la vie sociale*. In February, with British and French appeasement of Germany set to fail, Nardal published a manifesto "on behalf of the sisters of the various French colonies" and called for the women of black Africa to safeguard French colonial territories.[145]

As anti-colonial uprisings swept across the Caribbean, Nardal wrote an article in the French weekly *Je suis partout,* a right-wing publication blaming unrest in the French Antilles on communists.[146] Despite her willingness to collaborate with communists defending Ethiopia, Nardal always maintained distance from communists in the Antilles, seeing them as anti-colonial agitators.[147] That Nardal held differing views about communists in France and in the French Antilles demonstrates how her political activism depended on the issue at stake and the geographical context. These particularities show how Nardal could be effective in creating coalitions across different political groups but remain independent in her thinking. Similarly, not being officially affiliated with any one specific organization gave Robeson relative flexibility. When Spain descended into civil war, for example, she practiced anti-fascist internationalism by travelling to express solidarity with the victims of fascism.

"WE GO TO SPAIN": ESLANDA ROBESON'S SPANISH TRIP

As with her travel to Africa, political as well as personal reasons contributed to Eslanda Robeson's decision to sojourn to Spain. In "We Go to Spain," Robeson's narrative about her thirty-day Spanish experience, she boasts, "I have some Spanish blood myself, and way back, my ancestors, the Cardozos, came from Spain, to America, and settled there. I had always wanted to see Spain, and to know the Spanish people."[148] For Robeson the journey was partly to learn more about her Spanish identity and history. Travelling alongside the Robesons was the feminist and writer Charlotte Haldane, who was a war correspondent, a member of the Communist Party, and the head of the International Brigade Dependents and Wounded Aid Committee in London.[149] Fernando Castillo, a Spanish English-speaking driver and guide, escorted the trio safely through Spain and developed a long-term friendship with the family.[150]

Eslanda and Paul Robeson were not the only African American activists to travel to Spain. In 1937, Langston Hughes ventured there to report on African American involvement for the *Afro-American*. Louise Thompson Patterson, Thyra Edwards, and brigade nurse Salaria Kee also travelled to Spain. Patterson and Edwards formed links with progressive European women, while Kee ended up marrying an Irish ambulance driver for one of the brigades.[151] Although the experiences of Eslanda Robeson and these women differed, they had a similar impact and sharpened her anti-fascist critique.

Robeson filled "We Go to Spain" with important insights into the trials and tribulations of the civil war. In the narrative she discusses friendship, violence, survival, chaos, destruction, and religion. The first stop on their trip was Barcelona: "a handsome city, built on hills, by the sea, with great, wide boulevards, and avenues, and fine cross streets."[152] Next, the group visited hospitals and a prison for women on the outskirts of Valencia, which Robeson thought was more like a sanatorium.[153] In the capital, Paul Robeson brought music to the military by singing to soldiers in English and Spanish. The visitors met "keen, and aware and sturdy spirited" African American soldiers, including Roderigo from Harlem, A. M. from Oklahoma, Oliver Ross from Baltimore, Frank Warfield from St. Louis, Gibbs from Chicago, and Clark Bringle from Ohio.[154] Although they did not meet, the Robesons learned of the experiences of Oliver Law. He was an army officer from Chicago who rose to command the Lincoln-Washington Battalion. A member of the American Communist Party, Law chaired Chicago's South Side chapter of the International Labor Defense and led the Hands Off Ethiopia campaign.[155] His troops considered him to be "the best battalion commander in Spain" before he died from his injuries on the battlefields of Brunete.[156] Law's story inspired the Robesons, and Paul wanted to make a film about him but lacked the funding.

Eslanda Robeson's narrative presents a complex view of Republicans' reaction to violence. After hearing news that the government had responded to fascist air raids on the civilian population by bombing Saragossa, "a gasp of horror went up from all the Spaniards and their faces showed great mental protest against this terrible thing which had been done." In contrast, Robeson admits, "Paul, Charlotte, and I were elated, and our first reaction was 'that'll learn 'em.' But, gradually, we began to realize their point of view" because many Spaniards had relations on both sides of the war divide.[157] Being in Spain enabled Robeson to comprehend the significance of pacifism to the Republican cause. In the years to come, she would take up the cause of peace with greater zeal.[158]

Striking similarities existed between the way Robeson encountered Spain and the Soviet Union, especially when it came to racism. A decade after her Spanish trip, Eslanda Robeson informed an audience at an International Brigade meeting in Boston that neither she nor Paul "felt any barrier because of race or color."[159] The Spanish people "accepted Paul as a brother, because they knew he was interested in them, had spoken for them, was working for them, and had come to sing to them; but they accepted me as a sister because they said, I was Spanish ... and I belonged."[160] Castillo, their Spanish guide, had also assured the Robesons that the Spanish "lack all sense of color prejudice, and are actually proud of whatever boorish [sic] blood they have."[161] Although the Robesons claimed that they did not encounter racism, African American soldiers, who were mistaken for Moroccans fighting for Franco, certainly experienced it. The Loyalists took an active role in race baiting through their war propaganda, relaying messages of black savagery through the imagery of the Moors.[162]

In February 1938, the Robesons returned to London, confident that the Republicans would prevail. But by the year's end, the Republicans had suffered major losses and Franco's fascist rule would endure for forty years. Nonetheless, the Robesons followed events in Spain closely throughout their lives and remained committed to promoting the Republican cause.

. . .

The Italian invasion of Ethiopia and the Spanish Civil War were major turning points for all three of these women, who worked in various ways through networks under the umbrella of anti-fascist and black internationalism. Nardal forged pragmatic and flexible connections with communists, radicals, pacifists, and women's groups, building a transnational coalition in support of Ethiopia. Her activism also linked to her faith and demonstrates that she understood the crisis through a religious lens, practicing Christian internationalism. The crisis also increased her interest in African politics, and her involvement in women's and religious groups gave her space to air her conservative colonial views.

Marson's work at the legation gave her an intimate involvement in the war, as did her role as Selassie's secretary and her travel to the LoN. Her hectic work schedule, the emotional consequences of war, and the loss of friends triggered health problems that would recur throughout her life. Marson's calls for racial unity and race consciousness on her return to Jamaica in the late 1930s are evidence of how she coupled her practice of black internationalism with Jamaican nationalism.

Meanwhile, Robeson's travels to sub-Saharan Africa and Spain were acts of solidarity that deepened her anti-colonial and anti-fascist politics and expanded her black internationalist connections. For all the women, the events strengthened their interest in Africa, showing that the continent's past and present culture was central to the overlapping black, feminist, Christian, and anti-fascist internationalisms they practiced. And as an even larger war beckoned in 1939, the scope for these race women internationalists to practice varied internationalisms increased.

Una Marson, *Tropic Reveries*. Courtesy of the National Library of Jamaica.

Una Marson at the BBC. Courtesy of the National Library of Jamaica (top).

Una Marson at the BBC, London, World War II. Courtesy of the National Library of Jamaica (bottom).

Eslanda Robeson, London, 1920s. Courtesy of the Moorland-Spingarn Research Center, Manuscript Division, Howard University, Washington, DC.

Eslanda Robeson at the United Nations. Courtesy of the Moorland-Spingarn Research Center, Manuscript Division, Howard University, Washington, DC.

LA FEMME DANS LA CITE

REVUE MENSUELLE DU RASSEMBLEMENT FÉMININ
PARAISSANT A FORT-DE-FRANCE (MARTINIQUE)
Directrice : P. NARDAL.
Rédaction — Administration provisoirement : 32 rue Ernest Deproge
Tirage : 1.100 exemplaires.

CINQ FRANCS   NUMÉRO VINGT-TROIS

La Femme dans la cité, front cover. Archives départementales de la Martinique (ADM), Fort-de-France, Martinique. Photograph by author.

PAULETTE NARDAL NOUS A QUITTÉS

Vendredi 15 février, une grande dame antillaise s'en est allée, une grande figure de notre musique, Paulette Nardal. Le 30 mars 1981, Télé 7 Jours Martinique lui consacrait une couverture et quatre pages où Mme Nardal se confiait et présentait la chorale Joie de Chanter qu'elle avait fondée en 1954. Je vous propose de redécouvrir aujourd'hui ce document d'archives.

Mardi matin, neuf heures et demi ; j'ai rendez-vous avec une grande dame de la Martinique.
Je pousse l'énorme porte en fer forgé de cet immeuble de la rue Schœlcher qu'elle m'avait indiqué au téléphone. Je grimpe jusqu'au premier étage et j'aperçois dans l'embrasure de la porte d'entrée de son appartement.
Paulette Nardal m'accueille d'un large sourire. Je ne l'imaginais pas autrement. D'un geste solennel, elle m'indique le passage. Et je me retrouve dans ce salon de la rue Schœlcher en compagnie d'une de ces vraies femmes de cœur et d'esprit qui ont contribué à la formation de l'élite martiniquaise.
Paulette Nardal, est née au François à la fin du siècle dernier. Son père, Paul Nardal, ingénieur des Ponts et Chaussées et l'auteur, peu de gens s'en souviennent, du reservoir d'eau de l'Ermitage à Fort-de-France, du clocher du Robert et du clocher de l'ancienne église du François.
Sa mère, née Achille, est la sœur du colonel Louis-Achille dont le stade à Fort-de-France porte le nom.

La vie de Paulette Nardal a été grandement marquée par l'influence de ses parents. Elle a souvent rendu hommage au «courage silencieux de sa mère, à l'intelligence et à la générosité de son père».
«Grâce à nos parents, a-t-elle ou l'occasion d'écrire, nous avons baigné dans une atmosphère d'entente éclairée par la foi et par la beauté intérieure».
Atmosphère musicale également : «Ma mère était organiste, mon père flûtiste. Mon enfance était donc baignée de musique. Il y avait toujours autour de moi un groupe de jeunes gens et de jeunes filles s'intéressant à cet art... Mes parents organisaient à la maison des séances de musique ou encore des concerts.
La voix est claire, posée ; l'éloquence facile. Paulette Nardal me tend un dossier qu'elle avait préparé à mon intention. Un dossier sur sa vie... Des documents exceptionnels.
Voici une photo, jaunie, du groupe «Antillea» qui est devenu plus tard «Chorale de la J.E.C.» puis «Chorale de Mademoiselle Nardal».

«Mais à cette dernière assonance, explique-t-elle, j'ai préféré l'appellation «Joie de chanter».
Une réussite monumentale, cette chorale. Et plus d'un quart de siècle après, elle nous en donne le secret comme un message pour la jeunesse : «On a voulu créer la beauté & je crois qu'on a travaillé en ayant toujours en vue la perfection.
Je lui pose alors l'inévitable question du répertoire de «Joie de chanter» : pourquoi avoir voulu dès le départ introduire le négro-spiritual ? Réponse mille fois répétée : «J'ai toujours pensé au négro-spiritual parce qu'en France j'avais eu la chance d'écouter des groupes faisant une telle musique. J'en ai gardé alors l'inspiration. Le negro-spiritual est un moyen d'atteindre la perfection... lorsque toutes les voix se fondent en une seule et que les choristes oublient leur personnalité pour ne noyer dans l'ensemble avec la seule idée de créer la beauté».
Vêtue de noir, Paulette Nardal est assise au bout de la table officielle. Dans un décor de plantes vertes et de fleurs magnifiques, elle écoute religieusement le discours de Marcel Lucien, vice-recteur. A ses côtés, Monsieur le préfet Lambertin et Mgr Henri Varin de la Brunelière. Mais quelle cérémonie relate donc cette photo ?
«C'était lors de la remise de la cravate de Commandeur du mérite national du Sénégal. Une véritable fête familiale».
Une marque d'estime du président Léopold Sedar Senghor. En 1976, elle recevait les insignes de Chevalier de la Légion d'Honneur. La rencontre de Paulette Nardal avec les écrivains de la négritude se fait à Paris

lorsqu'après des études classiques à Fort-de-France la jeune Martiniquaise part alors en métropole achever une formation universitaire pour l'obtention d'un diplôme d'études supérieures de langue. Elle est d'ailleurs une des premières étudiantes noires à être inscrites à la Sorbonne. Elle fonde donc dans cette période la «Revue du monde noir» avec Félix Eboué. Quelques années plus tard, on la retrouve conférencière internationale puis secrétaire parlementaire. Au cours de la seconde guerre, elle est victime d'un torpillage en Bretagne.
Cruellement mutilée, elle est désormais invalide à 75%. Après la guerre, elle travaille au secrétariat de l'O.N.U. aux Etats-Unis puis rentre au pays pour enseigner à nouveau l'anglais. En même temps, Paulette Nardal collabore aux journaux «La Paix» et «L'Information», puis fonde le «Rassemblement féminin», association créée dans le but de permettre aux femmes, qui venaient d'accéder au droit de vote, de se préparer à leur futur rôle civique et social. C'est le «Rassemblement féminin» qui a inauguré la Fête des mères en Martinique, le 23 mai 1948, et qui a lancé le concours de la plus jolie biguine devenu maintenant concours de la chanson créole.
L'œuvre de Paulette Nardal est impressionnante. La chanson, la polyphonie, le journalisme, la conférence, elle avait le souci constant de favoriser la communication entre les hommes, entre les cultures, entre les civilisations.
Une œuvre résumée avec maladresse et imprécision dans cet épais classeur que j'ai mis entre les mains. Des émotions, pour la mémoire, coincées sur du papier jauni.
Encore un regard d'admiration sur tel article de journal relatant une remise de médaille, un coin d'article sur «Joie de chanter» à Fort-de-France, à Reims ou à Vincennes. Des feuilles manuscrites et le double d'un discours où un homme a écrit : «Je souhaite ardemment que le rappel de votre vie constitue par lui-même un message d'avenir, en tant déjà qu'il constitue un faisceau de souvenirs d'une densité exceptionnelle».

"Paulette Nardal nous a quittés." File 25/J5/10, Archives departementales de la Martinique, Fort-de-France, Martinique. Photograph by author.

Une grande figure martiniquaise...
Paulette Nardal est morte

Paulette Nardal, s'est éteinte samedi dernier à 10h20, à l'hôpital de La Meynard. Avec elle, disparaît une femme de grand caractère et d'une immense générosité dont l'idéal était de servir et de se rendre utile.

On ne saurait oublier, son action en faveur de la femme martiniquaise, pour que celle-ci tienne dans la société la place à laquelle elle avait droit.

Femme de grande culture, elle fut secrétaire parlementaire, rédactrice de plusieurs revues et professeur d'anglais. Musicienne, c'est à elle qu'on doit la chorale « Joie de Chanter ». Paulette Nardal était officier des Palmes académiques, Chevalier de la Légion d'honneur et Commandeur de l'Ordre national de la République du Sénégal.

On ne saurait ici, dans la place qui nous est impartie, avoir la prétention de raconter toute la vie de Paulette Nardal, il nous faut pourtant, parcourir cette longue vie, d'un survol rapide pour en découvrir la richesse et les aléas.

LA FAMILLE

Paule —ce n'est que par la suite qu'on l'appellera Paulette— est née au François en octobre 1896 —où son père Paul Nardal, était ingénieur des Ponts-et-Chaussées qui, de par sa fonction, était chargé de tout le secteur de cette commune.

C'est dire, que la famille Nardal, suivit les pérégrinations dues aux fonctions du chef de famille, jusqu'à ce que celui-ci soit affecté à Fort-de-France, comme second du Chef de service des travaux publics. Sont donc nées au François : Emilie (devenue Mme Fortuné, décédée il y a 3 ans), et Paule.

Naissèrent ensuite : Alice (musicienne, notre Tante Alice »), puis Jeanne (professeur de lettres, devenue aveugle) puis Lucie (professeur de mathématiques et de sciences, ex-directrice du Collège de jeunes filles), Cécile (Mme Vve Marie-Magdeleine, infirmière et sage-femme) et Andrée (pianiste, décédée la première, en Guadeloupe, 10 jours après son mariage, avec Roland Boisneuf).

On retrouve Paule, au Pensionnat Colonial, à Fort-de-France où elle obtient son Brevet supérieur : elle passera ensuite, ce qui correspond à cette époque pour les jeunes filles au baccalauréat, le diplôme d'Études secondaires.

C'est alors, qu'elle part pour la France pour y « faire l'anglais ». L'anglais chez les Nardal, est un penchant naturel —on eut dans la famille un oncle agrégé d'anglais à 23 ans qui, en son temps, fut le plus jeune agrégé en cette langue, Monsieur Louis Achille.

L'approche de l'anglais, a encore été facilité, pour les Nardal par le fait qu'ils avaient des amis sainte-luciens, chez qui ils allaient, tout comme eux venaient en Martinique, à l'occasion des vacances.

A Paris, elle passe son diplôme d'Études supérieures mais elle n'enseignera pas. Elle est là, en quelque sorte, la représentante d'un groupe d'Antillais et elle est « le contact » dans la capitale de nombreux noirs américains que lui adresse le cousin Louis Achille qui est aux USA. C'est en cette période qu'elle crée « La Revue du Monde noir ». Paule était alors secrétaire parlementaire (faisant en autres des traductions d'anglais, pour les journaux de Galan dou Diouf, député du Sénégal.

Elle fait la connaissance de Senghor qu'elle présente à René Maran, ex-administrateur des Colonies. Elle rencontre aussi le jeune, Aimé Césaire. Elle évolue dans un milieu d'intellectuels, auprès de qui elle ne cesse de s'enrichir de ce que ceux-ci lui apportent, de leur culture et de leur personnalité.

Abordant les origines de la famille Nardal, nous y rencontrerons une très belle histoire d'amour entre un blanc, d'origine européenne et une jeune beauté africaine, « si belle nous dit Alice Nardal, qu'elle ne fut jamais esclave (sinon dans sa prime jeunesse) mais maîtresse de maison, chez elle, aux côtés de celui avec qui elle partageait la vie. Ils furent heureux et eurent beaucoup d'enfants, des garçons et des filles. » Notre trisaïeule nous précise encore Tante Alice, était une des filles de cette jolie fille de couleur, elle avait les cheveux chatain clair et les yeux bleus, c'est au moins, ce que rapportèrent tous ceux qui l'ont connue.

Cette belle se prénommait Adite et dans son quartier on l'appelait « Adite aux yeux bleus ». C'était une vraie Tanagra.

Adite et les siens, se situent sur le territoire du Lamentin. A sa mort, son compagnon jura de ne prendre aucune autre femme et il resta avec ses enfants qui portaient tous le nom de leur mère.

Du côté paternel, on trouve un très bel homme, originaire sans doute de la Côte d'Ivoire, grand, fin, solide, noir de type hindou. Un homme réaliste et de caractère, tel fut M. Nardal, le père des sept filles, on en jugera par ces propos que nous rapporte Alice « Je n'ai rien à vous laisser, dira-t-il un jour à ses filles, qu'une maison, il vous appartient de travailler comme sept garçons ». Précisons qu'à l'époque les femmes ne travaillaient pas.

L'ACCIDENT

Dans les années 30, Paule Nardal revient en Martinique. Elle donne des cours d'anglais à son titre d'institutrice et pourtant, elle ne se sent pas faite, pour l'enseignement, ni femme de lettre, ni journaliste, c'est pourtant du côté de l'expression écrite qu'elle va se tourner. On sait qu'à Paris elle vit de ses traductions d'anglais. Elle viendra en Martinique en 1939 pour y voir les siens mais à la France, Hitler déclare la guerre à la France. Paule Nardal se sent tenue de regagner son poste à Paris. Pour rentrer en France une seule voie, la voie maritime. Elle retient une place à bord d'un bananier. Le départ de celui-ci est prévu pour 16h. Elle se présente plus tôt, vers 15 heures.

Place Paulette Nardal, Fort-de-France, Martinique. Photograph by author.

3

Internationalisms during and after World War II, 1939–1949

As the Second World War mobilized and moved millions across the globe, it upended Robeson's, Marson's, and Nardal's lives. After eleven years of living in London, the Robesons returned to Harlem before relocating, in July 1941, to a large estate named The Beeches in Enfield, Connecticut.[1] While they were keen to escape wartime bombings, Una Marson, by contrast, decided to make London her home once again. Although her career had revived in Jamaica, she disliked her "dull and monotonous" life.[2] When the opportunity arose to return to London in 1938, through an invitation to provide testimony at the Moyne Commission, she eagerly grasped it. In the hearings, Marson suggested a tax on men who failed to take responsibility for their children but her opinion fell on deaf ears.[3] She later resumed her involvement in the League of Coloured Peoples and the British Commonwealth League (BCL) and raised funds for Jamsave.[4]

Around the same time that Marson was in Britain, so too was Paulette Nardal. Her journey there, however, was far more tragic. In July 1939, Nardal had returned home to Martinique following a commission from Georges Mandel, the minister of colonies, to write the screenplay for a government film, "Young Craftsmen of Cinema."[5] In September, after Adolf Hitler ordered the invasion of Poland, the forty-four-year-old Nardal boarded the SS *Bretagne* and headed back to France.[6] As the ship sailed past England, German bombers attacked it.[7] She recovered from her immediate injuries after an eleven-month stay in a hospital in Plymouth, but the injuries limited her mobility.[8] Nardal had taken most of her personal papers on her fateful journey, and the sea had destroyed them. Thanks to her cousin Louis Achille, who sent Nardal $350 that covered her medical bills and transportation back to Martinique via Liverpool, New York, and Puerto Rico, she returned to her Vichy-controlled home island in 1940.[9]

The onset of World War II reconfigured the black communities that Nardal, Marson, and Robeson had played a role in forging in interwar Europe. In France, the war and subsequent German occupation of parts of the country by the collaborationist, fascist Vichy regime headed by Philippe Pétain led to the dispersal of the black French population, with many returning to the colonies.[10] In Britain, many African and West Indian students also returned home, while others chose to stay but relocate to the north.[11] Yet while the Second World War dispersed blacks, more from the Caribbean and the United States came to Europe. As they had in the First World War, West Indians volunteered in vast numbers to play their part as British subjects in defeating Germany. Over 10,000 people from the British Caribbean, mostly men, volunteered in the armed services.[12] Around 500 West Indian service men and women arrived on Britain's shores, serving in various capacities, some in the Auxiliary Territorial Service, others in the Women's Auxiliary Air Force.[13] Around 1,000 from the Caribbean were hired to work in ordnance factories.[14] Black West Indians in Britain were joined by 130,000 black American GIs.[15] The increased presence of blacks raised concerns among those in the War Office, especially in relation to the racist treatment that black soldiers faced from white soldiers and the resident population, reports of which were frequently published in newspapers.[16] Authorities were also concerned about interracial relationships between black soldiers and white women and the increased number of mixed race children that were born of these relationships.[17]

After the war, concepts of "one world" and "global citizenship" would grow in popularity, capturing the new sense of global togetherness that was needed to heal the wounds of death, devastation, and genocide.[18] Building on these ideas, a raft of international organizations were created including the United Nations (UN), the International Monetary Fund, and the International Bank for Reconstruction and Development (later the World Bank). Following its official founding in October 1945, the UN, in particular, for Nardal and Robeson signalled the beginning of a new world: a new world free from war; a new world that extended freedom, liberty, and democracy to all. It symbolized feelings of hope and optimism that the second half of the twentieth century would differ from the first.

The decade 1939 to 1949 expanded Marson's, Nardal's, and Robeson's black, feminist, Christian, and liberal internationalism. In London, by 1941, Una Marson's career was taking a different route that found her at the heart of the British media. She broke through the glass ceiling and the color bar by becoming the first black woman employed by the BBC. She was appointed full-time program assistant and a year later producer for the radio program *Calling the West Indies*, a weekly show that broadcast West Indian servicemen's and servicewomen's messages home to their families and friends. While she did not have free rein to discuss her views on race or feminism on the radio, Marson's prominence at the BBC placed her in a position to cultivate racial unity and cooperation among West Indians and African Americans during the physical and psychological terrors of war that she would fall victim to.

When she arrived back in Martinique, Paulette Nardal resumed her anti-fascism by opposing the Vichy regime. But it was the political changes near the end of the war—namely, the extension of the franchise to women in 1944 and departmentalization in 1946—that galvanized her activism. Throughout and immediately after the war, Eslanda Robeson was the one who continued to travel regularly—throughout the United States and to Francophone Africa and China. This enabled her to spread black and feminist internationalism through the new coalitions she made with activists and politicians. The ways in which Nardal, Marson and Robeson expressed various internationalisms in newspapers and salons and by travelling and working with international organizations, particularly the UN, in the immediate aftermath of the war, show their continued involvement in the public sphere and the persistence of their practices as race women internationalists.

THE WAR YEARS 1939-1945

In a 1942 BBC broadcast, Una Marson informed her audience about the growing black presence in Britain. She observed that "the war has meant the end of the feeling of loneliness and isolation among West Indians who for one reason or another work and live in Britain. The people on the street have got used to seeing as many as seven or ten West Indians in uniform coming up to the flat which some of them regard as home from home."[19]

West Indian servicemen and servicewomen faced varying experiences in Britain, ranging from acceptance to rampant racism. Rather than admit that many faced difficulty, Marson presented a positive image of their experiences. But Marson knew all too well that despite the increase in numbers of blacks in Britain, hostility and racism continued. Many black soldiers, for instance, struggled to get housing.[20] Marson's role at the BBC required her to travel extensively throughout Britain, yet she was refused accommodation because of her race. Although she did not comment publicly on the experience, it was noted in her BBC employee file.[21] Yet Marson's observation that among West Indians there was an end to their "feeling of loneliness and isolation" had much to do with her building black internationalist connectivity between, in particular, West Indians and African Americans. Marson's home in Hampstead became, much like Nardal's Clamart salon, a space where blacks in Britain could interact, socialize, and discuss new political ideas.[22]

In her small flat in northwest London, which she shared with a Jamaican student, Linda Edwards, in the early 1940s, Marson hosted gatherings to which she invited blacks who were serving in the forces. These gatherings helped to foster

West Indian unity, which would become important to attempts to create a West Indies Federation (WIF), which Marson supported. In 1945 Trinidadian Ulric Cross praised "Marson's tactful leadership and generous hospitality" and commented that "in her flat in London and by reason of the mysterious chemistry of her personality, West Indians in England from varying islands have been knit together in a common brotherhood in which baser rivalries have yielded place to common aims."[23]

Marson also invited Maida Springer to her flat.[24] Springer travelled to England from the United States in 1945 as a delegate representing American labor, one of the first black women in this role.[25] During her seven-week stay, Springer met British women involved in war industries and influential Pan-African activists, including George Padmore, who would become her mentor. The BBC invited Springer to give a broadcast, where she met Marson, who later welcomed her to her flat.[26] Springer recounted in some detail the nature of Marson's gatherings, commenting that "Una was very selective about the people she invited—these were men who had a vision of the future, and they were looking to the day when they were going to have a country, not a colonial dependency. So it was very good talk at night. Very explosive talk! Had they been heard, they would all have been court-martialed."[27] Clearly, the radical circles that Marson was mixing with in the 1940s differed from the League of Colored Peoples, where she had been active in the 1930s. Springer's mention that most of the attendees were men reflects not only the larger number of black men in wartime London but also that Marson's gatherings were a space for the development of a decidedly masculinist vision of West Indian nationalism and independence, which she would later challenge. The fact that men were able to discuss these issues within a woman's home shows the importance of figures like Marson to Caribbean nationalism.

The West Indian servicemen who attended Marson's flat included Cross; Kenny Ablack, a broadcaster and pilot officer; and Thomas Wright. Wright fondly remembered that "Una spent enormous amounts of time and a good deal of her own slender resources in helping West Indians, and especially Jamaicans, when they got into some sort of a jam, which was often. . . . She had a good brain and was an able administrator, and all of us had a deep affection for her."[28] One of Wright's fellow servicemen, the Jamaican Dudley Thompson, developed a deep affection for Marson that turned into love.[29] But their brief relationship ended in heartbreak.

Marson's desire to create a welcoming environment for blacks in Britain was not limited to the gatherings in her flat. In 1941, she urged the Colonial Office to "consider setting up a special centre for West Indians only, preferably managed by a West Indian." The cultural center Marson had in mind would be a space for West Indians to live and interact with one another and "could show the people of this country that the West Indians had a culture of their own and could contribute to the intellectual and cultural activities of this country."[30] Although the idea was not taken up, it shows how keen Marson was to challenge the divisions among West

Indians from different islands and place culture at the heart of West Indian nationalism.

Although Marson was not able to talk frankly about race or racism at the BBC, she did have a platform to share information with white and black audiences about key Caribbean figures. On *Calling the West Indies,* Marson profiled and interviewed Harold Moody; his brother, the artist Ronald Moody; and Lily Jackson, the first Jamaican woman barrister.[31] She also featured interviews with Trinidadian Learie Constantine, who was appointed Welfare Officer in the Ministry of Labour in the North East.

In 1944, Marson branched out and helped to create *Caribbean Voices,* a twenty-five-minute broadcast on the BBC West Indian Service that aired Caribbean literature by promoting young writers and giving them a wider audience.[32] The show featured Trinidadian Neville Giuseppe, Barbadian John Wickham, and the Jamaican poet Ruth Horner.[33] After 1946, the show changed its format and grew in popularity under the direction of Irishman Henry Swanzy, becoming a launchpad for the careers of predominantly male Caribbean writers, including V. S. Naipaul, Sam Selvon, and George Lamming.[34] At the BBC, Marson also collaborated with other prominent figures, including George Orwell, with whom she corresponded and developed a friendship.[35]

Although Marson reached the peak of her career at the BBC, her success had repercussions. As the only black woman on the BBC payroll, the backlash Marson faced from whites and blacks, both Britons and West Indians, was severe. The white-led, London-based West India Committee disliked Marson's broadcasts and wanted more white West Indians interviewed on the shows. Established in the eighteenth century, the West India Committee had initially consisted of London merchants who lobbied for their rights and those of planters. In the twentieth century, it still promoted West Indian trade through members in the Caribbean and Britain.[36] In a BBC memo to her boss, John Grenfall Williams, Marson addressed the West India Committee's criticism, commenting that its feeling "it has the privilege of controlling anything to do with the West Indies is in the old tradition. I think it is possible for you, and all progressive peoples, to get them to realise that with the help of God the backward coloured peoples are now gradually able to take a hand in looking after themselves."[37] Marson's words reflect her understanding of the growing self-determinist ethos of West Indian nationalism, which she also saw as being linked to religion.

Yet some black West Indians resented Marson. An "anti-Marson faction" grew at Aggrey House, with some complaining that Marson favored Jamaicans, and disagreements about the content of her programs spurred attempts to oust her.[38] This shows how strong the perceived dominance of Jamaica as being representative of the Caribbean was among West Indians, as well as the island-wide tensions. Furthermore, Marson experienced ugly, racially charged incidents with coworkers

Joan Hilbert and Guianese classical musician Rudolph Dunbar, who had been popular during the Harlem Renaissance.[39] According to scholar James Procter, "competition, as much as contact and collaboration, characterized Marson's tenure at the corporation and ... these rivalries reveal distinct tensions and fault lines at play in the projection of a West Indian diasporic community."[40]

Despite the acrimony she faced, Marson was fortunate to have the support of the Colonial Office and her employers. One of her bosses, Dr. H. B. Morgan, wrote in a memo, "I have felt all along that it was our duty to support Miss Marson in every possible way because of her own inexperience and the very grave difficulties with which she is constantly faced.... Miss Marson on our instructions has taken great pains to see that West Indian broadcasts include so far as possible, representatives of all islands, though here again Jamaicans preponderate."[41] With this backing, Marson continued to work at the BBC, albeit in difficult circumstances. While working, she managed to write poetry and in 1945, her fourth collection, *Towards the Stars*, was published by the University of London Press. As in *The Moth and the Star*, racism served as a central theme, while other poems conveyed her fear and trauma relating to the experiences of war that all Britons had faced. As historian Amy Bell remarks, "Fear was central to the civilian experience of London during the Second World War."[42]

Although Marson's work and social life in London kept her very busy, after she left Hampstead, she lived alone in Bayswater, and the high death toll of the Blitz had a psychological effect on her mental and physical health.[43] Recalling the war years in the 1960s, Marson wrote that "those of us who witnessed the devastation could not help feeling that within our own hearts there were scars of loss and sorrow that would live on with us long after the physical scars were repaired."[44] Feeling a need to take respite from London and in order to improve her health, in the spring of 1945 Marson approached the BBC with a request to go to the Caribbean and conduct research for her broadcasts. They thought the idea sounded interesting and agreed to let her go. In July, she sailed to New York before heading first to Jamaica.[45]

At this time, a range of new political developments were afoot in her home island—namely, the introduction of adult suffrage and the beginning of two-party dominance between the People's National Party and the Jamaica Labour Party. Historian Claus Füllberg-Stolberg identifies universal suffrage and the drafting of a new constitution granting internal self-government as important steps that set the stage for decolonization.[46] During the war, other changes had taken place throughout the Anglophone region. The Colonial Development Act passed in 1940 was designed to address some of the acute challenges facing society and the economy that had sparked the late 1930s riots.[47] Between 1940 and 1945, the act provided the British West Indies with £1,800,000, £1,500,000 of which went to Jamaica due to its size and the mounting problems the island faced.[48] Yet these funds did not mitigate the severe consequences of the war throughout the Caribbean, which led, for instance, to problems with the export of sugar and bananas.

After visiting Jamaica, Marson headed to the Bahamas, Trinidad, British Guiana, Barbados, and Grenada. She met old friends like Audrey Jeffers and Grantley Adams (later prime minister of Barbados) and gave speeches at parties held in her honor.[49] Marson also briefly visited Washington, DC, and took part in a broadcast for the *West Indian Newsreel* in which British Guianese writer William Harris was the main presenter. In the capital she also met the Oxford-educated historian Eric Williams, who was then secretary of the Research Council of the Anglo-American Caribbean Commission and later would be the first prime minister of Trinidad and Tobago.[50] In total, she travelled more than two thousand miles, which took a toll on her physically.[51]

When Marson returned to London, exhaustion and melancholy soon set in, making it difficult for her to continue working. She sought the help of a psychiatrist and voluntarily entered Maudsley Hospital.[52] Because of her slow progress, Marson was transferred to St. Andrew's Hospital in Northampton. Here doctors certified her as a person of unsound mind and diagnosed her with schizophrenia. According to medical reports, Marson suffered from "delusions of persecution by a group of individuals, but she is unable to say who the members of this group are."[53] Marson later wrote about this period, reflecting that "my years at the BBC now seem like a dream—an exciting dream which ended in a nightmare when I got ill."[54] Marson's nightmare was the result of a combination of depression, stress, and loneliness, but it is important to bear in mind when trying to understand her condition that there was no "definitive causal explanation."[55] Her friend and fellow writer Stella Mead arranged for Jamaican writer Clare McFarlane, another friend of Marson's, who was visiting England in April 1946, to take her back to Jamaica.[56] He did and, for the next two years, Marson lived in a home for the mentally ill.

Although she was invited, Marson's illness prevented her from attending the October 1945 Pan-African Congress held in Manchester. This conference was far larger than the previous four held since 1900. Marson's presence at the conference would have raised discussion about black women's role within Pan-Africanism but, significantly, another Jamaican woman took the podium. This was Amy Ashwood Garvey, who declared, "Very much has been written and spoken of the Negro, but for some reason very little has been said about the black woman. She has been shunted into the social background to be a child-bearer. This has principally been her lot."[57] Marson, who possibly socialized at Ashwood Garvey's restaurant, the Florence Mills Club, while living in interwar London, would have certainly agreed with her comment, because the postwar era was a time when black women were becoming more vocal in openly challenging their erasure within Pan-Africanism.[58]

While Marson was in London forging black internationalism through fostering racial unity among diasporic blacks and West Indian nationalism, Paulette Nardal was back in Martinique. There she resisted the fascist regime that swept across the French Caribbean. The high commissioner for the French government in the Antilles was Admiral Georges Robert, who caved quickly into Pétain's Vichy regime.[59] Between 1939 and 1943, Allied forces blockaded around 10,000 mostly white Vichy troops in Martinique who increased racism on the island and introduced a regime of "denunciations, deportations, disappearances, executions, and murders."[60] According to historian Eric Jennings, one of the consequences of Vichy was that it amplified nationalism in the French Antilles because of its explicitly racist colonialism.[61]

During the war, rising poverty, violent racism, and food shortages caused many to leave Martinique.[62] It has been estimated that 5,000 Antilleans left the French Caribbean between 1940 and 1943 via canoe to St. Lucia and Dominica, including noted psychiatrist and anti-colonialist Frantz Fanon.[63] But the journey across the Caribbean Sea was arduous and many drowned. While the majority of Martiniquans decided to remain on the island, those who tried to challenge the Vichy regime were dealt with severely. Historian Kristen Stromberg Childers has stated that "dissidents were subject to harsh penalties if they were caught, and over 80 people were sentenced to death by military tribunals for attempting this escape. Others who were caught were sentenced to hard labor in prison camps in French Guyana."[64] Despite these circumstances, Nardal made the decision to remain on the island, and even though she knew the dangerous consequences of being caught, she covertly taught English to Martiniquans eager to leave.

Nardal's actions placed her alongside other activists and writers who challenged the Vichy regime, especially her friends who founded the literary surrealist cultural review *Tropiques* (1941–1945). This magazine was established by Aimé and Suzanne Césaire, both teachers at Schoelcher High School in Fort-de-France, and by other activist-educators such as René Ménil, Lucie Thésée, and Aristide Maugée. *Tropiques* not only undermined Vichy, but it also criticized French colonialism. Although only fourteen issues were published, literary scholar Daniel Maximin has called *Tropiques* "the most important literary review of the Antilles." Due to its discussion of colonialism, fascism, and racism, the journal suffered from censorship and was forced to end in 1945.[65] By this time the Free French army had made significant gains, and France's African and Caribbean empire was no longer under Vichy rule.[66]

Away from the main sites of battle, Eslanda Robeson continued to study at this time. She enrolled on a PhD program in anthropology at Hartford Seminary. She submitted a thesis entitled "The Negro Problem: An Approach to the Problem of Race Relations in the U.S.A. and a Suggested Solution" but she never received a PhD. She also used the war years to sojourn, venturing to Mexico, Central America, and various parts of the US South, where she met with old and new friends who shared her left-wing views, such as Ira and Gladys Reid and Lillian Smith.[67] Robeson's travels and connections with left-wing, anti-racist activists caught the attention of the Federal Bureau of Investigation (FBI), and in 1943 it began to monitor her activities as well as Paul's.[68]

Despite the surveillance under which she operated, Eslanda Robeson gave speeches about her travels in Europe and Africa to various organizations and colleges across the United States, where she expressed black internationalism. In 1943, she wrote an open letter to students at the historically black Fisk University in Tennessee, encouraging them to see themselves as part of a larger group of nonwhite peoples. Robeson declared, "In my travels about the world I have come to realize that we are not only lumped together as Negroes, 13 million of us, we are lumped together, in the world view, as Colored Peoples, which . . . includes the West Indian Negro, the African, the Chinese, the Indian and the Malayan."[69] These colored cosmopolitan sentiments came in the same year that Roi Ottley declared that African Americans "are feeling a great resurgence of racial kinship to other colored peoples of the world."[70] They were further expressed by other activists such as A. Philip Randolph, whose planned March on Washington two years earlier had intended to link "the interest of the Negro people in America to the interests of Negroes all over the world."[71] The march had been halted when Democratic president Franklin D. Roosevelt issued Executive Order 8802 in June 1941 banning discrimination in war industries and creating the Fair Employment Practice Committee.[72]

Among African American activists more broadly, World War II sparked the rise of the global Double Victory campaign for democracy at home and abroad.[73] In 1945, Robeson wrote in the opening of *African Journey* that discrimination affected all minorities, that racism affected the "the 390 million Indians in India, the problem of the 450 million Chinese in China, as well as the problems of all minorities everywhere."[74] The wider links between African American–based activists and those of other nonwhite people in different parts of the world reflected the growing interconnectedness between freedom struggles against racism and colonialism that would figure prominently in the postwar era and to which Robeson would continue to give voice through her involvement with the Council on African Affairs (CAA) and her later travels.[75]

THE WOMEN'S ASSEMBLY, *LA FEMME DANS LA CITÉ/ WOMAN IN THE CITY,* AND POSTWAR MARTINIQUE

As the Vichy regime and World War II were drawing to an end, Paulette Nardal seized on the political climate to practice feminist internationalism. In 1944, women in France and the French Antilles received the franchise, and it was ratified the following year. In 1946, *anciennes colonies* in the Antilles shifted their status from colonial outposts to being *départements d'outre mer* and a part of France.[76] According to literary scholar Nick Nesbitt, departmentalization replaced the "institutions of Third Republic colonialism such as the *colonial gouverneur* with structures systematically equivalent to those of the Metropole: the *préfet, conseil général,* and an identical legal code and judicial system."[77] Nesbitt challenges those who interpreted it as an assimilating force such as noted Martiniquan intellectual Edouard Glissant, who described departmentalization as "the most concrete form of fear and self-denial."[78] Nesbitt argues that departmentalization had less to do with cementing the centuries-long policy of assimilation and was more concerned with democratizing "colonial power structures."[79] Departmentalization aimed to equalize citizens in the colonies with those in France. This mirrors arguments made by Childers, who comments that "choosing French citizenship through departmental status was a means of making good on the promises of a universal, race-blind Republic and demanding that the special relationship between France and its *vieilles colonies* finally be turned more to Antilleans' advantage."[80]

Yet, departmentalization was not just about the role of France. The United States played a part too. Many Martiniquans feared that more US involvement in Martinique would see the transfer of an American Jim Crow style of racism to the island, similar to that during the nineteen-year occupation of Haiti between 1915 and 1934.[81] In the first half of the twentieth century, rumors abounded that the United States could annex part of the French Caribbean in exchange for cheaper repayments of debt owed from World War I.[82] In the end, most Martiniquans preferred to place their future with France.

In the 1960s, in a letter to Léopold Senghor's biographer, J. L. Hymans, Nardal voiced her opinion about Martiniquan independence, saying that Martiniquans' beliefs "are very compatible with our very deep attachment to France, our great country. We find the idea of independence for the Antilles stupid."[83] Although she did not favor Martiniquan independence due to her support of French colonialism, Nardal recognized the new and more important role the island would play as part of France. Rather than being a neglected island on the periphery, departmentalization cemented in Nardal's mind that Martinique would have a prominent part to play politically, socially, and culturally. Alongside the extension of women into the political and public sphere through the ballot, departmentalization provided Nardal with the ability to assert the importance of women's voices on issues affecting Martinique, France, and the wider world.

Nardal articulated this vision in the Women's Assembly/Rassemblement féminin, which she established in December 1944. The organization served as the Martiniquan branch of the French-based Women's Civic and Social Union/Union féminine civique et sociale. The Women's Assembly promoted middle-class women's engagement with politics and social work among working-class women. Nardal also founded and edited the Women's Assembly's monthly journal, *La*

Femme dans la cité/Woman in the City (1945–1951), and started a salon held at the home she shared with her sisters in Fort-de-France. This took place every second Thursday of the month.[84]

The inaugural issue of *La Femme dans la cité* printed the Women's Assembly diverse manifesto. The manifesto reflected idealistic aims as well as the many challenges facing Martinique. In it, the group stated its commitment to challenging alcoholism, immorality, tuberculosis, and the growth of slums. The Woman's Assembly dedicated itself to supporting laws that assisted working- and middle-class families. It sought to help produce peaceful relationships among people of different races and classes.[85] Healing bitter divisions within society was embedded in the Women's Assembly's mission "to create a new frame of mind favorable to the rapprochement of classes and races and to social progress; to undertake pressing social projects; to do civilizing work."[86] The Women's Assembly's ambitions derived from late nineteenth-century traditions of welfare reform, racial and class uplift, and the colonial civilizing mission.

Christianity was also central to the group's platform. The Women's Assembly desired "to translate the Spirit of the Gospels into deeds that motivates most of us." Nardal described the group's doctrine as the practice of "'Christian humanism."[87] Although Nardal's Catholicism shaped her pacifism, especially during the Italian invasion of Ethiopia, her work in Martinique with the Women's Assembly saw her more explicitly tie her activism to her faith. With Catholicism being practiced by the majority of Martiniquans, Nardal knew that the organization would gain more popularity and support from local religious leaders and Catholic women and men.

The Women's Assembly was not the only important women's organization in the postwar French Caribbean. In Martinique, the Union des femmes martiniquaises (UFM) was founded by activist Solange Fitte-Duval, a communist and educator who similarly supported the needs and rights of working- and middle-class women.[88] The Union des femmes de la Martinique was another active organization linked to communism; it was led by Jane Léro and its journal was *Femmes Martiniquaises*.[89] The Union des femmes françaises was composed of working-class women who tried to set up family assistance groups and child care facilities; it operated in Guadeloupe.[90] The creation of these organizations challenges "the fundamentally male projects of decolonization or self-determination" and demonstrates how women were critical to postwar politics in the French Caribbean.[91] Yet what made the Women's Assembly distinct was its publication.

According to T. Denean Sharpley-Whiting, *La Femme dans la cité* was "the first theologically and philosophically woman-centered liberationist journal in print" in the French-speaking Caribbean.[92] Nardal described it as "an instrument of moral and social progress for Martinique."[93] There are no figures for how many copies it sold or how wide its circulation was, although it can be assumed that it was distributed in Fort-de-France and possibly other parts of Martinique and perhaps Guadeloupe. In its pages, Nardal and other women involved in the Women's Assembly discussed a range of social, cultural, and political issues; shared food recipes; and gave fashion advice.[94] In particular, Nardal wrote numerous articles encouraging Martiniquan women to engage in social work, to vote, and to help solve problems facing their island.

In the inaugural edition, Nardal drew on gendered differences to articulate the important role that women could play in social work: "Owing to the physical and psychological differences that exist between man and woman," women's attachment to humanity "will be of a different kind, though not necessarily of lesser value because of its difference."[95] Nardal drew on what historian Karen Offen has called "relational feminism" to assert the importance of women. The key aspects of relational feminism include "the notion that there were *both* biological *and* cultural distinctions between the sexes, a concept of womanly or manly nature, of a sharply defined sexual division of labor, or roles, in the family and throughout society following from that 'difference.'" Relational feminism underpinned not only Nardal's writing but the ethos of the Women's Assembly more broadly.[96] In order to harness their distinct skills, Nardal said that women would need to "free ourselves from old prejudices, from lazy routines, in order to become familiar with social environments different from our own." Nardal directed her plea toward middle-class and elite Martiniquan women who, in trying to maintain their status, treated working-class women with less regard. The stigmatizing stereotypes attached to working-class women as disease-ridden, impoverished laborers ensured that some middle-class women kept their distance. But Nardal tried to persuade middle-class women to see the working and lower classes less as pathological paragons of backwardness and more as products of their environment, malleable to change. If middle-class women educated themselves about "problems concerning the family, the professions, the city," she believed they could extend the right hand of Christian fellowship to help vulnerable individuals.[97]

From its inception, the Women's Assembly implemented a number of programs for working-class women, and Nardal used the pages of *La Femme dans la cité* to detail them. The Women's Assembly opened a "course on Domestic Instruction for domestic workers, . . . an Association of Ladies of the House," and the "Layette Effort" intended to "obviate the lack of preparation of our less privileged fellow women citizens" and "educate the masses and raise their social status."[98] The Women's Assembly sponsored conferences, created social programs and health and child care centers, and put forward legislation to assist families and children.[99] Nardal informed readers that economic inequality and changing conditions in Martinique awakened middle-class women to their "social realities. They have understood that the realization of their duty requires the best preparation for the political role that they will be called to play. This is why they join, in greater numbers each day, the Women's Assembly, a group for . . . civil and social action."[100] Nardal's words illustrate that she understood women's engagement in social work as preparation for the greater political role they would play as enfranchised citizens.

In *La Femme dans la cité*, Nardal pleaded with women to exercise their vote. Newly enfranchised women in Fort-de-France cast their first votes in the 1945 mayoral election, when Aimé Césaire stood and won as a candidate for the Communist Party and then began to campaign to represent Martinique at the Constituent Assembly based in Paris.[101] Due to the Women's Assembly's apolitical stance, Nardal did not explicitly endorse Césaire in *La Femme dans la cité*. But she urged women to make their voices heard in the historic election. In the 1945 article "From an Electoral Point of View," she stresses that "the stakes are at this moment terribly high" because "political struggles in the Antilles no longer constitute a sport." The stakes were high because the vote would ensure Martinique's position within France and its future. With his middle-class background and European education, Césaire was considered a capable candidate to continue to promote Martiniquan interests in France. Nardal implored women to use their vote "to imprint on the collective effort toward social justice the mark of peace."[102] Nardal saw peace as an innately gendered and pressing concern, writing that "if, internationally speaking, the role of women is to strive in favor of upholding of peace, locally speaking, an immediate task is upon them. Faithful to their feminine vocation, they must be able to endeavor to maintain the electoral debates within the limits of civility. Instead of increasing men's passions with their own agitation, they will endeavor to exercise a calming influence."[103] For Nardal, women's promotion of peace in the voting arena would ensure the decorum and gentility of the electoral process. Arguing against those who saw women as unable to rationalize political issues like men, Nardal emphasized the soft feminine power of female voting.

By claiming women would calm agitated, angry men, Nardal unwittingly made it easier for detractors to argue that women took a frivolous approach to politics. She tried to silence these critics by admonishing that women will bring to political action "their fresh strength, but also their good sense and the sort of insight that daily connection with material realities offers."[104] Nardal recognized the significance of bringing women's emotions into politics but went on to caution, "May our reason check the flights of our feelings. . . . Loyalty, the spirit of conciliation, harmony is not only indispensable to the reconstruction of our great fatherland, France [but also] . . . to the future of our little country."[105] Nardal linked women's voting with ensuring the future stability and progress of Martinique and France.

The importance Nardal gave to women exercising their right to vote meant that she considered abstention a social crime. During the November 1946 election, when Martiniquans voted to appoint representatives for five-year terms, Nardal made a passionate plea to women: "I call upon all women who do not vote. To them I repeat: You have the opportunity to change all this by just leaving behind your lethargy for one day, namely by going to cast a vote at the ballot box for a candidate of your choice."[106] Nardal understood voting as essential to changing the world. In another article she asked, "Is it true that tens of thousands of women refuse to go drop a ballot in the ballot box on election day, refuse to 'remake the world,' to create History?" She wondered, "Are they not therefore aware of their eminent dignity as humans, of the possibility that they have been given to change the face of the world?" She answered her own question by remarking, "If this were true, I would give up hope for the women of my country."[107] Nardal's pessimism counterbalanced her optimism. She blamed abstaining women voters for present conditions on the island, asking more rhetorical questions: "How surprised would you be if I told you that you are partially responsible for the present-day situation that dissatisfies you? As most of you are Christian, you believe in the reversibility of mistakes; you profess that with Christ, all men form one single body in which all members are one. Why would it not be the same within the political realm?" She went on to lament, "If we suffer because social relations are presently dominated by hate, we should ask ourselves: What have we done to improve the fate of the people? Have we focused our attention on their poverty?"[108] Nardal's words blurred the religious and political divide, highlighting similarities between the two.

By 1951, however, even fewer women turned out to vote. In 1945, abstentions had been 30,000 and six years later they were 45,000. Nardal calculated that "given that Martinique has five women for every man, one may assert without risk of exaggeration that it is to female indifference that we must attribute this huge number of abstentions." Despite her repeated calls and the work of the Women's Assembly, Nardal argued that middle-class women "have, in effect, lost contact with the masses preyed upon by poverty and hatred. Facing blaring ignorance, astounding credulity, or perfidious sectarianism of certain milieus demands a rare courage."[109] In *La Femme dans la cité*, Nardal wrote about the lack of courage among Martiniquan women to address society's problems alongside other issues such as poverty, disease, and crime on the island.

In the late-1940s, still recovering from the economic damages caused by World War II and the Vichy regime, Martinique suffered from low wages, stagnation, and minimal jobs. The failing sugar industry increased levels of poverty and unemployment.[110] Even after departmentalization, Martiniquans faced political repression. In August 1947, Pierre Trouille was the first *préfet* to the island, and he "reproduced the arbitrary and authoritarian power of previous colonial governors." Yet civil servants and other workers "fought for the working conditions, labor protections, and social security benefits (including health, unemployment, and accident insurance, pensions and family allocations) promised by departmentalization" and organized successful strikes. The longest of these occurred in 1953 and enabled Martiniquans to increase their benefits, but challenges remained.[111]

To alleviate ongoing social and economic problems, Nardal argued that charity must "guide the activities of the State social worker, so that this social undertaking is actually effective."[112] Nardal went on to state that "social action, and its admirable accomplishments, is the modern form of charity and one of the faces of social justice."[113] She saw charity and social work as crucial to mitigating alcoholism, venereal disease, tuberculosis, overcrowded slums, and prostitution, and she informed readers of *La Femme dans la cité* about the various programs the Women's Assembly planned to create to assuage these problems. Funding for a welcome center for children with leprosy and other projects came from arts exhibits and the Colonial Commission. The governor of Martinique supported the Women's Assembly by approving its intention to "create a 'domestic center for disadvantaged mothers,' . . . a store where our poorest members could, at very low prices, purchase cloth and other sewing articles that we hope to obtain at a bulk discount."[114] The Women's Assembly also intended to start a course for young girls leaving primary school who planned to offer domestic help to middle-class women.[115]

Another way the Women's Assembly supported the education of girls was training them for employment after their education. According to Nardal, the lack of education in Martinique explained the apathetic nature of elite women and in the case of the working class accounted for their "ignorant and gullible" attitude, a comment that reveals Nardal's patronizing perspective towards the poor. To resolve these problems, Nardal suggested that the Women's Assembly and society as a whole "must first give them the taste for work and a sense of their own dignity." Nardal argued that a practical and arts-based curriculum was the best type of education. She recommended that "a large place should be made for art in the education of the people. . . . May the people of Martinique, once so amiable, again begin to sing and rediscover their smile. . . . The inspiration of folklorists too should be renewed."[116] Nardal's commitment to arts education would flourish in the 1950s and 1960s.

In *La Femme dans la cité,* Nardal encouraged her predominantly female readers to take an interest in issues facing not only Martinique and France; she also stressed the importance of paying closer attention to global issues. In one article, Nardal criticized the French-based curriculum in schools for not providing students with knowledge of international affairs. Nardal cautioned, "One should know better than to congratulate ourselves too much for the recent implementation of new metropolitan programs in island schools" because "notwithstanding the old curriculum, our children took little or no interest in questions of general interest, in the great problems the entire world today seeks to solve." Yet, Nardal remained confident that the new curriculum would encourage among students an interest in internationalism because it would "incorporate lectures on the Bank of France, atomic energy, new international institutions, etc., in addition to courses on civic education and moral development." Nardal hoped that the curriculum would help prevent students from "committing lamentable errors . . . which lead some girls to misinterpret, for example, the significance of a lecture on the United

Nations (which they confuse with the United States)."[117] Nardal was an enthusiastic supporter of the UN: "The world is transforming before our eyes," she said. "We are witnessing the birth of a new world."[118]

The importance Nardal placed on students being taught about the UN overlaps with Marson's plans to write booklets about the LoN to students in the Caribbean. Both women wanted Caribbean children to be taught about global politics through international organizations. Historian Mark Mazower has observed that "the utopianism that has attached itself to international bodies like the United Nations and its predecessor, the League of Nations, was certainly a vital aspect of their appeal."[119] However, Mazower also notes, as early as the UN's founding, others were skeptical, seeing the organization's aims as too broad and highly unrealistic.[120]

As an avowed admirer of the UN, Nardal informed her readers about the importance of the organization that she saw as "the living reality of human solidarity." She understood its pressing mission to "work toward the liberation of all Mankind. Liberation from the fear of injustice, and from poverty. Liberation from fear, first from the calamity of war; liberation from fear, born of the great fears of Men, which have led them to salutary decisions." The ways in which she envisioned the UN as liberatory demonstrates her utopian view of its power in undermining divisions among peoples and nations that contributed to the Second World War. She saw the postwar political climate that led to the UN as essential to promoting human rights, commenting, "The efforts of the allied nations allow every individual, regardless of race or religion, to live in material and ethical conditions that conform to human dignity."[121]

Nardal specifically drew readers' attention to the significance of the UN Charter, which, in Glenda Sluga's apt description, "confirmed the 'fundamental freedoms for all without distinction as to race, sex, language, or religion' and introduced a human rights orientation to the concept of social justice."[122] Nardal doled out lavish praise of the charter for promoting "great principles that are Christian principles." In the charter, Nardal envisioned "the symbol of the mystical Body of Christ actualized."[123] She would have been pleased that French women played their part, albeit in a small way, in the charter. French president Charles de Gaulle appointed Elisabeth de Miribel, a resistance fighter and member of his cabinet, to attend the meetings. His decision to appoint a woman to the male-dominated UN confirmed to Nardal his belief in the importance of women participating in global politics. Yet, Sluga has argued that the French government was against making women's equality a "point of international principle."[124] Only four of the 160 signatories of the UN Charter were women: Minerva Bernadino from the Dominican Republic, Bertha Lutz from Brazil, Wu Yi-Fang from China, and Virginia Gildersleeve from the United States.[125] The issue of female representation at the UN was something that Nardal would soon confront and that Robeson would later criticize.

Despite high hopes, the UN Charter remained weak, with many nation states circumventing its rules.[126]

Nonetheless, the opportunity for working for the organization was presented to Nardal in the shape of an invitation from her friend, the international civil servant Ralph Bunche. The two met at the Clamart salon while Bunche was in Paris conducting research for a doctoral thesis. Bunche was a skilled diplomat and the only African American member of the US delegation to the San Francisco meetings that led to the formation of the UN in 1945; he drafted chapters about the non-self-governing territories and the trusteeship system in the UN Charter and served as the first director of the UN Division of Trusteeship.[127] He invited Nardal to act as a delegate to the UN Department for Non-Autonomous Territories and the UN Commission on the Status of Women.[128] In the autumn of 1946, she boarded the passenger ship *Sarah R. Bell* bound for New York, where she lived between December 1946 and July 1948.[129]

At the UN, Nardal was able to practice liberal internationalism through her work in the department of non-autonomous territories where she attended meetings and lectures and interacted with delegates from different parts of the world.[130] She also practiced feminist internationalism through her involvement with the Sub-Commission on the Status of Women, which derived from the Human Rights Commission chaired by First Lady Eleanor Roosevelt. It quickly became an independent body and transformed into the Commission on the Status of Women in 1946.[131] The commission focused on "equality in marriage, monogamy, property, and guardianship of children, social and economic equality, equal opportunity in the domain of education, and the prevention of slave trafficking."[132] It sought to apply the notion of human rights to women through new ideas for legislative change.[133] Furthermore, the committee aimed to "raise the status of women irrespective of nationality, race, language, or religion to the equality of men in all fields of human enterprise; and to eliminate all discrimination against women in statutory law."[134] Apart from the letters Nardal wrote about her time in New York, there are limited sources about her experiences in the United States.[135] But she did comment on the fact that many of the issues raised by delegates to the commission were already part of the Women's Assembly's agenda.[136]

Indeed, the Women's Assembly saw itself as working within the context of growing feminist internationalism through the links it forged with other women's organizations across the world. In 1945, the Women's Assembly sent representatives from Martinique to Paris to attend the annual conference of the French-based Women's Civic and Social Union/Union féminine civique et sociale. With women from fourteen other countries, they "decided to work together to promote in the world more justice and more charity."[137] From the beginning, the organization had developed "relations with women from around the world, groups of black and white Americans (the American branch of the Committee for Women), The

Women's Civil and Social Union (Association of Social Catholics); general assemblies for Youth (Jeanne Canudo, a radical-socialist and free-thinker), Communist friends."[138] These alliances demonstrate the breadth of the Women's Assembly's global networks, which bridged ideological and geographical boundaries. Nardal also forged links with women in the Anglophone Caribbean following an invitation to attend a conference on women organized by the Coterie Workers in Trinidad and Tobago.[139] In July 1948, Nardal returned to Martinique and resumed her work with the Women's Assembly and *La Femme dans la cité*.

ROBESON'S SECOND AFRICAN JOURNEY

Two years earlier, in 1946, Eslanda Robeson had been travelling again, building black internationalist networks throughout Francophone Africa. A decade after her first trip and at the age of fifty, Robeson returned to her "old country" for a six-month sojourn. The desire to learn more about colonialism in postwar Francophone Africa and her interest in world politics motivated her travels.[140] In her diary, Robeson scribbled that "one of the most important issues in the future world is the quick progress of the colonial peoples."[141] There was one colonial who especially fascinated Robeson: the late Félix Éboué, whom she admired because he respected African traditions and seemed to have a different attitude towards Africans than his fellow middle-class elite Antilleans, and she planned to conduct research on him. Leopoldville was her first stop, and from there she would visit Brazzaville, the Congo River, Fort Sibut and Bangassou, Bambari and Bangui, Ruanda-Urindi and Chad.[142]

Robeson's journey occurred at a significant moment in the continent's history. During World War II, Africans had contributed in large numbers to manpower and labor.[143] In both the First and Second World Wars, French African soldiers had played major roles, including serving in the Armée d'Afrique, the army of French North Africa, and the Troupes Coloniales, commonly known as the Tirailleurs Sénégalais, which consisted of men from Madagascar and Indochina, as well as the West and Equatorial Africa federations.[144] In sub-Saharan African countries controlled by European powers, the war years saw rising tensions as communities suffered from food rationing, labor shortages, and false promises of change.[145] At the end of the war, Africans continued to reel in its atrocious aftermath. The mid-to-late 1940s saw a wave of labor strikes affecting Lagos in 1945 and Dar es Salaam in 1947.[146] These protests shaped anti-colonial nationalism, forcing colonial powers and the United States to take seriously the growing demands for direct rule, which heightened after India gained independence in 1947.

Many differences existed between Robeson's first and second trips to Africa. Unlike her 1936 sojourn, Robeson travelled alone and flew on an airplane, which she described as being like a "magic carpet." The 1940s saw a boom in passenger aviation and Robeson enjoyed the "powerful luxurious Pan American constellation plane" that took her from New York to Leopoldville in thirty-four hours.[147] One similarity between her first and second trips to Africa was that she continued to build new friendships that facilitated black internationalist notions of self-determination, anti-racism, and anti-colonialism.[148]

In the Belgian Congo, Robeson continued with her method of interviewing to gain insights on different perspectives relating to colonialism, inequality, and independence. In Elizabethville, she interviewed workers and Samuel Lutete, the Congolese manager of the Union Mission House, where she initially stayed when she arrived.[149] At the Union Mission House, she also met a group of Angolan men who informed her of conditions in the country and their lack of political rights. One interesting figure Robeson interviewed was a Jamaican-born ship captain, William St. John Straw. Later she published a collection of articles in the *Amsterdam News* about him and other West Indians who moved to the Congo in search of work.[150]

The next city Robeson visited was Brazzaville, the capital of French Equatorial Africa. At Government House in Brazzaville, Robeson met and interviewed the "tall, handsome, brilliant and charming . . . Mettis [sic]," Gabriel D'Arboussier, a Communist deputy from French Sudan and later an official at the UN.[151] D'Arboussier, the son of a "former French Governor and an African lady," helped Robeson understand the political changes taking place in Francophone Africa.[152]

During their conversation, the two discussed the new citizenship law that had recently passed. D'Arboussier explained to Robeson that "everyone is now a citizen of his own country, and all countries in the French Federation now belong to the French Union."[153] Although Robeson agreed that the "Citoyen Law may be really revolutionary in Africa," as an American she knew all too well about the limits of legal citizenship and confessed that "in the back of my mind I kept thinking: We Negroes also have laws enshrined in our Constitution and Bill of Rights, so I am not so optimistic as is Mr. D'Arboussier."[154] The two moved on to discuss the position of *évolués* in French Africa, and D'Arboussier voiced his opposition, saying, "the Evoluee [sic] system is a caste system, and we must fight it."[155]

The status of African women was another conversation they tackled. Robeson reported that D'Arboussier opined that "one of the very worst faults of French Colonial Policy was that it considered only the men, not the women." He went on to say that "the result was that we had some educated men who could not find educated women of their own to marry, but had to marry French women, or women of their own who were still in the same stage of development they were centuries ago."[156] D'Arboussier's comments showed his criticism of the gendered inequalities that underpinned European colonialism and partly explained the existence of interracial relationships, a topic that Robeson had previously discussed with Nardal. The fact that the topic of gender and interracial marriage were raised indicates Robeson's interest in grasping the consequences of colonialism on women's personal lives.

Their wide-ranging conversation also covered the relationship between the United States and Africa. D'Arboussier told Robeson, "I would like Americans to be interested in us, and to understand us" because "we are very conscious of what African civilization can contribute to Democracy as a whole, and we do not see our problem only in African terms, but in world terms."[157] D'Arboussier's desire in having Americans interested in Africa was based on his belief that the United States would have a positive influence on the continent. His words also articulate his sense that African affairs had global ramifications. Although D'Arboussier was married, Barbara Ransby hints that he and Robeson may have shared a brief romance.[158]

Another prominent figure Robeson interviewed in French Equatorial Africa was Jeanne Vialle. Born in the Congo, the daughter of a French businessman and an African woman from Gabon, Vialle was educated in the Congo and France. At nineteen years of age, she married a Frenchman, but the marriage did not last. Vialle struck Robeson as "very sturdily built, a pretty beige color, and (with) an attractive personality."[159] The two women discussed the position of African women in society. Vialle implored, "We must fight the African himself and Muslim religion and custom, and we must also fight the white commercial man.... All these are against liberty for the African woman." Robeson wondered if white women in France had any interest in Africa and African women. Vialle distinguished between white French women in France who "are much more interested in the colonial question and in African affairs than the colonial Frenchwomen, generally speaking." White French women in Africa tended to be more interested in the advancement of their husbands than of the Africans.[160]

Keen to learn more about Vialle's activism, Robeson inquired about her role in helping to form and then serve as secretary of the Women's Association of the French Overseas-Metropole Union/Association des femmes de l'union française outre-mer-metropole. Based in Paris, the organization sought to unite "all the women of the French Union, the West Indies, North Africa, Black Africa, Madagascar, Indo-China, and all the other overseas territories, who for six long years were separated from the metropolis, and who suffered from the racist methods of the Vichy regime."[161] The group resembled Nardal's Women's Assembly but was far more left-wing and had a diverse membership, including Suzanne Césaire, who served as a member of the Director's Committee. Robeson wrote that "Vialle is enthusiastic about the possibilities of the Association" and believes female unity will lead to female equality. In Vialle's words, "It will be wonderful if many women, all over the world, will work together for the liberation and equality of women."[162] Alongside her career as a journalist and activist, Vialle was active in party politics. In June 1946, she stood for the position of deputy to the Legislative Assembly as a Marxist Socialist, but she did not win. Both Vialle and Robeson believed that political corruption and Islamic conservatism were two of the reasons for her defeat.[163]

As she continued travelling, Robeson reached out to white and black colonial officials in Rwanda. When she visited Kisnego (Kinsenyi) and Usumbura, she interviewed Moïse Kapenda Tshombe.[164] Born in the Belgian Congo, Tshombe came from a large, poor family but became a business owner. He would later back the Belgians in the independence struggles and influence the assassination of Congolese leader Patrice Lumumba, whom Robeson deeply respected.[165] In Chad, Robeson managed to conduct research on Félix Éboué, who had died in Cairo in 1944 following a heart attack.

Robeson's time in the Belgian Congo and French Equatorial Africa saw her build new networks with activists that both widened her sense of racial solidarity with Africans and sharpened her understandings of the nuances of French colonialism, especially in relation to class, gender, and citizenship differences. Her travels also influenced her growing interest in international relations, which would become an important part of her journalism in years to come.

ROBESON IN CHINA—AFRO-ASIAN SOLIDARITY

Three years later, in 1949, Eslanda Robeson was on the move again. In September, she addressed the American Continental Congress for Peace in Mexico, and two months later, she attended the Women's International Democratic Federation (WIDF) meeting in Moscow.[166] Founded in 1945, at the first International Women's Congress in Paris, the WIDF promoted world peace and women's equal rights.[167] In December, she ventured for the first time to China to attend the Asian Women's Federation meeting in Beijing. Robeson went "as a reporter to gather first hand news from behind the 'Iron Curtain'" and as a representative of the Council on African Affairs (CAA), the Congress of American Women (CAW), and the Progressive Party, the third largest political party in the United States, in which she was actively participating.[168]

Ada Jackson, a black American Labor Party (ALP) activist from Brooklyn, a left-wing group Eslanda Robeson also supported, accompanied her to China.[169] The *Amsterdam News* claimed that Robeson and Jackson were the first African American women to visit China since the new Chinese government had been inaugurated three months earlier.[170] Jackson and Robeson's trip did not break the law, but their "actions were a dissident response to official US foreign policy," and the FBI monitored Robeson's movements. This was because the US government did not support Communist China and had put its weight behind the Nationalist group led by Chiang Kai-shek.[171] The United States identified Chiang as leader of Formosa, which was given membership in the UN. That Robeson visited China knowing that she would be monitored shows her willingness to challenge US foreign policy and her commitment to practicing various internationalisms.

Robeson's visit allowed her to learn about and support struggles for Chinese freedom, which she linked with those waged by black Africans, Americans, and West Indians. By stressing Afro-Asian solidarity, she widened further her practice of black internationalism.[172] In 1951, Eslanda Robeson published articles about her visit to China and her thoughts about the nation's politics and future in the newspaper *Freedom*.[173] Her husband had founded *Freedom* in 1950 and used it to counter press censorship of him. Harlem-born activist Louis Burnham edited the paper, which was an important publication for the views of radical and leftist black women like Eslanda Robeson, Louise Thompson Patterson, Vicki Garvin, Alice Childress, and Lorraine Hansberry.[174] *Freedom* lasted for five years, 1950–1955, and shared offices with the CAA. Its successor, *Freedomways* (1961–1985), continued with the newspaper's global and feminist politics, which Eslanda Robeson contributed to.[175]

In other articles about her experiences, Robeson informed readers about how Chinese men and women had won the fight to repossess their land and drive "the foreigners and the feudal lords off the mainland of China to Formosa, and set up their own Central Peoples Government."[176] She argued that these actions had consequences for black Americans: "Every Negro who has listened ad nauseum to talk about Freedom and Democracy, and got none of it; every Negro who has finally come to the conclusion, as the Asian and African people did, that next time he hears the slogans FREEDOM and DEMOCRACY he too will take them literally."[177] Despite the similarities between African American and Chinese freedom struggles against oppression, Robeson overlooked the significant differences in order to emphasize Afro-Asian unity.

While her experiences in China expanded Robeson's practice of black internationalism, they also saw her engage with feminist internationalism. During the conference Robeson "met, talked with, listened to, travelled with, and briefly lived with 165 Delegates representing 14 Asian countries, and 33 Observers representing Africa, Europe and the Americas—women Delegates officially representing, in all, 500 million women." Being with women from all across the world, in Robeson's words, "gave us a new feeling about women, about the importance of the role we women have to play in this new and changing world."[178] Although Robeson interacted with various women, one had a profound impact on her: Madame Sun Yat-sen, also known as Soong Ching-ling, who served as vice president of the People's Republic of China, president of the Chinese People's Relief Administration; she was the second wife of Sun Yat-sen, the leader of the 1911 revolution. Robeson admired Soong Ching-ling and described her as "World Woman Number One" because of "her deep sense of being not only one of the 250 million women of China, one of the 500 million people of China, but also one of and one with the billions of women and people of the world."[179] Robeson observed that Soong "had much to tell, but much to ask, because her deep concern for her own people is bound up with a deep concern for the people of the world."[180] Soong Ching-ling came to represent, for Robeson, the ideal activist who had empathy and compassion for women who did not share her privileges. Robeson's fondness for Soong is evidence of her commitment to the importance of interracial female friendship that strengthened Afro-Asian solidarity.

On her return to the United States in January 1950, Robeson held a press conference and called on Secretary of State Dean Acheson to visit China and observe conditions himself.[181] She participated in a speaking tour arranged by Louise Thompson Patterson and visited California, Ohio, St. Louis, and Detroit, insisting that the government formally recognize the People's Republic of China.[182] Additionally, she reached out to the Chinese diplomatic figures in New York including Kung Pu Shen, a member of the People's Republic of China Ministry of Foreign Affairs.[183]

MARSON'S RECOVERY

By 1948, a year before Robeson ventured to China, Una Marson was recovering. After moving back to Kingston, she revived her literary career by creating new relationships with African American writers, including Langston Hughes. When Hughes had visited Jamaica in October 1947, meeting writers for his upcoming anthology *Poetry of the Negro 1746–1949*, the still unwell Marson had missed the chance to see him.[184] Her friend the Jamaican writer Vivian Virtue, however, kindly introduced Hughes to Marson's poetry, which he admired, and he included two of Marson's poems in his anthology. To thank Hughes for this honor, Marson penned her first letter to him on November 20, 1948; in it, she shared some of the challenges she faced as a writer on an island where literary culture remained the preserve of the rich.[185]

A few months later, Hughes replied, sending Marson copies of *Ebony* magazine.[186] Founded by John H. Johnson, an African American businessman, the first issue of *Ebony* had been published in November 1945. The glossy monthly magazine combined gossip with news, entertainment, and politics specifically about blacks in America, and it became an instant success. In 1951, Johnson established an equally successful weekly magazine, *Jet*. Marson felt "very proud of these journals" but remained unhappy "about the magazines we are turning out in Jamaica."[187] If she were "twenty years younger," Marson said she would "start one now." But at the age of forty-three, Marson admitted, "After living in England for twelve years and particularly since my illness I find Kingston's heat very tiring and don't think I could do the rushing around that such a venture needs."[188]

Although she did not have the strength to start a new magazine, Marson did embark on a few projects. She confided to Hughes about a new book she was writing on "everyday life in Jamaica" and her travel plans: "If I live and all goes well I want to go to the 1951 London Exhibition and come to lecture and read some poetry in America after."[189] Neither plan came to fruition, but she did initiate a new project to develop Jamaican literature.

In 1949, Marson founded the Pioneer Press, which published affordable fiction and poetry by Jamaican authors for young readers with financial support from the *Daily Gleaner*. Marson worked with up-and-coming writers like Panama-born Jamaican Andrew Salkey. Through the Pioneer Press, Marson also revived the Readers and Writers Club in which she had participated in the early 1930s.[190] Unfortunately, the Pioneer Press did not last long. The initial enthusiasm for the project waned as financial difficulties arose when the *Daily Gleaner* ran out of money to support the venture.[191] The challenges she faced with the Pioneer Press also related to her unhappiness with living in Jamaica.

In the late 1940s and early 1950s, Marson wrote articles attacking politicians, bemoaning the lack of women's interest in literature, and detailing the negative aspects of cinema on youths.[192] Her criticism of Jamaican society was one of the reasons why Marson decided it was time, again, to leave. "To stay here in this depressing confusion is to stagnate and I'm getting on," she wrote to her BBC colleague John Grenfall Williams, a white South African medical missionary.[193] Seeking opportunities elsewhere, Marson decided to move to the United States. In a letter to the head of the Associated Negro Press (ANP), Claude Barnett, who was a committed Republican in Chicago, Marson wrote, "I am coming to America early next month. . . . I am very excited about this as it is really the first time I am going to stay in America."[194] The ANP was an influential press agency that put news about blacks in national and black newspapers.[195]

Marson had met Barnett and his wife when they visited Jamaica in the late 1940s. In his reply, Barnett excitedly wrote, "It is indeed good news to know that you are coming to America. One of your mental vigor and resolute determination to succeed will enjoy a visit here."[196] Marson's correspondence from Jamaica with Hughes and Barnett, in particular, is evidence that she was trying to reach out to prominent African American men in an attempt to not only develop her career but also practice black internationalism and promote Caribbean literature. In the early 1950s, she left Kingston Harbour and sailed to the United States.[197]

. . .

Thus, the war years saw Nardal, Marson, and Robeson expand their practices as race women internationalists. In London, Marson had continued to practice black internationalism by bringing together West Indians and African Americans at her home. However, at the BBC she had faced serious opposition that highlighted the difficulty of being a black woman working within a white-dominated media institution and trying to represent blacks. Her work at the BBC was also affected by divisions among black and white West Indians, undermining her attempts to foster West Indian unity. The impact of living in London during the war had a professional and personal cost for Marson, severely affecting her mental and physical health. Once her health had improved, Marson tried to build new links with

African Americans. In contrast to Marson, Nardal's anti-fascist activism had persisted during the Vichy regime as she covertly undermined its objectives. After the war, by establishing the Women's Assembly and *La Femme dans la cité* and working at the UN, she had more scope as an activist-intellectual to express relational feminism and practice liberal and feminist internationalism. Robeson, through her travels, despite government surveillance, continued her attempts to build more black internationalist connections in Francophone Africa. Her experiences in China also saw her practice black and feminist internationalism by forging interracial friendships and stressing the significance of Afro-Asian solidarity.

In the next decade, changes in Nardal's life would see her move away from being an activist-intellectual. For Robeson, the context of the Cold War would galvanize her practices as a race woman internationalist. By relocating to the United States, Marson believed she could reinvigorate her activism and writing. But her second stay in the country posed new and unexpected challenges.

4

Continuities and Changes, 1950–1966

The Cold War, civil rights protests, and decolonization served as the wider global political forces that came to shape Nardal's, Robeson's, and Marson's activism and thought between 1950 and 1966. In the United States, anti-communism especially impacted left-wing and black-led anti-colonial and anti-racist organizations.[1] As critiques of American racism and anti-colonialism became synonymous with pro-communism, leading leftists like the Robesons, W. E. B. Du Bois, and Claudia Jones became targets of the Red Scare. In addition, anti-colonial groups such as the Council on African Affairs (CAA), already monitored by the FBI, splintered. In response, more moderate groups like the NAACP fought to hold onto their influence by emphasizing anti-communism over anti-colonialism.[2] Yet despite the attacks on the black left, the Cold War energized progressives, especially Eslanda Robeson.[3]

As the Cold War gathered pace, so too did civil rights protests in the United States. The 1954 *Brown v. Board of Education* decision ruling that segregation in public schools was unconstitutional galvanized activists seeking to dismantle Jim Crow. Yet the violent backlash unleashed by white resistance through the growth of White Citizens' Councils and the lynching of fourteen-year-old Emmett Till in Mississippi in 1955 showed that segregationists were not going to acquiesce easily. Nonetheless, with more organizations like the NAACP forming coalitions with other church-based and student activist groups, this set the stage for further sit-ins, boycotts, riots, and marches throughout the country that were both inspired by and helped to encourage freedom movements in Africa. When Ghana gained its independence on March 6, 1957, this roused freedom struggles in other parts of the continent, so much so that by 1960 seventeen more countries had gained their independence. This led the United Nations to dub that year the "Year of Africa."

But the South African Sharpeville massacre that killed sixty-nine brought international attention to the brutal realities of the challenges facing black South Africans living under the repressive apartheid regime.

In the Anglophone Caribbean, unprecedented political shifts following the creation and quick failure of the West Indies Federation (WIF) paved the way for independence. In the Francophone region, unemployment grew, prompting many to migrate to Marseille and Paris in search of work. Similar patterns of migration occurred in Britain as the Conservative and Labour governments confronted what Jamaican folk poet Louise Bennett called "colonisation in reverse." The movements of African, Caribbean, and South Asian colonial and postcolonial subjects to Britain led to race riots, intensified housing discrimination, and precipitated police injustice.

The sixteen years between 1950 and 1966 saw a series of continuities and changes in Nardal's, Robeson's, and Marson's lives. In the case of Nardal, her work as an activist-intellectual lessened as she entered the cultural arena. Meanwhile, Robeson's travels to Trinidad, Britain, Ghana, and Germany expanded her practice of black and feminist internationalism. In this period, newspapers became an important space for her to voice internationalism. It was also a time when her views about equality widened to embrace a language of human rights.

By contrast, living in the United States imposed limitations for Marson. Her sense of isolation and being confronted with the daily realities of Jim Crow initially stifled her creativity and activism but renewed her Christian faith. Although Marson did not participate explicitly in anti-racist activism in the United States, she still engaged in transnational activism through her support for the WIF. Her Christian faith enabled her to work with interracial groups and spurred her interest in social work. Towards the end of her time in the United States, Marson was also able to resume her literary career, but the depression that began after the breakdown of her brief marriage halted her ability to write and work. On her return to Jamaica, Marson's political conservatism and romantic nostalgia for British culture kept her focused on national political issues and social work, but when she travelled to Israel, she was able to practice feminist internationalism. Overall, the final years of the three women's lives show the consistency of Robeson's practices as a race woman internationalist due to the varied networks she was involved in that influenced her travels and writings. Marson's practices as a race woman internationalist regressed but later grew, and Nardal's took on a different cultural expression.

NARDAL AND BLACK INTERNATIONALIST MUSIC

Paulette Nardal's involvement with *La Femme dans la cité* and the Women's Assembly lessened by the early 1950s. Low circulation and financial pressures forced the end of the magazine around 1952, but the Women's Assembly's activities continued in the 1950s and 1960s. As other women took leadership roles in the group, Nardal moved her attention away from the activist-intellectual terrain and began to focus on music. In the mid-1950s, Nardal became a member of the Society of Composers, Authors and Music Publishers/Societé des auteurs, compositeurs, et éditeurs de musique.[4] In 1954, she founded a choir called la Chorale de la jeunesse étudiante chrétienne, which became la Chorale de Paulette Nardal and later la Joie de chanter.[5] Through her involvement in the choir, Nardal wrote compositions and harmonies of folk tunes and began, as one journalist put it, "a new way of expression in the Martinican music world." The choirs centered on the study of Negro spirituals and folk songs.[6]

In interviews with journalists, Nardal reminisced about first learning about Negro spirituals in interwar Paris. These "true psalms of suffering," Nardal explained, expressed "rhythm that recalls Africa, the desire of heaven, the sadness of exile, the horror of their earthly condition but also invincible expectancy and the triumphant joy of Christians that transcends hatred." By bringing together spirituals with folk songs, Nardal helped rescue "some songs that fell into disuse." The choir was popular in Martinique and Guadeloupe and was described as having "great musical quality class, distinction [and] elegance."[7] Although in her later years she was no longer an activist-intellectual, Nardal's involvement with the choir shows that she still expressed cultural dimensions of black internationalism through music. By translating African American musical genres and lyrics with Martiniquan folk songs, Nardal expressed diasporic solidarity and connection to the history of slavery.

Furthermore, during the 1950s, Nardal remained engaged in other areas of Martiniquan civil society. She sat on the supervisory board of the local prison and the Association for the Protection of Children and Adolescents, which reflected her commitment to social work.[8] She also participated in the literary scene and served as a member of the selection committee on the Prix du roman des D.O.M., a literary prize for writers in the French Antilles.[9]

MARSON IN THE UNITED STATES

While Nardal was still actively participating in Martiniquan public life, Una Marson, in 1952, arrived in the United States, and her experiences of racism would have a prodigious impact on her faith. As soon as she arrived, she began putting pen to paper, noting her impressions. The first place Marson visited, with her cousin who lived in America, was the "tourist paradise of Miami." Like the rest of the Jim Crow South, segregation existed in Florida. Marson was warned by "most West Indians who had come to America through Jamaica" that Miami "was a good place to get out of." The city's racism left Marson distraught. While gazing out of the window, she saw a "bus passing by with all the dark skinned people sitting at the back." The sight gave her "a sickly feeling" in her stomach.[10] She was shocked by her reaction to segregated transport remarking, "Why, I had lived in Europe for over fifteen years ... and here was I gaping and surprised as though I had come with the idea that I would be startled and that everything was colossal in America."[11]

Marson continued to observe racism when she moved to the nation's capital. Although home to Americans, foreign diplomats, politicians, aides, and lobbyists, Washington, DC, also had a distinct racial hierarchy that resembled the Jim Crow South. In the city, Marson shared a room with an Italian woman sculptor in a student house, where she "met people from many parts of the world."[12] Yet as she visited different parts of Washington, DC, she observed that "practically half the population was coloured and ... apart from a large number of coloured Government employees, most of the waiting on and manual labour work was done by coloured people."[13] Of the capital's historically large black population, a disproportionately large number worked in low-paid government jobs and lived in the Northwest section of the city in the Shaw neighborhood. Howard University, situated near Shaw, had a number of civic clubs, such as the Phyllis Wheatley Young Women's Christian Association, built in the 1920s. Bars and restaurants began to flourish in the neighboring area of U Street, considered a second Harlem. The segregation throughout Washington, DC, meant that Marson "got a rude shock" when she was refused admission into a cinema, and she routinely struggled to find a diner that would serve her.[14]

Confronted with the emotional and psychological terror of incessant racism, Marson turned to religion. Although her father was a Baptist pastor and she had shared a close relationship with Harold Moody in London, attending church with his family, Marson was not a devout churchgoer. When she moved to the United States, however, her religious outlook changed. "In less than a month," she wrote, "I had a deep hurt down inside of me and I prayed continually to forgive and that the hearts of these people might be changed."[15] Marson's resolve to pray was similar to the message she had conveyed when she experienced racism in interwar London.

As Marson began to attend church regularly, she noticed the ways in which racism shaped religious practice too: "One thing that greatly puzzled me ... is the segregated church." She retold a story that illuminated the puzzle, saying that while she was "passing by a pleasant looking church ... an oldish lady was passing and I don't know what prompted me to ask her if this church was open to all people. She replied by telling me where I could find the nearest coloured church." Although she was subtly and sometimes not so subtly made to feel unwelcome in white churches, Marson visited one with a few of her friends. While there, she saw "a couple people staring at me, and one angrily. This I felt to be such intense dramatic irony that I could not keep away a smile from my face." As a foreigner, she stated, "I do not think it is possible for those who have accepted segregation in churches all their lives to understand what a shock this is to a visitor in whose mind a segregated Christian church is a contradiction in terms."¹⁶

Unwelcome in white churches, Marson "worshipped in a coloured church in Washington" but still "felt unhappy."¹⁷ She preferred to attend the few desegregated churches and "particularly enjoyed worshipping at the Church of the Saviour, an interracial ecumenical centre." Marson also attended prayer sessions at the "Fellowship House, Centre of the International Christian leadership." Yet, even in these Christian spaces, "there was only one thing that worried" Marson. "Almost invariably," she wrote "I was the only coloured person present." To Marson, this fact "did not seem reasonable . . . when half the population in Washington is coloured, and these groups are agreed that 'if we do not love our brother whom we see, how can we love God whom we have never seen?'"¹⁸

Marson had hoped that being in the United States would enable to her to be part of activist groups. Yet she found that "the intellectuals and professional people of colour seem rather a closed group. I am astonished to find there is no large Coloured Club or Centre interested in coloured visitors. . . . Perhaps they exist and I do not know of them." The closed nature of black-led organizations may have been informed by the repressive Cold War context that stifled diasporic links groups could forge. As a single black woman from outside the United States, Marson felt acutely conscious of her unwanted presence. She remarked that "as a coloured person I have found not only the white people wary of entertaining strangers among them, but the coloured people too." She knew that if her skin color had been white, she would have had more opportunities: "As a journalist, a humble poet and a professional radio woman I could make many more contacts and join in regular professional group life if I were white." But Marson did not express self-pity and though she realized that she was "missing a lot," she knew that so too were "the people who feel ill at ease with coloured people. We don't bite and we are just as human as they are."¹⁹

Nevertheless, she saw racial progress developing from the church rather than activist groups. Marson commented, for example, that while "everyone is insisting that things are improving, . . . it is to the Christian groups the visiting outsider looks for a lead in the solution of such problems."²⁰ She foresaw the significant role of organizations like the Southern Christian Leadership Conference.

Yet Marson did manage to forge friendships with Jamaicans at Howard University. Colloquially known as the "Negro Oxford," a term coined by Eric Williams, Howard University was the foremost of the historically black universities in the country. Its alumni and faculty included a who's who of notable black American public intellectuals, including Alain Locke, Zora Neale Hurston, historian Rayford Logan, and future president of Nigeria, Nnamdi Azikiwe. Others who worked at Howard included educator Lucy Diggs Slowe and the renowned international relations scholar Merze Tate.²¹

Marson did not study at Howard University but "met a couple of the Professors, ... one of these a Jamaican." She befriended "a woman professor in the Drama department" who invited her "to a couple of the plays she was responsible for producing at the Howard Drama Theatre."[22] Although she enjoyed visiting the theatre, a few plays she saw disturbed her. One "was about the return of a coloured soldier from the war and his struggle to get adequate employment. It seemed so tragic to me that I just sobbed myself ill. For days I was so depressed I did not know what to do with myself." Marson confronted the reality that "those Southern scenes of terror were constantly before me now. It was frightening. It was terrifying. . . . I asked about the play and understood it to be quite true to life."[23] Marson's words illustrate how open she was to voicing the extent to which racism affected her mental health.

Another important relationship Marson developed in the United States led to marriage. Marson married Peter Staples, an African American dentist, widower, and father of two daughters.[24] The exact date of the wedding is unknown but it is likely to have taken place in the mid-1950s.[25] What is known is that it lasted less than a year.[26]

While Marson struggled to be involved with black activist groups during her time in the United States, she gained further insight into how African Americans and Afro-Caribbeans lived by visiting areas like Brooklyn and Harlem. In the former district, she noticed "there were so many West Indians, or people looking like West Indians, on the trains that I felt that I had not left Jamaica! Why I was right home again except that no one said hello."[27] The unfriendliness Marson experienced in Brooklyn also existed in Harlem. This was a place she had romanticized for a long time, but when she visited, she disliked it immediately. "Harlem may have its charms," Marson noted, "but I did not find them." Her gloomy view of Harlem was rooted in her dislike of segregation. She commented that "life becomes broadened and enriched when people of all colours and races learn to live with each other as good neighbors."[28] To further her interest in the lives of blacks in America, Marson participated in social work. When she lived in Baltimore, "some members of our group joined with students from Morgan State University and went down to do manual work in the slums of Baltimore," she reminisced.[29]

During her time in the United States, Marson remained involved in Caribbean politics. Although little information exists, it appears that she spent two years working in a "West Indian Office connected with the Embassy."[30] Furthermore, she was especially supportive of the creation of the WIF. Inaugurated on January 3, 1958 in Trinidad, the WIF was a union of Caribbean countries that intended to ascend into an independent nation from Britain. The ten islands in the WIF were Jamaica, Barbados, Trinidad and Tobago, Antigua, Dominica, St. Christopher-Nevis-Anguilla, St. Vincent, St. Lucia, Montserrat, and Grenada. The WIF sat alongside the growing independence struggles waged by people of color. Historian Eric Duke argues that "efforts to create a federation in the British Caribbean were much more than merely an imperial or regional nation-building project. Federation was also a black diasporic nation-building endeavor intricately connected to notions of racial unity, racial uplift, and black self-determination."[31] Marson was committed to helping the WIF, commenting that "native West Indians living in this country and their well-wishers should organize themselves in an effort to support the newly formed federation."[32] She was the engineer behind the creation of the American Friends of the West Indies Federation (AFWIF) alongside supporters such as Rayford Logan, Adam Clayton Powell, and Michigan congressman Charles C. Diggs, who helped to create local chapters of the organization.[33] An informal meeting of the AFWIF took place in May 1958 at Powell's office in New York, which Marson attended.[34] She also published articles about the WIF in the *Sunday Washington Star*.[35] Marson's involvement with the AFWIF built on the gatherings she had held at her flat in wartime London and reflect her practice of black internationalism that was tied to Caribbean nationalism. It is unclear who else was involved in the group, but the fact that it attracted high-profile black politicians and its growth outside of New York suggest its broader significance for developing West Indian and black American alliances.

In the last two years of her stay in the United States, Marson also returned to formal education that ignited her creative writing. She enrolled for classes in writing for children at George Washington University and participated in a course in writing for the stage and television at the Catholic University Drama School. This career change demonstrated how Marson tried to expand her literary skills to appeal to different audiences, which paid off. Her stories "Harvest Thanksgiving Festival" and "Christmas on Poinsettia Island" were both published in the *American Junior Red Cross News*.[36] Yet by the late 1950s and early 1960s, Marson's depression returned, partly in response to the breakdown of her marriage, and she decided to sail home to Jamaica.[37]

NEW WORLD REVIEW, THE PROGRESSIVE PARTY, AND THE SOJOURNERS FOR TRUTH AND JUSTICE

While Eslanda Robeson was in China forging new links with women from across the world, Paul Robeson came under increasing attack from anti-communists in the United States. In 1949, he attended the Congress of the World Partisans of Peace. After delivering a speech on the need for world peace and cooperation, he ended his remarks with a discussion about the role of black and white workers in creating the wealth of America, stating that "we are resolved to share it equally among our children. And we shall not put up with any hysterical raving that urges us to make war on anyone. . . . We shall not make war on the Soviet Union."[38] The Associated Press deliberately misquoted this relatively harmless statement and claimed that Robeson said, "It is unthinkable that American Negroes would go to war on behalf of those who have oppressed us for generations against a country [the Soviet Union] which in one generation has raised our people to the full dignity of mankind."[39] This controversial statement led to a widespread backlash against Paul Robeson in both the mainstream and black press.

The misquoted speech also led to a government investigation, and the State Department decided to seize Paul's and Eslanda's passports.[40] The confiscation of the Robesons' passports occurred because they refused to sign an affidavit stating they were not members of the Communist Party. It sparked an international protest movement known as the Committee to Restore Paul Robeson's Passport, which was based in London.[41] Between 1950 and 1958, Paul and Eslanda Robeson could not leave the United States, which damaged Paul Robeson's career and decreased their family income.[42]

Despite the backlash, Eslanda Robeson continued to voice her progressive views through writing. In 1949, her third book, a series of conversations with writer Pearl Buck titled *American Argument,* was published. Robeson was introduced to Buck after reading her 1931 novel, *The Good Earth,* a story about family life in China before the First World War, which was awarded the Pulitzer Prize in 1932. Buck came from a family of American missionaries and had spent her childhood in China in the 1900s. Buck chose to collaborate with Robeson because she "best fulfilled my need to find someone with a fine mind, the ability to laugh, a triumphant person ... and, above all, an American who had lived here most of her life and yet had been abroad enough to know that no one country makes the world."[43]

The eleven chapters of *American Argument* focus on their respective upbringings and backgrounds, American identity, gender differences, education, humanism, Russia, freedom, international relations, and children. Both women agreed on a number of topics, like the importance of education, the complexities of marriage, and the necessity of peace. But they clashed over communism. Buck remarked that "every Communist I have ever met in any country has been a simple person whose thinking was fairly stereotyped."[44] Robeson challenged Buck by comparing white American attitudes about communism and their beliefs about blacks saying, "Americans have already had their minds made up for them about the Russians and about the Soviet system.... White Americans have already had their minds made up for them about the Negro, and no matter what evidence we offer—scientific, statistical, factual—they turn a deaf and prejudiced ear, and refuse to listen and to be convinced by facts."[45]

Buck remained staunchly anti-communist despite Robeson's continued stress on the importance of mutual cooperation between all countries. Yet Buck admired Robeson's sense of solidarity with others across the world, writing that "Eslanda will not let herself be merely an individual. She sees in herself every Negro in the United States, every poor white in a poll-tax Southern state, every black man, woman, and child in Africa, every untouchable in India, every colonial in

Indonesia, and Indo-China, every woman anywhere who longs for equality."[46] This description illuminates the many alliances Robeson felt with oppressed groups. While the two women differed on communism, within four years of the publication of *American Argument,* Robeson confronted the opposing ideologies of the United States and Soviet Union directly.

In 1953, the Senate Committee on Government Operations' Permanent Subcommittee on Investigations, headed by Joseph McCarthy, called her to testify because her two books, *Paul Robeson: Negro* and *African Journey,* were considered "un-American" and this along with her friendships with communists and travel to the Soviet Union created questions about whether she was or ever had been a Communist.[47] At the hearing, Robeson refused to answer direct questions about whether she belonged to the Communist Party. Robeson's refusal to feel threatened by anti-communist pressure was reflected in her involvement with the National Council of American-Soviet Friendship (NCASF). She sat on its board of directors and worked with its associated publication *New World Review.*

Established in 1951, *New World Review* succeeded the journal *Soviet Russia Today.*[48] The left-leaning newspaper was sympathetic to the USSR, and many of its editorials expressed pro-communist, anti-colonial, and radical views. Its editor, activist Jessica Smith, had travelled to the Soviet Union as early as 1922 and had ties to the Communist Party. A number of black leftists and radicals who had links with Smith contributed to *New World Review,* including Vicki Garvin, Thelma Dale Perkins, George Murphy Jr., Elizabeth Moos, Shirley Graham Du Bois, Alice Childress, and Halois Moorhead.[49] Robeson mixed with many of these figures, but her position with *New World Review* was more official: she was appointed the editorial consultant on issues relating to colonialism and African Americans.[50] She began writing regularly for it in 1951 and received an office at the UN press section in New York.

Like Nardal, Robeson admired the UN. In 1945, as a representative of the CAA, Robeson had attended the meetings that led to the creation of the UN.[51] "Working in San Francisco," Robeson remembered, "was for me a fantastic experience ... for I was a NOBODY, dipping into the business of the making of a NEW WORLD."[52] Robeson believed that the UN and its charter transformed ideas about citizenship, stating, "We Americans are not just American citizens any longer—we are also World Citizens."[53] Robeson's understanding of world citizenship was not in conflict with her status as an American citizen, but complemented it.[54] World citizenship, asserts political theorist Derek Heater, "imposes the need to know about and understand world issues as well as local and national ones, and to be concerned about, even involved in, the problems facing the planet and its inhabitants, especially the most disadvantaged."[55] Robeson practiced liberal, black, and feminist internationalism in print through the articles she wrote for *New World Review* on the UN and African and Asian independence struggles.

In the *New World Review*, Robeson shined a spotlight on the role of women at the UN. "It is unfortunate, but true, that our general press pays too little attention to the activities, and important contributions, of the women at the United Nations," Robeson argued. In 1954, she informed readers about the UN's eighth annual session of the Commission on the Status of Women. The commission consisted of women from the Dominican Republic, Byelorussia, Haiti, France, Cuba, the Soviet Union, the United Kingdom, Poland, Iran, Venezuela, China/Formosa, Lebanon, Pakistan, Burma, and the United States. These delegates, Robeson wrote, represented "women throughout the world and they deal with vital matters."[56] During its three-week session, the commission passed many resolutions, including two "on the principle of equal pay for equal work for men and women workers."[57] It announced that "the International Convention on the Political Rights of Women had now received its sixth ratification, and would therefore come into force on July 7th, 1954." Robeson outlined the Convention, which stated that women shall be allowed to "vote in all elections on equal terms with men; that they shall be eligible for election to publicly elected bodies; and that they shall be entitled to hold public office and to exercise all public functions." Although Robeson delighted in seeing women in leadership roles at the UN, she avidly looked forward to the time when "women, appointed by their governments, will sit, side-by-side with men, in the top policy-making bodies of the United Nations—in the Security, Trusteeship, and Economic and Social Councils."[58] Robeson wanted women to influence all sectors of the UN.

She did not shy away from criticizing the gender inequality that prevented the organization from achieving it. At the twelfth General Assembly, in 1957, Robeson recorded that "there were 36 women representatives from 27 Nations; . . . 12 of the women were full delegates, and 24 were alternates." Most of "these women enjoy considerable prestige in their countries," and she named a few prominent figures: Golda Meir (foreign minister of Israel), Ulla Lindstrom (minister of state for Sweden), Georgette Ciselet (Belgian senator), Z. V. Mironova (deputy mayor of Moscow), Angie Brooks (assistant attorney general of Liberia), Laili Roesad (deputy chief of the Ministry of Foreign Affairs of Indonesia), Gloria Addae (research economist in the Ministry of Trade and Development of Ghana), Taki Fujita (president of the League of Women Voters of Japan), and Indian activist Tarkenshwar Sinha.[59] Robeson stressed the advantages of having more women at the UN because she believed that men's dominance explained "why some of its important discussions continue to be unrealistic, impractical and futile." Robeson believed that "women, with the day-to-day direct working responsibility for the children, the family, the home, and the budget are inclined to be, often forced to be, much more down-to-earth and common sensical than men."[60] Similar to Nardal, Robeson drew on relational feminism to show the value of women's skills in the political arena.[61]

At the UN Robeson made contacts with a number of influential women and developed a particularly close friendship with Indian diplomat Vijaya Pandit,

Jawaharlal Nehru's sister. Robeson had met Pandit with Nehru, who was also a good friend of hers, in London in 1938.[62] Pandit shared similar interests with her brother, and in the 1940s, while she was imprisoned for her political views, her two daughters Nayantara (Tara) and Chandralekha (Lekha) studied at Wellesley College in Massachusetts and stayed with the Robeson family at The Beeches.[63] A pioneer in the male-dominated political and diplomatic field, Pandit was the first Indian woman to hold a post in the cabinet. In the 1940s she served as the Indian ambassador to the Soviet Union, the United States, Britain, and Spain. Between 1946 and 1968 she headed the Indian delegation to the UN, and in 1953 she was appointed the first woman president of the UN General Assembly.[64] Robeson's friendship with Pandit, as with Soong Ching-ling, shows how important interracial friendship was in the formation of Afro-Asian solidarity.

In *New World Review*, Robeson informed her audience about changes taking place at the UN, in particular relating to the influence of newly independent countries in Asia and Africa, which she hoped would challenge the power of Western countries. In October 1955, she argued that "the formerly quiet, assured, occasionally arrogant voices of the Colonial Powers are not so confident these days; the often meek voices of the Small Nations are taking on a new courage, determination and purpose." The new determination of the smaller nations displayed itself when the Algerian War was discussed. While France and its allies insisted that the UN did not have a right to discuss Algeria because it was a national matter for France, the smaller powers won the right to address the Algerian question at the tenth General Assembly. As a result, "France 'walked out' of the General Assembly because she cannot, or will not, face a discussion of the situation in Algeria."[65] Robeson saw this triumph as a sign that the UN would become an organization in which newly independent nations could wield power.

Robeson also wrote about key figures from Asia and Africa who could reshape debates at the UN, one of whom was her friend Krishna Menon, whom she had met in 1930s London. Considered "one of the most important diplomats in the world" in those days, Menon served as India's chief delegate to the UN.[66] Born in India in 1897 and raised in a middle-class family, Menon joined the Indian Nationalist Movement at a young age and campaigned for home rule. In the late 1920s he moved to England to study at University College London, then London School of Economics, and later read law at Inner Temple. During this time, Menon joined the English Fabian Socialists and served as secretary of the India League, a group that campaigned for Indian independence from 1929 to 1947. Extolling Menon's intelligence, "dignity, courage and confidence," Robeson remarked on how his personality and politics caused tension with his Western counterparts, who "find it very hard to take heed, calmly, of what Mr. Menon says; and they find it much harder to agree with him." Robeson explained the reasons behind this, saying that a few years before, Menon was "speaking from a soap box in London's Hyde Park;

Jawaharlal Nehru ... was in prison, and the British ... thought patronizingly, that they could afford to treat them as agitators and crackpots." With Nehru now prime minister and Menon serving as his foreign minister, Robeson opined that "the old type of conservative diplomat finds himself more and more helpless, isolated, out of the stream of things."[67] What made Menon a "new type of diplomat" was not just his political views but also that "his mind, temperament and interests are ready and eager to consider anything and everything, in all its aspects."[68]

Robeson's admiration for Menon was similar to what she felt for the leader who had hosted the historic Bandung Conference the previous year. That conference had brought together twenty-nine nations from Asia, Africa, and the Middle East. The host of the conference, the first president of Indonesia, Ahmed Sukarno, called the meeting "the first international conference of colored peoples in the history of mankind."[69] They met "to promote cooperation among the nonaligned nations of the Third World; to deliberate about such common problems as colonialism and racism; and to advocate world peace."[70] At the conference, members endorsed the strategy of nonalignment to assert their neutrality in the Cold War.[71]

In *New World Review*, Robeson reported on President Sukarno's first US state visit in 1956. She described him as "55 years old, small, compact, and handsome. An engineer by training (Bandung Technical College), a scholar, philosopher, and celebrated orator, a successful practical politician." Robeson gushed that his "speeches made an important contribution to the urgently needed 'agonizing reappraisal' of our foreign policy" and should be taken seriously.[72] For Robeson, Menon and Sukarno showed that emerging Third World leaders would reshape global politics by shifting the power balance at the UN.

As the UN expanded, more countries challenged South African apartheid. While US president Dwight Eisenhower refused to condemn racism in the US South or South Africa, Eslanda Robeson argued, "Colored Americans will be very glad to learn that ... the United Nations, and many of its Members think ... that race conflict anywhere, and in particular race conflict in South Africa, is a very grave danger in the world today."[73] Robeson denounced Eisenhower's hypocrisy, stating that he considered "the situation of the Hungarian refugees, and indeed the situation of the South Koreans and the Formosans, so important that he sent the Vice-President, the Army, and the Navy, respectively, to 'protect' these distant peoples; while not even the local police, let alone the F.B.I. and Federal troops were used to protect Colored American citizens right here in our own Southland from organized assault, bombing, dynamiting and shooting."[74] Robeson's criticism of Eisenhower's lack of interest in US racism (despite his intervention at Little Rock Central High School earlier in the year when Arkansas governor Faubus tried to prevent nine black pupils from entering the high school) and global racism chimed with many black Americans, but she optimistically saw the UN as a potential leader on this issue. She informed readers about the

"Special Political Committee" meetings that UN members held in the first two weeks of January 1957. If "Colored Americans had packed the public galleries to listen to the debate," Robeson believed that "they would have been greatly heartened by what they would have heard." At the meeting, some of the delegates from the Bandung Conference and socialist nations "declared flatly that unless racial discrimination was outlawed and put an end to, civil and racial war in the world might result."[75]

Alongside writing for *New World Review*, Robeson also participated in leftwing and radical political circles. Although she had campaigned for Roosevelt's reelection in 1944, by the end of the decade she cofounded the Progressive Party, formed in Philadelphia in July 1948 by former Democratic vice president Henry Wallace.[76] That year, Wallace ran his presidential election campaign promising peace and civil rights. Robeson followed Wallace on an eighteen-city peace tour.[77] Robeson also stood for elected office and campaigned for Connecticut secretary of state.[78] On Election Day, Wallace received less than 3 percent of the popular vote and no electoral votes.[79] Robeson also lost her race.[80] Accusations that the Progressive Party had ties to the Communist Party thwarted Wallace's political campaign.[81] Wallace left the Progressive Party in 1950 because of the debate over communism.[82] That year Robeson entered the political fray again and ran for US Congress as a third-party candidate although she received only 2,300 votes.[83] In 1948 the Progressive Party, which was committed to including black candidates on its tickets, had run forty-five for state and local offices.[84] Indeed, black American women played significant roles in the party's grassroots organization.

Shirley Graham Du Bois and Charlotta Bass were two other African American women involved with the Progressive Party.[85] Around the same time, these women, along with Robeson, were also central figures in Sojourners for Truth and Justice (STJ), a black feminist internationalist organization that supported civil rights and anti-colonialism and was established in 1952.[86] The group sprang out of an event held in September 1951, when over a hundred African American women, as part of a Sojourn for Truth and Justice protest, travelled to Washington, DC, to demand justice for racial abuse.[87] Other radical black women involved in Sojourners for Truth and Justice included the actress Beulah Richardson (Beah Richards) and activists Louise Thompson Patterson, Alice Childress, and Yvonne Gregory. According to Erik S. McDuffie, STJ was "the only organization of its kind formed during the entire Old Left period ... [that] forged a leftist, gendered vision of diaspora that viewed black women as the vanguard for radical global social change."[88] The group supported cases that were major miscarriages of justice such as those facing Rosa Lee Ingram and her children, sentenced to imprisonment for the killing of their white neighbor; W. Alphaeus Hunton, a leader in the CAA jailed for his left-wing activism; Willie McGee, who was sentenced to death in

Mississippi in 1945 following a false rape accusation by his white female lover; the Martinsville Seven; and the Trenton Six, "a group of men sentenced to death in 1948 for allegedly killing a white shopkeeper."[89]

The STJ was committed to building transnational connections with South African women in the African National Congress Women's League.[90] In a letter to South African women trade unionists who had launched a campaign against the restrictive pass laws, Bass and Patterson said: "We have been inspired by the example of militant action on the part of African women. We realize that our fight for freedom in the United States is inextricably linked to the struggle against the tyranny of the white supremacists not only in South Africa but throughout the entire continent."[91] They went on to underscore that "we further recognize that these struggles for full freedom on the part of colored women in Africa, Asia and in the United States must lead to the complete emancipation of women throughout the world."[92] Although STJ had not many more than one hundred members, it preceded the interracial and international solidarity with women of color in later groups like the Third World Women's Alliance (TWWA) of the 1970s and 1980s in its articulation of an emerging third-world women's movement.[93] Its quick demise was sparked by FBI infiltration in it and other black leftist groups that members belonged to, yet Robeson's involvement with STJ demonstrates that she was part of a larger cohort of progressive black women who practiced black feminist internationalism.[94]

THE NEW WEST INDIAN NATION

In 1957, when restrictions on Eslanda and Paul Robeson were lifted so that they could visit places where a passport was not needed, one of the first invitations Eslanda accepted was to attend the founding of the WIF in Trinidad. Black US newspapers saw the WIF as a key part of global black politics alongside the rising tide of independence struggles waged by people of color in Africa and Asia. The *New York Amsterdam News* noted in an editorial that "the advent of the Federation of the West Indies marks another milestone in the continued emergence of the people of African descent all over the world into positions of leadership and authority."[95] Robeson's visit to Trinidad reflects her interest in the Caribbean as "a site for transnational and diasporic black nation-building efforts beyond Africa."[96] It also provided her with a chance to practice black and feminist internationalism.

Robeson observed the "historic and memorable meeting" with delegates from as far away as Pakistan and Ghana, as well as other Americans like Powell.[97] In articles about her time in Trinidad, Robeson reported that she found the WIF's membership "historically significant" because it was "overwhelmingly Negro in composition," along with an Indian minority.[98] Robeson hoped that "the diverse elements of this very interesting and attractive multi-racial society . . . will continue to submerge their widely different interests, traditions and customs, and join together to build a healthy, happy, prosperous nation, unified in its diversity."[99]

During her stay, Robeson met leading political figures, like Grenadian journalist Theophilus Albert Marryshow, architect of the WIF, known as the "father of the federation." She also delivered speeches at the public library in Port-of-Spain.[100] She gave special attention to meeting women's organizations and leaders. Historians Alice Colón and Rhoda Reddock have argued that in the postwar years most women's political activism in the Caribbean took place through women's groups that were part of national political parties.[101] Robeson addressed the Women's League of the People's National Movement, the center-left political party founded by Eric Williams in 1955 and the Communication Services and General Workers Union, a trade union for women.[102] She also spoke at an "all-day Rally" to a group of female welfare and social workers that "is just now crystallizing, and is called THE CARIBBEAN WOMEN'S ORGANIZATION IN THE MAKING." This group was "inter-racial, inter-Island, and represents all aspects of welfare and social work." Marson's long-time friend, the Trinidadian activist Audrey Jeffers served as the tentative chairman of the group while J. D. Ramkeeson acted as tentative secretary. At the rally, Robeson discussed the subject "children are the future." Other speakers included poet Louise Bennett, "Dr. Marjorie Bean of Bermuda, Mrs. Phyllis Allfrey of Dominica and Minister of Social Affairs for THE WEST INDIES, and Mrs. Janet Jagan, Minister of Housing in British Guiana."[103]

It was the first time that Robeson had met many of these women, and she took an immediate liking to Bennett. She also got a chance to spend more time with the one figure she did know well, her fellow American Janet Jagan. Raised in a Jewish family in Chicago, Jagan had met her husband, Indo-Guianese Cheddi Jagan, when he was studying in the United States. After their wedding, Cheddi and Janet Jagan returned to British Guiana, where they helped to establish the People's Progressive Party, a leading left-wing political party. In the early 1950s, when Janet Jagan had briefly visited the United States, she had arranged to meet the Robesons. Following their meeting, Janet Jagan and Eslanda Robeson formed a close friendship based on their mutual political interests and views.[104] After the death of Cheddi Jagan in 1997, Janet Jagan served as prime minister and then president of independent Guyana, becoming the first woman ever to do so.

Although Robeson wanted the WIF to transform into a permanent nation, it did not. Regional hierarchies, personality clashes, and racial, ethnic, and religious tensions led to its end on May 31, 1962, following a referendum in Jamaica the previous year, where 54 percent voted to leave, leading to the beginning of island-wide independence in the Anglophone Caribbean.[105] Yet the time Robeson spent time in Trinidad speaking to and building links with emerging women's organizations, along with her role with STJ, reflected the significance feminist organizing had come to have for her activism.

MARSON'S CONSERVATIVE JOURNALISM IN JAMAICA

After recovering from depression, Una Marson resumed writing articles. In them, she discussed a range of topics that were not strictly linked to her practices as a race woman internationalist but that were important for giving voice to her growing conservative views regarding changes taking place in Jamaican society such as independence as well as marriage, social welfare, and labor. In the article "Building National Culture," she told the story of a friend who "protested to me that he would do his utmost to root out everything planted by British Colonialism and its brainwashing influence of white superiority to the vast majority of black peoples of our land."[106] When Marson stated that this would be impossible to enact, "he accused me of being one of those who had been brain-washed and suggested that if I did not wish to accept the reign of the black man, . . . I and others who thought like me could go elsewhere." The reference to the "reign of the black man" demonstrates how some strands of Jamaican nationalism were linked to black male patriarchy, leaving little room for women to voice their concerns.

Marson later reported that her "suggestion that the flag was a misfortune and the National Anthem a tragedy only heaped down more coals of fire on my head."[107] While she was not against Jamaican independence, she cautioned against blaming Jamaica's problems on British colonialism. It is interesting to note Marson's contradictory views on decolonization. As a supporter of the WIF and the People's National Party (PNP) who sought independence, Marson's views on how independent Jamaica should understand its past and relationship to Britain revealed her altered views on colonialism. In her opinion, "Jamaica is too small and too poor an island to begin its national life with a determination to purge the dominant elements of its past, repudiating its history, . . . abusing and denying a culture which is the only one by which we have grown."[108] In this comment Marson overlooked Jamaica's African past and culture, which she had tried to promote in the 1930s.

She rhetorically asked, "Did the British settlers in the early years of slavery, which by the way they did not initiate, think the African slaves were bad and ugly?" Her rather problematic answer was that the "early history of the West Indies records many expressions of admiration for these people," and she added that "there was some amount of admiration in the lust that started with the impregnation of women who were moral according to their own traditions."[109] Here, Marson overlooked the violence of sexual relationships between enslaved women and their masters.

Marson went on to place herself in the history of slavery, commenting that "it is mostly from the strains of this blending that my friend, myself, and countless Jamaicans now climbing unto the ranks of the middle class and proving to be successful leaders had their start." She continued by arguing that "thousands of slaves who showed ability, intelligence and leadership were freed during slavery and jumped unimpeded on the ladder of progress. It was the white missionaries who helped to educate and settle them in freedom."[110] However, Marson failed to consider the agency of slaves in their own emancipation struggles, an argument that C. L. R. James had stressed in his 1938 study of the Haitian Revolution, *The Black Jacobins*.[111] She also overlooked the fact that many formerly enslaved did not easily progress and many stayed trapped within the poor lower classes. Marson further absolved the violence of British colonialism and transatlantic slavery by offering a Whiggish interpretation of history, stating that "it was neither the fault of the British nor the Africans that they found themselves in the juxtaposition of master and slave. In fact it was history repeating itself for the British were once slaves of the Romans."[112] Her views overlooked the differences between Roman slavery and the race-based nature of the transatlantic system.

Marson faced difficulty publishing this article because of its pro-British stance. Despite the conservatism of the *Daily Gleaner*, it endorsed the ideas of Alexander Bustamante, who expressed right-leaning but pro-independence views. Yet Marson's article reveals the extent to which she and other members of the black middle class from different islands of the Caribbean tried to assert the positive implications of British colonialism and history in the newly independent region. After meetings in London with the secretary of state of the colonies in February 1962, Bustamante, as leader of the Jamaica Labour Party (JLP), reached an agreement for independence to begin on August 6 that year.[113] As a supporter of the PNP, Marson expressed disappointment that the JLP won that year's election.[114] Unlike Amy Jacques Garvey, who tried to push the PNP to consider ways to close the race and the class divide, Marson did not actively participate in the PNP.[115] Although she remained on the outskirts of party politics, Marson warned that "it will be a long time before all the people of this young nation will fully understand and succeed in living up to the implications of independence," showing her lack of optimism for post-independence politicians.[116]

Another unpublished article Marson wrote centered on marriage. Eschewing her feminist politics, she called for a law stipulating "that married women with children up to the age of ten should not be allowed to go out to full time work away from home. Exceptions to be made in cases of the illness or other incapacity of the husband."[117] Marson supported her reactionary idea by arguing that "in the mad rush for equality women have lost the respect and consideration of many of their menfolk."[118] She encouraged women to "give marriage a chance and let the careers go to single women. Choose a career, yes, in the early training against being a spinster or a widow. But marriage is a career, or should be."[119] Marson's thoughts on marriage serve as an interesting counterpoint to her own personal life. After her separation from Staples, Marson's idea of marriage as a career indicates that she may have regretted the choices she had made in her relationships with men in the past. Her words also resonated with the narrative of marriage in Jamaica, where the number of married women declined as cohabitation and having children outside of wedlock rose. The colonial government saw these types of relationships, especially common among lower-class women, as immoral, and it instilled marriage as a respectable middle-class norm, which independence leaders also promoted.

While these controversial articles remained unpublished, Marson managed to get other pieces published in the *Daily Gleaner* and its sister paper, the *Sunday Gleaner*. In February 1961, she wrote about the recent move of the YMCA and YWCA buildings from downtown Kingston. She believed that these civic and Christian organizations fostered an active nationalism and urged young people to "visit these organizations, seek membership, take part in the programmes and learn to associate with and serve one another with love. Thus . . . the new Jamaica will be building a sturdier citizenship."[120] In her attempt to serve other Jamaicans with love, Marson rejoined Jamsave (Jamaica Save the Children Fund) as executive secretary and used the pages of the *Sunday Gleaner* to publicize the organization in order "to increase our numbers of subscribers."[121]

Since its founding in 1938, Jamsave had grown and had successfully raised funds to build three play centers in Kingston. Through Jamsave, Marson advocated better living conditions for Rastafarians and helped to establish the Foreshore Road Infant Centre for Rastafarian children.[122] But she remained frustrated with the professionalization of social work. Writing under her pen name "The Torch," she admitted "getting a bit impatient with people who need to research for seven months to find out what is obvious. I suppose getting to know the area and winning people over is important but when one starts with the knowledge of urgent needs, the planning and persuasion should not be too long drawn out."[123] In her article, Marson described a meeting with a British social worker who visited Jamaica. In their discussions about London's East End, the social worker "explained that the area has been thoroughly worked over and was no longer a centre for visitors and workers who were interested in social problems."[124] By comparing London's East End with conditions in Jamaica, Marson hoped to show that positive changes and the alleviation of class divisions could occur in places long neglected by the colonial government and in need of attention by the independent government.

Despite the range of Marson's writings, as well as her social work, she remained unpopular in the new nation. Delia Jarrett-Macauley has said, "Visiting community centres, social organisations and clubs, her strong social conscience struck people as endearing and rare. But in Kingston her conservative views increasingly marked her as out of step with the times."[125] While Marson's conservativism cost her popularity and public recognition, it reflects how the context of independence altered her political views. But by contrast, Robeson remained very much engaged in left-wing politics and international debates.

THE ROBESONS IN LONDON, 1958–1962

When Eslanda and Paul Robeson's passports were returned in 1958, they protested their confinement by returning to the city they had called home during the interwar years, which gave her further opportunities to practice black and feminist internationalism.[126] The London the Robesons returned to in 1958 differed dramatically from the one they had left in 1939. Since the arrival of the *Empire Windrush* on June 22, 1948, at Tilbury Docks, which brought five hundred mostly male West Indians to Britain, their presence had raised the issue of immigration and employment to the forefront of British politics. In July 1948, the Labour government passed the British Nationality Act with the backing of the Conservative Party.[127] The act intended to protect the security of the British Commonwealth and enshrined in law that "all colonial citizens had the status of a British subject—and thus the right to live and work in Britain."[128] Unexpectedly, by 1958, around 200,000 men and women from Pakistan, India, and the Caribbean had come to Britain.[129] That year violent anti-black riots erupted in Notting Hill. In response, Claudia Jones founded the *West Indian Gazette*, later renamed the *West Indian Gazette and Afro-Asian Caribbean News* to embrace the larger diasporic community. It became an important publication that detailed black global news and, in particular, served as a rallying call for anti-racist activists in Britain. Like most black newspapers, the *West Indian Gazette and Afro-Asian Caribbean News* suffered financially, and Jones was not in a salaried position as editor.[130] Nevertheless, the *Gazette* office in Brixton, home to an expanding West Indian population, acted as an advice bureau for black people as well as a discussion forum for visiting black political figures, such as Norman Manley and Martin Luther King Jr.

The greater presence of blacks in postwar Britain reshaped debates about immigration, citizenship, and empire that Eslanda Robeson would participate in. According to historian Kennetta Hammond Perry, "as Afro-Caribbean migrants made choices to exercise their imperial citizenship and rhetorically and symbolically insist that 'London is the place for me' by journeying to the 'Mother country' and asserting their rights to belong, they made race, and more precisely, the problem of racism a subject of public dialogue and political debate.... [They] remapped the very boundaries of what is meant to be both Black and British."[131] The Robesons soon become involved in black British politics through an internationalist lens.

With their base in London, the couple also continued to travel, venturing to the Soviet Union later in the year, where they reconnected with friends. In December 1958, Paul Robeson received an invitation to the All-African Conference in Ghana but could not attend because of prior performing engagements. Eslanda Robeson went in his place, reporting on events for the Associated Negro Press, which allowed her to practice black and feminist internationalism.[132]

On her first visit to independent Africa, Robeson found the Accra Conference very "exciting and rewarding." With around "200 delegates from 50 organizations (trade unions and political parties) from 20 countries," discussions at the conference "centered upon how the African people, in unity and close co-operation, can put aside their internal differences and work together to bring an end to Colonialism."[133] The conference took place after the First Conference of Independent African States was held in Accra in April 1958. Both conferences attempted to forward continental unity and present a "United States of Africa."[134] George Padmore organized the Accra conference, and Congolese leader Patrice Lumumba served as co-chair. At the conference, Robeson met African leaders whom she had written about in *New World Review,* including Lumumba, Kenyan trade unionist Tom Mboya, and Malawian leader Hastings Banda.[135] Robeson remarked on the uniqueness of the conference, commenting that "for the first time in modern history Africans from North, East, Central, South and West Africa met in conference on African soil to discuss African Affairs." She noted that "the United States sent more observers than any other country—more than 30, eleven of whom were Negroes." She reasoned that it was because "Americans did not want to miss the boat at Accra, as they did at Bandung."[136]

Although the conference aimed to present unity, tensions existed. Nigeria had not yet gained its independence, and with a much larger population than Ghana, many of its leaders did not want to be subordinate to their close neighbor. Debates raged over the use of violence versus nonviolence in independence struggles; some non-English speaking delegates complained that translators were inadequate; and Sudan did not attend because the recently installed military government under General Aboud promoted a pro-Western bias.[137]

Robeson was aware of tensions but returned to her constant critique of "the absence of women at the Accra Conference."[138] In total, "there were only eight official women delegates, and only two women addressed the plenary sessions." The two women were Martha Ouandie, who told "the terrible story of French colonialism now rampant in Cameroons, and Shirley Graham Du Bois [who] read the clear, forceful, constructive message to the conference from her husband." Robeson stressed, "A whole population cannot be properly mobilized if half of it is officially ignored."[139] Her continual insistence on asking the gender question shows her criticism of the masculinity inherent in the "big-man" politics of African independence that weakened claims about postcolonial equality.[140] At the conference, she not only reunited with Graham Du Bois but also formed links with other women attendees, including Nigerian activist Mallama Gambo, Egyptian feminist Saiza Nabarawi, radical Indian activist Geeta Mukherjee, and Maida Springer.[141] After the conference, she flew back to London via Nigeria, Kano, and Barcelona.[142]

Although Robeson did not disclose the news publicly, at this time doctors had diagnosed her with cervical cancer and later uterine cancer.[143] In January 1959, she went to the Soviet Union to undergo radiotherapy. Paul Robeson was also ill, suffering from depression. He too travelled to the Soviet Union to receive treatment. For the remaining years of his life, despite his revived career, his depression endured.[144] After their treatments, the Robesons returned to London and resumed their activism.

Eslanda Robeson threw herself into working among black internationalist political organizations challenging racism in Britain, Africa, and other parts of the African diaspora. She was part of campaigns that sprang up following the racist murder of thirty-two-year-old Antiguan-born carpenter Kelso Cochrane. His death and the fact that his white killers were known to the police but were not arrested and imprisoned sparked outrage among blacks in Britain. At the Kelso Cochrane Memorial meeting, Eslanda Robeson delivered a searing speech, reminding her audience of the wider implications of his death: "If a man can be attacked and killed because he is colored, this is of very [sic] concern to every West Indian, African, Indian, Negro, and Asian, wherever he may be."[145]

In the early 1960s, Robeson further expanded her activism and engaged in anti-apartheid protest. To mark the one-year anniversary of the Sharpeville massacre, Claudia Jones organized an anti-apartheid protest in Trafalgar Square, which Robeson attended. In her speech, Robeson reminded the crowd that "the reason the Murders at Sharpeville are important to the world is because they exposed, once again, the EVILS and DANGERS of Racial Discrimination, Segregation and Oppression."[146] She specifically called on women to take part in the anti-apartheid struggle, saying that "no human progress is possible without them."[147] Robeson connected the fight for anti-apartheid in South Africa to housing discrimination in Britain, suggesting that landlords and landladies "would do well to treat all prospective tenants as Human Beings. One never knows when a black student may return later as a President or a Prime Minister of a Free Nation." Robeson explicitly invoked the language and politics of human rights: "Let us bombard Governments, Ministers, the United Nations, and everybody everywhere to make sure that Human Beings enjoy freedom, Equality and Human Rights."[148] Her speech reflects that her internationalism and thoughts on equality had grown more inclusive. Blacks and whites applauded her speech, but she and others faced heckling from the racist members of the group Keep England White, and by the end of the rally thirty people had been arrested.[149]

But the event did help to bring the issue of apartheid to a broader public. So too did the continuing activism by Jones, who organized a hunger strike in support of those indicted in the Rivonia trial, including Nelson Mandela.[150] As television coverage of the horrors of apartheid became more widespread in the 1970s and 1980s and Mandela became a cause célèbre, there was a growth in anti-apartheid activism among blacks and whites in Europe and the United States.[151]

After her speech, Robeson halted her activism when news of Paul Robeson's attempted suicide in March 1961 in Moscow reached her. Eslanda rushed to Russia to help take care of her husband and son, who were together at the time.[152] Paul's Soviet doctors recommended that he receive tranquilizers. By October 1961, Paul's condition had not improved, and Eslanda Robeson made the difficult decision to admit him to the Priory in London, a psychiatric facility where he received "debilitating electroconvulsive therapy," which affected his physical and mental mobility.[153] Paul Robeson spent a number of periods during the next two years at the Priory, with Eslanda frequently visiting him.

Alongside taking care her husband, Eslanda Robeson joined Jones in helping to establish more women-centered groups—namely, the All African Women's Freedom Movement (AAWFM).[154] The left-leaning Pan-African group held its first event, African Women's Day, in December 1961 at the State Ballroom Hall. In her speech, Robeson remarked, "As a member of our great African family, indeed as a member of the greater non-white family in our world, I am of course very much interested and concerned with our family joys and sorrows and our many problems. . . . I am especially happy [to] . . . belong to this new organization . . . because I do believe that women have an important and urgent role to play in our new World."[155] Due to her work with the AAWFM, Robeson accepted invitations to participate in other activist groups. In April 1962, she spoke to the Committee of African Organisations (CAO) at its forum "The Role of Women in the Emancipation of Africa."[156] The CAO comprised a number of groups, including the West African Students' Union, the "Uganda People's Congress, the Zanzibar nationalist party, the Basutoland African Congress, the Somali Student Association, and the Society of African Culture."[157] That month, Robeson also addressed the audience at the Africa Day Meeting held at Festival Hall, organized by the Movement for Colonial Freedom (MCF), another group in which she participated. Robeson described the MCF as "a Bridge between the Old Dream world of Colonial Subjection and the New Real World of Afreedom *[sic]* and Equality for all."[158] Like the CAA, the MCF aimed to "properly inform the people of Britain about conditions in Africa."[159]

In July 1963, Robeson left London and headed to Germany to attend the trial in absentia of Hans Globke, a Nazi collaborator.[160] The following month her cancer recurred and she was informed that further treatment was futile. She and Paul entered the Buch Clinic in East Germany for treatment.[161] In the midst of her declining health, in August, Robeson received exciting news that she had been awarded the Clara Zetkin medal from the Council of Ministers from the German Democratic Republic for her "services in the struggle for peace and human equality."[162] During the 1930s, Zetkin had been a leading communist, anti-fascist, and feminist.[163] That month, from their hospital beds in Berlin, Eslanda and Paul watched the historic March on Washington. They both regretted being unable to attend, but Eslanda wrote that she and Paul "could almost feel ourselves there, in person.... We certainly felt ourselves an intimate part of this history."[164] Although unwell, she continued trying to fulfil speaking obligations.

In November, Robeson visited Leipzig to attend the International Documentary Film Festival and continued to forge black and liberal internationalist connections "with the African and other foreign students and faculty members of the Herder Institute, the foreign department of Leipzig [Karl Marx] University."[165] Later, she addressed the assembly and spoke about current racial conditions in the United States as well as her time travelling in Africa and writing about the UN. In December, she spoke at a forum at Humboldt University in Berlin on the topic "the Negro in the United States" and planned to build links with Jeanne Martin Cissé from Guinea. Martin Cissé served as the General Secretary of the All-African Women's Organization, "which [was] composed of twenty-three African national organizations with headquarters at Bamako, Republic of Mali."[166] Additionally, Martin Cissé was "a member of the Third Committee (Human Rights), representing Guinea in the Social and Humanitarian sessions" at the UN and in 1963 participated as an observer at the Status of Women Commission.[167] Robeson described Martin Cissé as "beautiful, with lovely skin and fine features and with brains and charm as well."[168] The two women discussed "the possibility of establishing contacts between Negro women in America and women of Africa, for the exchange of news and views, in order to develop understanding, friendship and cooperation."[169] This highlights Robeson's continuing commitment to creating alliances with black women across national borders.

Next, Robeson visited the Händel School in Berlin, where she shared news about the United States, Africa, the UN, and similarities between Jewish and African American integration as well as ways to connect with black children in schools.[170] Later, she ventured to the Fritz Heckert Trade Union College, which trained young people to become labor organizers. The college included around fifty African students from many parts of the continent, and she discussed race relations in Europe and Africa.[171] All the activities Robeson undertook in Germany show how, towards the end of her life and despite her poor health, she remained committed to forging multiracial and transnational connections. After their stay in Germany at the end of 1963, the Robesons returned to the United States.[172]

During the last two years of Robeson's life, she attended gatherings in honor of her and Paul's work and wrote about the civil rights movement, but health problems persisted.[173] In August 1965, Robeson returned to Beth Israel hospital.[174] On December 13, two days shy of her seventieth birthday, she died. Paul Robeson could not visit her because he was unwell in Philadelphia. Pauli, his wife, Marilyn, and their two children, David and Susan, held a private service, and later Eslanda was cremated.¹⁷⁵ Tributes from friends and family mourning her loss poured in from nearly every corner of the world.

MARSON IN ISRAEL AND LONDON

A year before Robeson's death, Una Marson's social work and former activism attracted the attention of Israel's foreign minister, Golda Meir, who invited her to attend a seminar for women leaders at the Mount Carmel International Training Centre for Community Services in Haifa and a conference in Jerusalem, "The Role of Women in the Struggle for Peace and Development."¹⁷⁶ Founded in 1960, the Mount Carmel Training Centre was a "permanent education centre for women."¹⁷⁷ After Meir's trip that year to West Africa, she created development programs for women. The first conference took place in 1961 and attracted over sixty delegates from different parts of the global South and Europe. The next meeting sought to build on the progress of the first by bringing together female nurses, politicians, and social workers.¹⁷⁸

Delighted with the invitation, Marson quickly packed her belongings, and her sojourn revived her practices of feminist internationalism through the networks and friendships she made. In November 1964, she arrived in Tel Aviv and exclaimed, "I had always said . . . that if ever I reached the Holy Land, I would bow down and kiss the earth, and I did too. I had no idea what would happen in the month ahead, but I was in the Holy Land and it was sure to be good."¹⁷⁹ At the seminar in Haifa, "Social and Cultural Integration in Urban Areas," Marson was one of over fifty delegates from the Caribbean, Africa, Latin America, and Asia. She spoke about the challenges that independent Jamaica faced and learned lessons from other delegates about policies and practices that could be implemented to improve the developing world.¹⁸⁰ While at the conference, she also visited a range of places, such as Upper Galilee, Nazareth, Beer-Sheba, and the Dead Sea, with other women.¹⁸¹ On November 29, she was in Jerusalem for the three-day international conference, where she was one of eighty-four women from forty-nine countries. The theme of the conference was "the role of women in the struggle for peace and development."¹⁸² She left the conference invigorated, insisting that "the future of the developing countries depends to a great extent on the progress and contribution of their women."¹⁸³ Geographically closer to London than she had been in nineteen years, Marson decided to pay the city where she spent "twelve of the most eventful and satisfying years of [her] life" a visit for one month.¹⁸⁴

In a February 1965 article in the *Sunday Gleaner*, Marson reflected on her experiences in London. When she had arrived in December 1964, what first struck her was that "everything seemed so peaceful and quiet that I just sat back and let the solid peace and security of this lovely old city sink again into my heart. I couldn't see a single crater or damaged building."[185] By the 1960s, remnants of the Second World War were slowly being wiped away. The peace and security that Marson found in London was complemented by the numerous reunions she had with friends, including Stella Mead, the photographer Erica Koch, her former neighbors, and Learie Constantine.[186]

In London, Marson's diary was packed. She visited the Save the Children Fund's office and the BBC Broadcasting House in Oxford Circus, where writer Andrew Salkey interviewed her for the Caribbean service. Another Caribbean writer she reconnected with was Vivian Virtue, who organized what Marson described as "a delightful party for me at which I met many West Indian writers."[187] On Christmas Day, Marson spent "a delightful day with Andrew, his wife and two lovely children." Among the guests were George Lamming, and she described "the conversation" as "lively, amusing and informative."[188] At the BBC she enjoyed the opportunity to discuss the Mount Carmel Training Centre on the popular radio show *Women's Hour*.[189] She also visited the cinema and the West End and enjoyed seeing *Lawrence of Arabia* and *Becket,* the French version of *Murder in the Cathedral*.[190] When Marson learned of T. S. Eliot's death, with whom she had collaborated when she worked at the BBC, she and Mead attended his funeral.[191]

Marson marvelled at all the things that appeared the same when she had lived in the city in the 1930s and 1940s. In Trafalgar Square, for instance, "nothing seemed changed." When she entered one of her "old haunts," Lyons Corner House, "it was much smarter inside and the prices were a great deal higher. But the atmosphere was the same." Yet the one striking change that Marson observed in London was the "several dark-skinned guards at the underground stations . . . and there was much more colour in the surging crowd of London's West end."[192] She expressed joy in seeing "my people looking smart and efficient as they work in tubes and buses. I have talked to them whenever possible, in restaurants, rest rooms, shops, post offices, and street cleaning." She summarized the attitude of these West Indians by saying many of them told her, "It is all right, but they would sooner be home in the sunshine IF there was work."[193] In the article, Marson glossed over the difficulties many West Indians and other nonwhite colonials faced in Britain, which she was well aware of.

Although her visit to London coincided with Martin Luther King Jr.'s, she did not meet him or meet with prominent black activists that Robeson had worked with. However, she heard debates by the Campaign Against Racial Discrimination (CARD), a group of blacks, whites, and South Asians formed around 1964, determined to challenge racism and repeal the 1962 Commonwealth Immigration Act.[194] Marson hoped "inter-racial relations will be improved by the formation of CARD and that wisdom, tact and patience will temper their anxiety to bring about better conditions for all coloured immigrants" in Britain.[195] Yet CARD was unable "to reckon with the germinating seeds of a more strident and unabashedly Black political consciousness that made demands of the state just as it implicated the Government in perpetuating anti-Black racism and White supremacy ... [which] ultimately led to the eventual demise of the organization" in the late 1960s.[196]

After a month in London, Marson returned to Haifa to work at the Mount Carmel Training Centre. Her role was to "assist in the work there among Asian and African and Latin American women."[197] This would have seen Marson working with women's organizations in these continents and with development programs to ensure that the needs of women, children, and families were being addressed by their respective governments. The director, Mina Ben-Zwi, was fond of Marson but wary of her coming back to work given her age, increasingly high blood pressure, and the physical demands of the job. But Marson reassured Ben-Zwi of her good health. She also reassured Ben-Zwi that the job's minimal financial reward was acceptable because she had "never had a great concern about money."[198] Three months into her job in Haifa, Marson received news from the British Council that she had received funding to begin a project charting social development research in Jamaica. Unfortunately, this became another project that Marson neither started or finished. At this time, her melancholy reappeared, rendering her unable to work. Although she wanted to go back to London, Ben-Zwi and doctors in Haifa convinced Marson to return to Jamaica. Her flight departed on April 10 and after spending time recovering at home with her older sister Ethel, she entered Kingston Hospital.[199] After ten days in hospital, on May 6, Marson died after a heart attack.[200]

Following her death, tributes streamed in from friends and organizations Marson had worked with, including the YWCA, the Jamaica Teachers Association, and Jamsave.[201] In honor of Marson, Jamsave started the Una Marson Memorial Infant Centre in Trench Town, and the Mount Carmel Training Centre began a scholarship for a Jamaican woman to attend the annual leaders' seminars.[202]

A year after Marson's death, Paulette Nardal received recognition for her contribution to Negritude by Léopold Senghor, who awarded her the Commander of the National Order of the Republic of Senegal/Commandeur de l'ordre national de la république du Sénégal.[203] Paulette Nardal and her sister Lucy were also awarded the French Légion d'honneur.[204] In later decades, Nardal was less active in public life in Martinique than she had been but she remained a popular, well-known figure. In 1985, at the age of eighty-nine, she passed away. The following year, the Municipal Council renamed Place Fénélon in the center of Fort-de-France Place Paulette Nardal in recognition of the contribution she had made to her island and beyond.[205]

. . .

Towards the latter stages of their lives, changes and continuities shaped Robeson's, Marson's, and Nardal's practices as race women internationalists. Of the three, it was Robeson who most consistently used travel to Trinidad, Britain, Ghana and

Germany and her writings in *New World Review,* even within the hostile Cold War context and in spite of her illnesses, to express black, liberal, and feminist internationalism. This was also a period when Robeson began to articulate the importance of human rights that stemmed from and became an important part of her internationalism.

The 1950s saw changes in Marson's ability to practice race women's internationalism. In the United States, her religious faith increased, which influenced her involvement in social work. Her time in the United States did also allow her to practice black internationalism through her critical role in forming the AFWIF. After her recovery from depression, her journalism centered on Jamaica and conservatism. But when she ventured to Israel, this provided her with a chance to practice feminist internationalism with women from different parts of the world.

This period saw Nardal move away from activist-intellectual work, but she remained engaged in cultural expressions of black internationalism through music. Furthermore, her continued involvement within the public sphere saw her gain more recognition for her involvement in French and Martiniquan politics and culture. The varied experiences of the three women between 1950 and 1966 attest to the complex changes and continuities based on differing contexts and personal life experiences that shaped their practices as race women internationalists.

Conclusion

Tracing the entangled lives of Eslanda Robeson, Paulette Nardal, and Una Marson has shown the complex and varied ways in which their travels facilitated their creation and participation in the transnational black public sphere, leading to their involvement in political, social, and cultural networks. This enabled their multidimensional practices as race women internationalists evidenced through their travels, writings, activism, and friendships where they engaged with interconnected internationalisms: namely, black, feminist, anti-fascist, liberal, conservative, and Christian. This, in turn, saw them contribute to the politics of racial destiny that underpinned global freedom struggles against fascism, racism, sexism, and colonialism.

The myriad internationalisms Nardal, Marson, and Robeson practiced reflect the diversity of intellectual history "black woman style." The trio drew on their lived experiences and shared their ideas in the pages of newspapers, books, poetry, plays, and short stories and in speeches. In particular, Nardal and Marson opened up their homes, which became critical contact zones for discussions about colonialism, departmentalization, and decolonization. Within these spaces and the other networks they interacted in, all three women voiced left-leaning, conservative, progressive, and radical views that further demonstrate the ideological heterogeneity that informed their internationalism.

Placing the three figures together from the 1920s to the 1960s has highlighted the similarities and differences between their activism and ideas and how they adapted over time. In the 1930s and 1940s, Una Marson's involvement with Pan-African black internationalist groups like the League of Coloured Peoples and her experience living in wartime London and working at the BBC led her to stress the need for race consciousness and racial unity among blacks. It was in feminist international organizations in interwar London where she was able to discuss racism and sexism and air her anti-colonial critiques. By the 1950s, and especially during and after her time in the United States, Marson began to express more socially conservative views on women's roles and marriage that perhaps mirrored some of the personal challenges she faced in life. Her time in the United States did see her engage in community activism through social work and contribute to Caribbean politics by forming the AFWIF, which provides evidence of her practice of black internationalism and Caribbean nationalism. Her criticism surrounding Jamaican independence in the early 1960s reveals the extent to which she did not fully embrace the anti-British stance that arose within radical circles at the end of empire in the Caribbean. Her trip to Israel, albeit short, allowed her to resume practicing feminist internationalism through the politics of development. For the majority of her life, Marson suffered from bouts of depression that interrupted her ability to work. The fact that she regularly sought help and spent time away from the spotlight reflects how she and her circle of friends and family worked hard to support her health and recovery.

Paulette Nardal's moderate conservative views were a staple throughout her life but they did not limit her from creating alliances with anti-colonials and radicals during the Italian invasion of Ethiopia and practicing black, Christian, and anti-fascist internationalism. When she returned to Martinique during the war, Nardal built on her participation in black internationalism in Europe by establishing the Women's Assembly and *La Femme dans la cité*. This allowed her to engage in feminist internationalism. Her time at the United Nations also saw her engage with liberal and Christian internationalism. Even when she was not active as an activist-intellectual after the late 1950s, her musical work remained expressive of black internationalism.

In interwar Europe, Eslanda Robeson was active in left-wing radical politics, which only grew as the decades wore on. Her numerous sojourns across the world, the friendships she developed with key African and Asian postcolonial leaders, her writings in newspapers like *New World Review*, her involvement with international organizations like the UN and progressive groups like the Sojourners for Truth and Justice (STJ) all enabled her to, unlike Marson and Nardal, consistently practice black, feminist, and liberal internationalism due to the varied activist networks she was involved in. Taking an expansive look at the women's lives across multiple contexts and time periods reveals how critical networks and networking within the transnational black public sphere was to their practices as race women internationalists.

The group biography method has illuminated further the nuances of their migratory subjectivities and the impact of travel. Travelling could in some cases hinder, while in other instances fuel their activism and thought. In the case of

Robeson, the US state and British colonial officials saw her travels as subversive and dangerous, showing the politicized and radical nature of black women's sojourns. These women's movements across the world has further illustrated the overlapping linkages between the internationalist contact zones of London, Paris, and New York with Kingston, Fort-de-France, Cape Town, and Brazzaville.

Nardal, Marson, and Robeson were part of a wider group of race women internationalists that continued in the latter half of the twentieth century and beyond. Following the publication of her 1969 autobiography, *I Know Why the Caged Bird Sings*, Maya Angelou was propelled into the national and international spotlight and became something of a spokesperson for black women in America and beyond. As someone who travelled frequently and spent time living abroad, Angelou identified as a self-styled "renaissance woman" who expressed solidarity with the struggles of all blacks and women across the world and especially those in the global South. Her serial autobiographies and empowering poems became a vessel through which the experiences of black diasporic women were voiced and a space for her to express race women's internationalist sentiments.

Other figures such as Vicki Garvin, Audre Lorde, and Angela Davis can be identified as race women internationalists due to their international travels and the fact that their activism was based on challenging globally interconnected inequalities surrounding racism, sexism, militarism, colonialism within and outside of America. Artist-activists like Nina Simone and Miriam Makeba sang and spoke as race women internationalists through their music, fashion styles, and involvement in civil rights, black power, and anti-apartheid movements. Building on STJ, the rise of black feminist organizations in the 1960s and 1970s in the United States, such as the Combahee River Collective and the Third World Women's Alliance, and in Britain, such as the Organisation of Women of Asian and African Descent and Southall Black Sisters, provided additional spaces for race women internationalists.[1]

In the Caribbean, the impact of Marson and Nardal and other black women activists are reflected in the rise of the Caribbean feminist movements seen through the formation of, to give one example, the regional non-governmental organization the Caribbean Association for Feminist Research and Action (CAFRA) in April 1985, a "progressive feminist orientated network of Caribbean feminists and feminist organizations."[2] CAFRA aims to reach all areas of the Caribbean and promotes "regional actions, campaigns, research projects, cooperation and collaboration."[3] There are many other island-wide, political, religious, racial, and ethnic women's groups that operate in the Caribbean and grew in the late 1960s alongside the rise of the women's movements in the United States and black power.[4] Yet, although feminist and women's organizations exist throughout the Caribbean, many have experienced uneven development due to the political, economic, social, and cultural challenges that continue to affect attempts to create gender equality.[5] This book has sought to add more recognition due to Nardal, Marson, and Robeson by seeing them as important figures within a larger genealogy of race woman internationalists who have been committed to, in various ways, challenging inequalities within global freedom struggles.

NOTES

Unless otherwise indicated, all translations from the French are mine.

ABBREVIATIONS

Manuscript collections frequently cited use the following abbreviations:

ADM	Archives departementales de la Martinique, Fort-de-France.
APP	Archives de la Préfecture de police, Paris.
BBC	BBC Written Archives Centre, Caversham, Reading.
BNF	Bibliothèque nationale de France, François Mitterrand, Paris.
BRBM	Beinecke Rare Book and Manuscript Library, Yale University, New Haven, CT.
CAOM	Centre des archives d'outre-mer, Aix-en-Provence.
EGRP	Eslanda Goode Robeson Papers, Moorland-Spingarn Research Center, Howard University, Washington, DC.
PERC	Paul and Eslanda Robeson Collection, Moorland-Spingarn Research Center, Howard University, Washington, DC.
PRO	Public Record Office, National Archives, Kew, Richmond, Surrey.
SLOTFOM	Service de liaison avec les originaires des territoires français d'outre-mer, CAOM.
TWL	The Women's Library, London School of Economics.
UMP	Una Marson Papers, National Library of Jamaica, Kingston.

PREFACE

1. See Anthony Bogues, *Caliban's Freedom: The Early Political Thought of C. L. R. James* (London: Pluto Press, 1997); H. V. Carby, *Race Men* (Cambridge, MA: Harvard University Press, 1998); Paul Buhle, *C. L. R. James: His Life and Work* (London: Allison and Busby, 1986); Selwyn Cudjoe and William E. Cain, eds., *C. L. R. James: His Intellectual Legacies* (Amherst: University of Massachusetts Press, 1995); Anna Grimshaw, ed., *The C. L. R. James Reader* (Oxford: Blackwell, 1992); Christian Høgsbjerg, *C. L. R. James in Imperial Britain* (Durham, NC: Duke University Press, 2014); James Hooker, *Black Revolutionary: George Padmore's Path from Communism to Pan-Africanism* (New York: Praeger, 1967); Fitzroy Baptiste and Rupert Lewis, eds., *George Padmore: Pan-African Revolutions* (Kingston, Jam.: Ian Randle, 2009); and Leslie James, *George Padmore and Decolonization from Below: Pan-Africanism, the Cold War, and the End of Empire* (Basingstoke, UK: Palgrave Macmillan 2015). Marc Matera, *Black London: The Imperial Metropolis and Decolonization in the Twentieth Century* (Berkeley: University of California Press, 2015), pp. 100–144, pays more attention to black women.

2. Una Marson, "Feminism," *Public Opinion* (10 April 1937), p. 10.

3. Paulette Nardal to Jacques Louis Hymans, letter, 17 November 1963, in Jacques Louis Hymans, *Léopold Sédar Senghor: An Intellectual Biography* (Edinburgh: Edinburgh University Press, 1971), p. 36.

4. My work builds on and is indebted to the excellent foundational work of the following writings: Delia Jarrett-Macauley, *The Life of Una Marson, 1905–65* (Manchester: Manchester University Press, 1998); T. Denean Sharpley-Whiting, *Negritude Women* (Minneapolis: University of Minnesota Press, 2002); Emily Musil, "La Marianne Noire: How Gender and Race in the Twentieth-Century Atlantic World Reshaped the Debate about Human Rights" (PhD diss., University of California Los Angeles, 2007); Barbara Ransby, *Eslanda: The Large and Unconventional Life of Mrs. Paul Robeson* (New Haven: Yale University Press, 2013); and Emily Musil Church, "In Search of Seven Sisters: A Biography of the Nardal Sisters of Martinique," *Callaloo: A Journal of African Diaspora Arts and Letters* 36, no. 2 (2013), pp. 375–90.

INTRODUCTION

1. Anna Julia Cooper, *A Voice from the South* (1892; repr., New York: Oxford University Press, 1988), p. 31. Capitalization and italics in the original.

2. For more on racial uplift and black intellectual leadership, see Kevin K. Gaines, *Uplifting the Race: Black Leadership, Politics, and Culture in the Twentieth Century* (Chapel Hill: University of North Carolina, 1996).

3. Michelle Mitchell, *Righteous Propagation: African Americans and the Politics of Racial Destiny after Reconstruction* (Chapel Hill: University of North Carolina Press, 2004), p. xix.

4. Cooper, *Voice from the South*, p. 3.

5. For more on clubwomen in general, see Deborah Gray White, *Too Heavy A Load: Black Women in Defense of Themselves, 1894–1994* (New York: Norton, 1999). See also Vivian M. May, *Anna Julia Cooper, Visionary Black Feminist: A Critical Introduction* (New York: Routledge, 2007); Linda O. McMurry, *To Keep The Waters Troubled: The Life of Ida B. Wells* (New York: Oxford University Press, 1998); Mary Church Terrell, *A Colored Woman in a*

White World (1940; repr., Amherst, NY: Humanity Books, 2005); Joan Quigley, *Just Another Southern Town: Mary Church Terrell and the Struggle for Racial Justice in the Nation's Capital* (New York: Oxford University Press, 2016); Brittney C. Cooper, *Beyond Respectability: The Intellectual Thought of Race Women* (Urbana: University of Illinois Press, 2017); Lisa G. Materson, "African American Women's Global Journeys and the Construction of Cross-ethnic Racial Identity," *Women's Studies International Forum* 32 (2009): pp. 35–42; Michelle Rief, "Thinking Locally, Acting Globally: The International Agenda of African American Clubwomen, 1880–1940," *Journal of African American History* 89, no. 3 (Summer 2004): pp. 203–22; Joyce A. Hanson, *Mary McLeod Bethune and Black Women's Political Activism* (Columbia: University of Missouri Press, 2003); Nicholas Grant, "The National Council of Negro Women and South Africa: Black Internationalism, Motherhood and the Cold War," *Palimpsest: A Journal of Women, Gender, and the Black International* 5, no. 1 (2016): pp. 59–87; Kate Dossett, *Bridging Race Divides: Black Nationalism, Feminism, and Integration in the United States, 1896–1935* (Gainesville: University Press of Florida, 2008); Erik S. McDuffie, *Sojourning for Freedom: Black Women, American Communism, and the Making of Black Left Feminism* (Durham, NC: Duke University Press, 2011); Dayo F. Gore, *Radicalism at the Crossroads: African American Women Activists in the Cold War* (New York: New York University Press, 2011); Gregg Andrews, *Thyra J. Edwards: Black Activist in the Global Freedom Struggle* (Columbia: University of Missouri Press, 2011); Yevette Richards, *Maida Springer: Pan-Africanist and International Labor Leader* (Pittsburgh: University of Pittsburgh Press, 2000); Yevette Richards, *Conversations with Maida Springer: A Personal History of Labor, Race, and International Relations* (Pittsburgh: University of Pittsburgh Press, 2004); Patricia A. Schechter, *Exploring the Decolonial Imaginary: Four Transnational Lives* (New York: Palgrave Macmillan, 2012); Gerald Horne, *Race Woman: The Lives of Shirley Graham Du Bois* (New York: New York University Press, 2000); Ula Y. Taylor, *The Veiled Garvey: The Life and Times of Amy Jacques Garvey* (Chapel Hill: University of North Carolina Press, 2002); Tony Martin, *Amy Ashwood Garvey: Pan-Africanist, Feminist, and Mrs. Marcus Garvey No. 1, or, A Tale of Two Amies* (Dover, MA: Majority Press, 2007); Minkah Makalani, "An International African Opinion: Amy Ashwood Garvey and C. L. R. James in Black Radical London" in *Escape from New York: The New Negro Renaissance Beyond Harlem*, ed. Davarian L. Baldwin and Minkah Makalani (Minneapolis: University of Minnesota Press, 2013), pp. 77–101; Carole Boyce Davies, *Left of Karl Marx: The Political Life of Black Communist Claudia Jones* (Durham, NC: Duke University Press, 2008); Carole Boyce Davies, *Claudia Jones: Beyond Containment: Autobiographical Reflections, Essays and Poems* (Banbury, Oxfordshire, UK: Ayebia Clarke, 2011); Adelaide M. Cromwell, *An African Victorian Feminist: The Life and Times of Adelaide Smith Casely Hayford, 1868–1960* (London: Frank Cass, 1986); Constance Agatha Cummings-John, *Memoirs of a Krio Leader*, ed., introduction, and annotation, LaRay Denzer (Ibadan, Nigeria: Humanities Research Centre, 1995); Marc Matera, *Black London: The Imperial Metropolis and Decolonization in the Twentieth Century* (Berkeley: University of California Press, 2015), pp. 111–21; Cheryl Johnson-Odim and Nina Emma Mba, *For Women and the Nation: Funmilayo Ransome-Kuti of Nigeria* (Urbana: University of Illinois Press, 1997); and Judith A. Byfield, "From Ladies to Women: Funmilayo Ransome-Kuti and Women's Political Activism in Post–World War II Nigeria," in *Toward an Intellectual History of Black Women*, ed. Mia Bay, Farah Jasmine Griffin, Martha S. Jones, and Barbara D. Savage (Chapel Hill: University of North Carolina Press, 2015), pp. 197–213.

6. Emma Robinson-Tomsett, *Women, Travel and Identity: Journeys by Rail and Sea, 1870–1940* (Manchester: Manchester University Press, 2013), pp. 1–2.

7. Lara Putnam, *Radical Moves: Caribbean Migrants and the Politics of Race in the Jazz Age* (Chapel Hill: University of North Carolina Press, 2013).

8. On the black public sphere, see Catherine R. Squires, "Rethinking the Black Public Sphere: An Alternative Vocabulary for Multiple Public Spheres," *Communication Theory* 12, no. 4 (2002): pp. 440–67.

On the public sphere, see Jürgen Habermas, *The Structural Transformation of the Public Sphere: An Inquiry into a Category of Bourgeois Society*, trans. Thomas Burger (Cambridge, MA: MIT Press, 1989).

For feminist and class critiques of the concept, see Joan B. Landes, *Women and the Public Sphere in the Age of the French Revolution* (Ithaca, NY: Cornell University Press, 1988); and Craig J Calhoun, ed., *Habermas and the Public Sphere* (Cambridge, MA: MIT Press, 1992).

For a select overview of global civil society, see John Keane, *Global Civil Society* (Cambridge, UK: Cambridge University Press, 2001); Mary Kaldor, *Global Civil Society: An Answer to War* (Cambridge, UK: Polity Press, 2003); and Gordon Laxer and Sandra Halperin, eds., *Global Civil Society and Its Limits* (Basingstoke, Oxfordshire, UK: Palgrave Macmillan, 2003).

For a historical approach to the concept, see Andrew Arsan, Su Lin-Lewis, and Anne-Isabelle Richards, "Editorial: The Roots of Global Civil Society and the Interwar Moment," *Journal of Global History* 7, no. 2 (2012): pp. 157–65; and Benedict Anderson, *Imagined Communities: Reflections on the Origin and Spread of Nationalism* (London: Verso, 1983).

9. Nico Slate, *Colored Cosmopolitanism: The Shared Struggle for Freedom in the United States and India* (Cambridge, MA: Harvard University Press, 2012).

10. Slate, p. 2.

11. Treva B. Lindsey, *Colored No More: Reinventing Black Womanhood in Washington, DC* (Urbana: University of Illinois Press, 2017), p. 9.

12. Earl Lewis, "To Turn as on a Pivot: Writing African Americans into a History of Overlapping Diasporas," *American Historical Review* 100, no. 3 (1995): pp. 765–87; Nikhil Pal Singh, *Black Is a Country: Race and the Unfinished Struggle for Democracy* (Cambridge, MA: Harvard University Press, 2005), especially pp. 101–33; and Mitchell, *Righteous Propagation*, p. 8. While Mitchell's foundational work explores the politics of racial destiny among race women and men in the United States, the concept was also debated outside America's borders and beyond the late nineteenth and early twentieth century.

13. For more on the working-class expressions of black internationalism, see Putnam, *Radical Moves*, pp. 123–52. For a working-class black woman's engagement with black internationalist feminism, see Keisha N. Blain, "For the Rights of Dark People in Every Part of the World: Pearl Sherrod, Black Internationalist Feminism, and Afro-Asian Politics during the 1930s," *Souls: A Critical Journal of Black Politics, Culture, and Society* 17, no. 1–2 (2015): pp. 90–112.

14. James Weldon Johnson, "Harlem: The Culture Capital," in *The New Negro: Voices of the Harlem Renaissance*, ed. Alain Locke (1925; repr., New York: Atheneum, 1992), p. 301.

15. Farah Jasmine Griffin, *Harlem Nocturne: Women Artists and Progressive Politics During World War II* (New York: Basic Civitas, 2013), p. x; and Johnson, "Harlem: The Culture Capital," p. 301.

16. Fiona I. B. Ngô, *Imperial Blues: Geographies of Race and Sex in Jazz Age New York* (Durham, NC: Duke University Press, 2014), p. 13; and Wallace Thurman and William Jourdan Rapp, "Few Know Real Harlem, the City of Surprises: Quarter Million Negroes Form a Moving, Colorful Pageant of Life," in *The Collected Writings of Wallace Thurman: A Harlem Renaissance Reader*, ed. Amritjit Singh and Daniel M. Scott III (New Brunswick, NJ: Rutgers University Press, 2003), p. 67.

17. Barbara Ransby, *Eslanda: The Large and Unconventional Life of Mrs. Paul Robeson* (New Haven, CT: Yale University Press, 2013), p. 28.

18. Ransby, pp. 28–33.

19. Gary Wilder, *The French Imperial Nation-State: Negritude and Colonial Humanism between the Two World Wars* (Chicago: University of Chicago Press, 2005), p. 160.

20. Shireen K. Lewis, *Race, Culture, and Identity: Francophone West African and Caribbean Literature and Theory from Négritude to Créolité* (Oxford: Lexington Books, 2006), p. 64.

21. Emily Musil, "La Marianne Noire: How Gender and Race in the Twentieth-Century Atlantic World Reshaped the Debate about Human Rights" (PhD diss., University of California Los Angeles, 2007), p. 17.

22. Musil, p. 17.

23. Musil, p. 17.

24. Delia Jarrett-Macauley, *The Life of Una Marson, 1905–1965* (Manchester: Manchester University Press, 1998), p. 19.

25. Jarrett-Macauley, pp. 20–23.

26. Henrice Altink, *Destined for a Life of Service: Defining African-Jamaican Womanhood, 1865–1938* (Manchester, UK: Manchester University Press, 2011), p. 182.

27. Jarrett-Macauley, *Life of Una Marson*, p. 26.

28. Jarrett-Macauley, p. 30.

29. Una Marson, "Our Debut," *Cosmopolitan* 1, no. 1 (May 1928): p. 2.

30. On respectability and black women in the United States, see Evelyn Brooks Higginbotham, *Righteous Discontent: The Women's Movement in the Black Baptist Church* (Cambridge, MA: Harvard University Press, 1993); and Victoria W. Wolcott, *Remaking Respectability: African American Women in Interwar Detroit* (Chapel Hill: University of North Carolina Press, 2001).

31. See Una Marson, "Have married women taken the wrong turning?," n.d., p. 5, folder 12, MS 1944 B, Una Marson Papers, National Library of Jamaica, Kingston (hereafter UMP).

32. Ransby, *Eslanda*, p. 80.

33. Ransby, p. 62.

34. Una Marson, "Discovering America," n.d., p. 3, folder 12 MS 1944 B, UMP.

35. Jarrett-Macauley, *Life of Una Marson*, p. 38.

36. Ransby, *Eslanda*, pp. 164–65.

37. Carole Boyce Davies, *Black Women, Writing and Identity: Migrations of the Subject* (New York: Routledge, 1994), p. 4; and Davies, *Left of Karl Marx*, pp. 20–25.

38. Davies, *Black Women, Writing, and Identity*, p. 3.

39. Myriam J. A. Chancy, *Searching for Safe Spaces: Afro-Caribbean Women Writers in Exile* (Philadelphia: Temple University Press, 1997), p. xi. For more on the impact of travel on identity, see James Clifford, *Routes: Travel and Translation in the Late Twentieth Century* (Cambridge, MA: Harvard University Press, 1997).

40. Mary Louise Pratt, *Imperial Eyes: Travel Writing and Transculturation*, 2nd ed. (New York: Routledge, 2008), p. 8.

41. Davies, *Black Women, Writing and Identity*, p. 66. See Gloria Anzaldúa, *Borderlands/La Frontera: The New Mestiza* (San Francisco: Aunt Lute, 1987).

42. Katherine McKittrick, *Demonic Grounds: Black Women and the Cartographies of Struggle* (Minneapolis: University of Minnesota Press, 2006), p. xviii.

43. Eslanda Goode Robeson, *African Journey* (New York: John Day, 1945), p. 13.

44. Dossett, *Bridging Race Divides*, p. 2, 6.

45. Leah Rosenberg, "The New Woman and 'The Dusky Strand': The Place of Feminism and Women's Literature in Early Jamaican Nationalism," *Feminist Review* 95, no. 1 (2010): pp. 47–48, p. 45.

46. Una Marson, "Editorial," *Cosmopolitan*, May 1928, p. 5. For more on *The Cosmopolitan*, see Belinda Edmondson, *Caribbean Middlebrow: Leisure Culture and the Middle Class* (Ithaca, NY: Cornell University Press, 2009), pp. 21–49.

47. Rhoda Reddock, "Diversity, Difference, and Caribbean Feminism: The Challenge of Anti-Racism," *Caribbean Review of Gender Studies: A Journal of Caribbean Perspectives on Gender and Feminism* 1 (April 2007): p. 11.

48. Ransby, *Eslanda*, pp. 252, 264.

49. McDuffie, *Sojourning for Freedom*.

50. Deborah K. King, "Multiple Jeopardy, Multiple Consciousness: The Context of a Black Feminist Ideology," *Signs: Journal of Women in Culture and Society* 14, no. 1 (1988): pp. 42–72.

51. Dossett, *Bridging Race Divides*, p. 12; and Patricia Hill Collins, *Black Feminist Thought: Knowledge, Consciousness, and the Politics of Empowerment* (Boston: Unwin Hyman, 1990), pp. 31–39.

52. Jarrett-Macauley, *Life of Una Marson*. Marson's time in the interwar era has been well documented in a number of works. See Alison Donnell, "Una Marson: Feminism, Anti-Colonialism and a Forgotten Fight for Freedom," in *West Indian Intellectuals in Britain*, ed. Bill Schwarz (Manchester, UK: Manchester University Press, 2003), pp. 114–31; Altink, *Destined for a Life of Service*; Imaobong D. Umoren, "This Is the Age of Woman: Black Feminism and Black Internationalism in the Works of Una Marson, 1928–1938," *History of Women in the Americas* 1, no. 1 (2013): pp. 50–72; Anna Snaith, *Modernist Voyages: Colonial Women Writers in London, 1890–1945* (Cambridge, UK: Cambridge University Press, 2014), pp. 152–74; Matera, *Black London*, pp. 121–44; Ransby, *Eslanda*; T. Denean Sharpley-Whiting, *Negritude Women* (Minneapolis: University of Minnesota Press, 2002); Musil, "La Marianne Noire"; and Paulette Nardal, *Beyond Negritude: Essays from Woman in the City*, trans., introduction, and notes, T. Denean Sharpley-Whiting (Albany: State University of New York Press, 2009).

53. Work on black women's internationalism builds on earlier black Atlantic and African diasporic scholarship. See for instance, Robert Farris Thompson, *Flash of the Spirit: African and Afro-American Art and Philosophy* (New York: Vintage, 1983); Paul Gilroy, *The Black Atlantic: Modernity and Double Consciousness* (London: Verso, 1993); Tiffany Ruby Patterson and Robin D.G. Kelley, "Unfinished Migrations: Reflections on the African Diaspora and the Making of the Modern World," *African Studies Review* 43, no. 1 (April 2000): pp. 11–45; Brent Hayes Edwards, "The Uses of Diaspora," *Social Text* 19, no. 1 (66,

Spring 2001): pp. 45-73; and Sidney J. Lemelle and Robin D. G. Kelley, eds., *Imagining Home: Class, Culture, and Nationalism in the African Diaspora* (London: Verso, 2004).

For more on black internationalism, see Penny M. Von Eschen, *Race against Empire: Black Americans and Anticolonialism, 1937-1957* (Ithaca, NY: Cornell University Press, 1997); Brenda Gayle Plummer, *Rising Wind: Black Americans and U.S. Foreign Affairs, 1935-1960* (Chapel Hill: University of North Carolina Press, 1996); Brenda Gayle Plummer, ed., *Window on Freedom: Race, Civil Rights and Foreign Affairs, 1945-1988* (Chapel Hill: University of North Carolina Press, 2003); James H. Meriwether, *Proudly We Can Be Africans: Black Americans and Africa, 1935-1961* (Chapel Hill: University of North Carolina Press, 2002); Brenda Gayle Plummer, *In Search of Power: African Americans in the Era of Decolonization, 1956-1974* (New York: Cambridge University Press, 2013); Winston James, *Holding Aloft the Banner of Ethiopia: Caribbean Radicalism in Early Twentieth-Century America* (New York: Verso, 1998); Marc S. Gallichio, *The African American Encounter with China and Japan: Black Internationalism in Asia* (Chapel Hill: University of North Carolina Press, 2000); Kate A. Baldwin, *Beyond the Color Line and the Iron Curtain: Reading Encounters between Black and Red, 1922-1963* (Durham, NC: Duke University Press, 2002); Sharpley-Whiting, *Negritude Women*; Brent Hayes Edwards, *The Practice of Diaspora: Literature, Translation and the Rise of Black Internationalism* (Cambridge, MA: Harvard University Press, 2003); Tina M. Campt, *Other Germans: Black Germans and the Politics of Race, Gender, and Memory in the Third Reich* (Ann Arbor: University of Michigan Press, 2005); Michelle Ann Stephens, *Black Empire: The Masculine Global Imaginary of Caribbean Intellectuals in the United States, 1914-1962* (Durham, NC: Duke University Press, 2005); Susan D. Pennybacker, *From Scottsboro to Munich: Race and Political Culture in 1930s Britain* (Princeton, NJ: Princeton University Press, 2009); Jennifer Anne Boittin, *Colonial Metropolis: The Urban Grounds of Anti-Imperialism and Feminism in Interwar Paris* (Lincoln: University of Nebraska Press, 2010); Frank Andre Guridy, *Forging Diaspora: Afro-Cubans and African America's in a World of Empire and Jim Crow* (Chapel Hill: University of North Carolina Press, 2010); Minkah Makalani, *In the Cause of Freedom: Radical Black Internationalism from Harlem to London, 1917-1939* (Chapel Hill: University of North Carolina Press, 2011); Putnam, *Radical Moves*; and Matera, *Black London*.

54. Sharpley-Whiting, *Negritude Women*; Davies, *Left of Karl Marx*; Dayo F. Gore, Jeanne Theoharis, and Komozi Woodard, eds., *Want to Start a Revolution? Radical Women in the Black Freedom Struggle* (New York: New York University Press, 2009); McDuffie, *Sojourning For Freedom*; Gore, *Radicalism at the Crossroads*; Cheryl Higashida, *Black Internationalist Feminism: Women Writers of the Black Left, 1945-1955* (Urbana: University of Illinois Press, 2011); Tanisha Ford, *Liberated Threads: Black Women, Style, and the Global Politics of Soul* (Chapel Hill: University of North Carolina Press, 2015); Keisha N. Blain, "'We Want to Set the World on Fire': Black Nationalist Women and Diasporic Politics in the New Negro World, 1940-1944," *Journal of Social History* 49, no. 1 (2015): pp. 194-212; Blain, "For the Rights of Dark People in Every Part of the World," pp. 91-112; Keisha N. Blain, "'Confraternity among All Dark Races': Mittie Maude Lena Gordon and the Practice of Black (Inter)nationalism in Chicago, 1932-1942," *Palimpsest: A Journal on Women, Gender, and the Black International* 5, no. 2 (Fall 2016): pp. 151-81; Keisha N. Blain, *Set the World on Fire: Black Nationalist Women and the Global Struggle for Freedom* (Philadelphia: University of Pennsylvania Press, 2018); Keisha N. Blain and Tiffany Gill, eds., "To Turn

This Whole World Over: Black Women's Internationalism in Historical Perspective" (under review); Nicholas Grant, *We Shall Win Our Freedoms Together: African Americans and Apartheid, 1945–1960* (Chapel Hill: University of North Carolina Press, 2017); Annette Joseph-Gabriel, *Decolonial Citizenship: Black Women's Resistance in the Francophone World* (forthcoming); and future works by Dayo Gore.

The rise of black women's internationalism sits alongside the growth in the field of internationalisms more broadly; see Glenda Sluga, *Internationalism in the Age of Nationalism* (Philadelphia: University of Pennsylvania Press, 2013); and Glenda Sluga and Patricia Clavin, eds., *Internationalisms: A Twentieth-Century History* (Cambridge, UK: Cambridge University Press, 2017). It also links to the rise in work on other types of internationalism like religion. For a recent book that explores black Christian internationalism, see Sarah Azakansky, *This Worldwide Struggle: Religion and the International Roots of the Civil Rights Movement* (New York: Oxford University Press, 2017).

55. Carol B. Conaway and Kristin Waters, eds., "Introduction," in *Black Women's Intellectual Traditions: Speaking Their Minds* (Hanover, NH: University Press of New England, 2007), p. 3. For an earlier articulation on black women's intellectual history through the field of black women's studies, see Gloria T. Hull, Patricia Bell-Scott, and Barbara Smith, eds., *All the Women Are White, All the Men Are Black but Some of Us Are Brave: Black Women's Studies* (New York: Feminist Press, 1982); and its sequel, Stanlie M. James, Frances Smith Foster, and Beverly Guy-Sheftall, eds., *Still Brave: The Evolution of Black Women's Studies* (New York: Feminist Press, 2009). For an anthology of the writings of Caribbean women intellectuals, see Veronica Marie Gregg, *Caribbean Women: An Anthology of Non-Fiction Writing, 1890–1980* (Notre Dame, IN: University of Notre Dame Press, 2005).

56. Mia Bay, Farah Jasmine Griffin, Martha S. Jones, and Barbara D. Savage, eds., "Introduction: Toward an Intellectual History of Black Women," in *Toward an Intellectual History of Black Women* (Chapel Hill: University of North Carolina Press, 2015), p. 4. For a recent work that focuses on African American women's intellectual history and traditions, see Cooper, *Beyond Respectability*. The larger interest in black women's intellectual history from a US and African diasporic framework overlaps with the rise in work on global intellectual history; see Samuel Moyn and Andrew Sartori, eds., *Global Intellectual History* (New York: Columbia University Press, 2013).

57. Bay, Griffin, Jones, and Savage, "Introduction," p. 4; and Cooper, *Beyond Respectability*, p. 16.

58. Ula Y. Taylor, "Street Strollers: Grounding the Theory of Black Women Intellectuals," *Afro-Americans in New York Life and History* 30, no. 2 (July 2006): pp. 154; and Renate Holub, *Antonio Gramsci: Beyond Marxism and Postmodernism* (New York: Routledge, 1992).

59. Lizabeth Paravisini-Gebert and Ivette Romero-Cesareo, eds., "Introduction: Traveling the Margins of Caribbean Discourse," in *Women at Sea: Travel Writing and the Margins of Caribbean Discourse* (New York: Palgrave, 2001), p. 2. For more on black women's experiences of travel in fiction and travel narratives, see Farah Jasmine Griffin, *"Who set you flowin'?": The African-American Migration Narrative* (New York: Oxford University Press, 1995); Farah Jasmine Griffin and Cheryl J. Fish, eds., *A Stranger in the Village: Two Centuries of African-American Travel Writing* (Boston: Beacon Press, 1998); and Cheryl J. Fish, *Black and White Women's Travel Narratives: Antebellum Explorations* (Gainesville:

University Press of Florida, 2004). For a study of black women performers who travelled, see Jayna Brown, *Babylon Girls: Black Women Performers and the Shaping of the Modern* (Durham, NC: Duke University Press, 2008).

60. For a theoretical discussion of the politics of friendship, see Leela Gandhi, *Affective Communities: Anticolonial Thought, Fin-de-Siècle Radicalism, and the Politics of Friendship* (Durham, NC: Duke University Press, 2006).

61. Musil, "La Marianne Noire," pp. 40–41.

62. Darlene Clark Hine, "Rape and the Inner Lives of Black Women in the Middle West: Preliminary Thoughts on the Culture of Dissemblance," *Signs: Journal of Women in Culture and Society* 14, no. 4 (1989): p. 915.

63. Cooper, *Voice from the South*, p. 121

1. BLACK AND FEMINIST INTERNATIONALISM IN INTERWAR EUROPE, 1920-1935

1. Marilyn Lake and Henry Reynolds, *Drawing the Global Colour Line: White Men's Countries and the International Challenge of Racial Equality* (Cambridge: Cambridge University Press, 2008), p. 307. See also W. E. B. Du Bois, *The World and Africa* (1946; repr., New York: International Publishers, 1978), pp. 11–12.

2. Jennifer Ann Boittin, *Colonial Metropolis: The Urban Grounds of Anti-Imperialism and Feminism in Interwar Paris* (Lincoln: University of Nebraska Press, 2010), p. 74.

3. Michael Goebel, *Anti-Imperial Metropolis: Interwar Paris and the Seeds of Third World Nationalism* (New York: Cambridge University Press, 2015), p. 10.

4. Tyler E. Stovall, *Paris Noir: African Americans in the City of Light* (New York: Houghton Mifflin, 1996), p. 31.

5. Gary Wilder, *The French Imperial Nation-State: Negritude and Colonial Humanism between the Two World Wars* (Chicago: University of Chicago Press, 2005), p. 157.

6. On the experiences of blacks and immigrants in interwar France, see Michel Fabre, *From Harlem to Paris: Black American Writers in France, 1840–1980* (Urbana: University of Illinois Press, 1991); Stovall, *Paris Noir*; Jody Blake, *Le tumulte noir: Modernist Art and Popular Entertainment in Jazz-Age Paris, 1900–1930* (University Park: Pennsylvania State University Press, 1999); Petrine Archer-Straw, *Negrophilia: Avant-Garde Paris and Black Culture in the 1920s* (London: Thames and Hudson, 2000); Brett A. Berliner, *Ambivalent Desires: The Exotic Black Other in Jazz-Age France* (Amherst: University of Massachusetts Press, 2002); Clifford D. Rosenberg, *Policing Paris: The Origins of Modern Immigration Control between the Wars* (Ithaca, NY: Cornell University Press, 2006); Sue Peabody and Tyler Stovall, eds., *The Color of Liberty: Histories of Race in France* (Durham, NC: Duke University Press, 2003); Darlene Clark Hine, Tricia Danielle Keaton, and Stephen Small, eds., *Black Europe and the African Diaspora* (Urbana: University of Illinois Press, 2009); Wilder, *French Imperial Nation-State*; Boittin, *Colonial Metropolis*; Tricia Danielle Keaton, T. Denean Sharpley-Whiting, and Tyler Stovall, eds., *Black France/France Noire: The History and Politics of Blackness* (Durham, NC: Duke University Press, 2012); and T. Denean Sharpley-Whiting, *Bricktop's Paris: African American Women in Paris between the Two World Wars* (Albany: State University of New York Press, 2015).

7. Wilder, *French Imperial Nation-State*, p. 5.

8. Wilder, p. 157; see also Philippe Dewitte, *Les mouvements nègres en France, 1919–1939* (Paris: L'Harmattan, 1985); and James Spiegler, "Aspects of Nationalist Thought among French-speaking West Africans, 1921–1939" (DPhil diss., University of Oxford, 1968).

9. Wilder, p. 157.

10. Claire Oberon Garcia, "Black Women Writers, Modernism, and Paris," *International Journal of Francophone Studies* 14, no. 1–2 (2011): p. 29. There is no evidence of their meeting, but it is likely given their social circles.

11. Barbara Ransby, *Eslanda: The Large and Unconventional Life of Mrs. Paul Robeson* (New Haven, CT: Yale University Press, 2013), p. 49; and Eslanda Robeson diary, October 15, 1925, box 16, Eslanda G. Robeson Papers, Moorland-Spingarn Research Center, Howard University, Washington, DC (hereafter EGRP).

12. For an excellent study on late nineteenth- and early twentieth-century networks of Indian and British encounter through travel and literature in the British empire, see Elleke Boehmer, *Indian Arrivals 1870–1915: Networks of British Empire* (Oxford: Oxford University Press, 2015).

13. Hakim Adi, *West Africans in Britain, 1900–1960: Nationalism, Pan-Africanism, and Communism* (London: Lawrence and Wishart, 1998), p. 2. For more on Black British history, see Peter Fryer, *Staying Power: The History of Black People in Britain* (London: Pluto Press, 1984); Gretchen Holbrook Gerzina, *Black London: Life before Emancipation* (New Brunswick, NJ: Rutgers University Press, 1995); Gretchen Holbrook Gerzina, ed., *Black Victorians, Black Victoriana* (New Brunswick, NJ: Rutgers University Press, 2003); Jeffrey Green, *Black Edwardians: Black People in Britain, 1900–1914* (New York: Frank Cass, 1998); Laura Tabili, *"We Ask For British Justice": Workers and Racial Difference in Late Imperial Britain* (Ithaca, NY: Cornell University Press, 1994); C. L. Innes, *A History of Black and Asian Writing in Britain, 1700–2000* (Cambridge: Cambridge University Pres, 2002); Sukhdev Sandhu, *London Calling: How Black and Asian Writers Imagined a City* (London: Harper Collins, 2003); Bill Schwarz, ed., *West Indian Intellectuals in Britain* (Manchester: Manchester University Press, 2003); Kathleen Chater, *Untold Histories: Black People in England and Wales during the Period of the British Slave Trade 1610–1807* (Manchester: Manchester University Press, 2009); Marc Matera, *Black London: The Imperial Metropolis and Decolonization in the Twentieth Century* (Berkeley: University of California Press, 2015); and Kennetta Hammond Perry, *London Is the Place for Me: Black Britons, Citizenship, and the Politics of Race* (New York: Oxford University Press, 2015).

14. Barbara Bush, *Imperialism, Race, and Resistance: Africa and Britain, 1919–1945* (London: Routledge, 1999), p. 205.

15. Adi, *West Africans in Britain*, p. 13.

16. Adi, p. 14.

17. Tabili, *"We Ask for British Justice,"* p. 136.

18. Tabili, p. 137.

19. Jacqueline Jenkinson, *Black 1919: Riots, Racism, and Resistance in Imperial Britain* (Liverpool: Liverpool University Press, 2009), p. 1.

20. Winston James, "The Black Experience in Twentieth-Century Britain," in *Black Experience and The Empire*, ed. Phillip D. Morgan and Sean Hawkins (Oxford: Oxford University Press, 2004), p. 357.

21. James, p. 347.

22. Eslanda Goode Robeson, *African Journey* (New York: John Day, 1945), p. 13.

23. J. M. MacKenzie, *Propaganda and Empire: The Manipulation of British Public Opinion, 1880–1960* (Manchester: Manchester University Press, 1984), p. 108. For more on the exhibition, see Sarah Britton, "'Come and See the Empire by the All Red Route!': Anti-Imperialism and Exhibitions in Interwar Britain," *History Workshop Journal* 69, no. 1 (2010): pp. 68–89; and Daniel Mark Stephen, *The Empire of Progress: West Africans, Indians, and Britons at the British Empire Exhibition, 1924–25* (Basingstoke, UK: Palgrave Macmillan, 2013).

24. Daniel James Whittall, "Creolising London: Black West Indian Activism and the Politics of Race and Empire, 1931–1948" (PhD diss., Royal Holloway, University of London, 2012), p. 108; and Adi, *West Africans in Britain*, p. 25.

25. Judith R. Walkowitz, *Nights Out: Life in Cosmopolitan London* (New Haven, CT: Yale University Press, 2012), p. 3.

26. Ransby, *Eslanda*, pp. 50–51.

27. Ransby, pp. 50–53. For more on Americans in France, see Brooke L. Blower, *Becoming Americans in Paris: Transatlantic Politics and Culture between the World Wars* (New York: Oxford University Press, 2011).

28. Delia Jarrett-Macauley, *The Life of Una Marson, 1905–1965* (Manchester: Manchester University Press, 1998), p. 45.

29. Una Marson, "The America I have discovered—Miami and Washington," n.d., p. 1, folder 12, MS 1944B, Una Marson Papers, National Library of Jamaica (hereafter UMP).

30. Matera, *Black London*, p. 4.

31. Michael O. West, William G. Martin, and Fanon Che Wilkins, "Preface," in *From Toussaint to Tupac: The Black International since the Age of Revolution*, ed. Michael O. West, William G. Martin, and Fanon Che Wilkins (Chapel Hill: University of North Carolina Press, 2009), p. xi.

32. Michelle Ann Stephens, *Black Empire: The Masculine Global Imaginary of Caribbean Intellectuals in the United States, 1914–1962* (Durham, NC: Duke University Press, 2005), p. 6. For more on black internationalism, see West, Martin, and Wilkins, p. xi; Robin D. G. Kelley, "'But a Local Phase of a World Problem': Black History's Global Vision, 1883–1950," *Journal of American History* 86 (1999): pp. 1045–77; Brent Hayes Edwards, *The Practice of Diaspora: Literature, Translation and the Rise of Black Internationalism* (Cambridge, MA: Harvard University Press, 2003); Minkah Makalani, *In the Cause of Freedom*; and Matera, *Black London*.

33. Kenneth W. Warren, "Appeals for (Mis)recognition: Theorizing the Diaspora," in *Cultures of United States Imperialism*, ed. Amy Kaplan and Donald E. Pease (Durham NC: Duke University Press, 1993), pp. 392–406; Tiffany Ruby Patterson and Robin D. G. Kelley, "Unfinished Migrations: Reflections on the African Diaspora and the Making of the Modern World," *African Studies Review* 43, no. 1 (April 2000): pp. 11–45; and Edwards, *Practice of Diaspora*.

34. Emily Musil, "La Marianne Noire: How Gender and Race in the Twentieth-Century Atlantic World Reshaped the Debate about Human Rights" (PhD diss., University of California Los Angeles, 2007), p. 114.

35. Boittin, *Colonial Metropolis*, p. 141.

36. Wilder, *French Imperial Nation-State*, pp. 166–167.

37. Boittin, *Colonial Metropolis*, p. 135.

38. Boittin, p. 136.

39. Boittin, p. 135.
40. Boittin, p. 144.
41. Boittin, p. 38.
42. Paulette Nardal, "Une femme sculpteur noire," *La Dépêche africaine* 3, no. 27–28 (August and September 1930): p. 5; and Shireen K. Lewis, *Race, Culture, and Identity: Francophone West African and Caribbean Literature and Theory from Négritude to Créolité* (Oxford: Lexington Books, 2006), p. 60.
43. Paulette Nardal, "Le nègre et l'art dramatique," *La Dépêche africaine* 1, no. 3 (May 1928): p. 3.
44. See Paulette Nardal, "Musique nègre: Antilles et AfraAmérique," *La Dépêche africaine*, June 20, 1930, p. 5; and Paulette Nardal, "Le nouveau bal nègre de la glacière," *La Dépêche africaine*, May 30, 1929, p. 3.
45. Rachel Gillet, "Jazz Women, Gender Politics, and the Francophone Atlantic," *Atlantic Studies: Global Currents* 10, no. 1 (2013): pp. 109–30.
46. Paulette Nardal, "In Exile/En exil," *La Dépêche africaine,* December 15, 1929, p. 6; translation in T. Denean Sharpley-Whiting, *Negritude Women* (Minneapolis: University of Minnesota Press, 2002), p. 116.
47. Nardal, p. 6.
48. Nardal, p. 6.
49. Jennifer M. Wilks, "Black Modernist Women at the Parisian Crossroads," in *Escape from New York: The New Negro Renaissance beyond Harlem,* ed. Davarian L. Baldwin and Minkah Makalani (Minneapolis: University of Minnesota Press, 2013), p. 228.
50. Garcia, "Black Women Writers," p. 40; Gillet, "Jazz Women, Gender Politics," p. 121.
51. Fabre, *From Harlem to Paris,* p. 121.
52. Alice Nardal studied music in Paris between 1923 and 1930 as did Andrée; see Musil, "La Marianne Noire," p. 29. Two other Nardal sisters, Cécile and Lucie, also lived briefly with their other sisters and attended the Clamart salon. Comité d'action ethiopienne, August, 17, 1935, p. 1, file BA 2177 A/S, Archives de la Préfecture de police, Paris (hereafter APP).
53. Musil, "La Marianne Noire," pp. 110–52.
54. Louis T. Achille, "Préface," in *La Revue du monde noir/The Review of the Black World 1931–1932: Collection complète no. 1 á 6* (1932; repr., Paris: Jean-Michel Place, 1992), p. xv, translated in Boittin, *Colonial Metropolis,* p. 150. In the 1920s, Achille attended the University of Paris, where he received degrees in English before taking up a professorship of French at Howard University in Washington, DC; he remained a prolific writer throughout his long career. For more, see Musil, "La Marianne Noire," p. 31.
55. Wilder, *French Imperial Nation-State,* p. 174.
56. Achille, "Préface," p. xv.
57. Raisa Rexer, "Black and White and Re(a)d All Over: *L'Étudiant noir,* Communism, and the Birth of Negritude," *Research in African Literatures* 44, no. 4 (2013): pp. 1–14; and Edwards, *Practice of Diaspora,* p. 178.
58. Sharpley-Whiting, *Negritude Women,* p. 11.
59. Wilder, *French Imperial Nation-State,* p. 5.
60. Kevin K. Gaines, *American Africans in Ghana: Black Expatriates and the Civil Rights Era* (Chapel Hill: University of North Carolina Press, 2006), p. 32.
61. Sharpley-Whiting, *Negritude Women,* p. 36.

62. Sharpley-Whiting, pp. 33, 36.
63. Boittin, *Colonial Metropolis*, p. xxv.
64. Wilder, *French Imperial Nation-State*, p. 157.
65. Wilder, pp. 157–58.
66. Eslanda Goode Robeson, "Black Paris," *Challenge*, June 1936, pp. 9–12.
67. Boittin, *Colonial Metropolis*, pp. 151–52.
68. Paulette Nardal and Jeanne Nardal, "Our Aim" (1931), in *La Revue du monde noir/ The Review of the Black World 1931–1932*, p. 4, in Fabre, *From Harlem to Paris*, p. 151. Jane Nardal often published under the name Jeanne Nardal.
69. On the Scottsboro trial, see James A. Miller, *Remembering Scottsboro: The Legacy of an Infamous Trial* (Princeton, NJ: Princeton University Press, 2009); and Susan D. Pennybacker, *From Scottsboro to Munich: Race and Political Culture in 1930s Britain* (Princeton, NJ: Princeton University Press, 2009).
70. See Paulette Nardal to Alain Locke, 6 octobre 1931, box 164–174, Alain Locke Papers, Moorland-Spingarn Research Center, Howard University, Washington, DC.
71. Musil, "La Marianne Noire," p. 115; and Jane Nardal to Alain Locke, December 27, 1927, Alain Locke Papers.
72. Paulette Nardal, "La femme de couleur dans l'ordre social," *Le Soir colonial*, 1930, p. 5, quoted in Musil, "La Marianne Noire," p. 177.
73. Paulette Nardal, "Awakening of Race Consciousness," *Review of the Black World* 6 (April 1932), reprinted in *La Revue du Monde Noir/The Review of the Black World 1931–1932*, p. 25.
74. Nardal, p. 25.
75. Sharpley-Whiting, *Bricktop's Paris*, p. 107; Patricia A. Morton, *Hybrid Modernities: Architecture and Representation at the 1931 Colonial Exposition, Paris* (Boston: MIT Press, 2009).
76. Elizabeth Ezra, *The Colonial Unconscious: Race and Culture in Interwar France* (Ithaca, NY: Cornell University Press, 2000), p. 22.
77. Nardal, "Awakening of Race Consciousness," p. 25.
78. Nardal, p. 29.
79. Robeson, "Black Paris," p. 9.
80. Robeson, p. 10. For more on Nardal's views on interracial relationships, see Sharpley-Whiting, *Negritude Women*, pp. 77–78.
81. Erik S. McDuffie, *Sojourning for Freedom: Black Women, American Communism, and the Making of Black Left Feminism* (Durham, NC: Duke University Press, 2011), p. 120.
82. Robeson, "Black Paris," p. 11.
83. Nardal, "Awakening of Race Consciousness," p. 30.
84. Wilks, "Black Modernist Women," p. 227.
85. Nardal, "Awakening of Race Consciousness," p. 31.
86. Nardal, p. 31.
87. Nardal, p. 31.
88. See Jane Nardal, "Internationalisme noir," *La Dépêche africaine*, February 15, 1928, p. 5, translated in Sharpley-Whiting, *Negritude Women*, pp. 105–7.
89. Wilder, *French Imperial Nation-State*, p. 179; and Léon Damas, "Entretien avec Léon-Gontran Damas," May 1977, in Daniel Racine, *Léon-Gontran Damas: L'homme et l'oeuvre* (Paris: Présence Africaine, 1983), p. 200.

90. Goebel, *Anti-Imperial Metropolis*, p. 76.
91. Goebel, p. 76.
92. Boittin, *Colonial Metropolis*, p. 151; and Sharpley-Whiting, *Negritude Women*, p. 57.
93. Wilder, *French Imperial Nation-State*, p. 179; and Ministre de la Guerre chargé de l'intérim du Ministère des Colonies to Gouverneur général de l'Afrique occidentale française, September 17, 1931, 21 G-44, Archives nationales de l'Afrique occidentale française, Paris.
94. Paulette Nardal, "Guignol ouolof/The Wolof Puppet," *L'Étudiant noir* 1 (March 1935): pp. 4–5; and Wilks, "Black Modernist Women," p. 233.
95. Edwards, *Practice of Diaspora*, p. 186.
96. Boittin, *Colonial Metropolis*, p. 168.
97. Boittin, p. 168; Musil, "La Marianne Noire," p. 200; and "Paulette Nardal, l'âme de la perfection," *Carib-Hebdo*, n.d., p. 24. The researcher was unable to find Nardal's articles in *Le cerf*.
98. David Killingray, "'To Do Something for the Race': Harold Moody and the League of Coloured Peoples," in *West Indian Intellectuals in Britain*, ed. Bill Schwarz (Manchester: Manchester University Press, 2003), p. 52.
99. Jarrett-Macauley, *Life of Una Marson*, p. 46.
100. Killingray, "'To Do Something for the Race,'" pp. 55–56.
101. Matera, *Black London*, p. 38.
102. Una Marson, "Problems of Coloured People in Britain," n.d, p. 1, box 1944C, UMP, quoted in Alison Donnell, "Una Marson: Feminism, Anti-Colonialism, and a Forgotten Fight for Freedom," in Schwarz, *West Indian Intellectuals in Britain*, p. 120.
103. Marson, "Problems of Coloured People," p. 1.
104. Marson, p. 1.
105. Una Marson, "Little Brown Girl," in *The Moth and the Star* (Kingston, Jam.: self-pub., 1937), pp. 11–13.
106. Marson, pp. 11–13.
107. Marson, pp. 11–13.
108. Jarrett-Macauley, *Life of Una Marson*, p. 48.
109. Una Marson, "Current Comments," *New Cosmopolitan*, April 1931, p. 20. In 1931, Marson changed the title of *The Cosmopolitan* to *New Cosmopolitan*.
110. Adi, *West Africans in Britain*, pp. 15–19; Jenkinson, *Black 1919*, p. 7; and Matera, *Black London*, p. 29.
111. Jenkinson, p. 8.
112. Killingray, "'To Do Something for the Race,'" p. 61
113. Anne Spry Rush, *Bonds of Empire: West Indians and Britishness from Victoria to Decolonization* (Oxford: Oxford University Press, 2011), p. 107.
114. *The Keys* 1, no. 1 (1933): p. x.
115. Killingray, "'To Do Something for the Race,'" p. 63.
116. Matera, *Black London*, p. 48.
117. Matera, p. 53.
118. Matera, pp. 55–56.
119. Rush, *Bonds of Empire*, p. 108.
120. Jarrett-Macauley, *Life of Una Marson*, p. 71.

121. Pennybacker, *From Scottsboro to Munich*, p. 34, citing *Daily Worker*, July 1, 1932, p. 2; and *Daily Worker*, July 4, 1932, p. 2.
122. Jarrett-Macauley, *Life of Una Marson*, pp. 69–70.
123. Una Marson, "At What a Price?," unpublished playscript, LCP1933/47, Lord Chamberlain's Plays, Manuscript Collections, The British Library, London.
124. Jarrett-Macauley, *Life of Una Marson*, pp. 53–54.
125. *The Keys*, 1, no. 3 (January 1934): p. 43.
126. Jarrett-Macauley, *Life of Una Marson*, p. 54.
127. *The Keys* 1, no. 1 (1933): pp. 1–2.
128. *The Keys* 1, no. 4 (April–June 1934): p. 70; and Jarrett-Macauley, *Life of Una Marson*, p. 54.
129. Una Marson, "Nigger," *The Keys* 1, no. 1 (1933): p. 9.
130. Una Marson, *News Chronicle*, June 15, 1934, repr. in *The Keys* 2, no. 1 (July–September 1934): p. 17.
131. Una Marson, "London Calling," act 1, scene 1, p. 11, unpublished playscript, 1937, MD1944A-D, UMP.
132. Marson, act 1, scene 1, p. 11.
133. Marson, act 2, scene 1, p. 5.
134. Marson, p. 4.
135. Marson, p. 9.
136. Elaine Campbell, "The Unpublished Plays of Una Marson," in *Anglophone- Karibik- USA*, ed. H. Michael Hoenisch and Remco van Capelleveen (Hamburg: Redaktion Gulliver, 1991), p. 111.
137. Una Marson, "Editorial," *The Keys*, 2, no. 3 (January–March 1935): p. 45.
138. Marson, p. 45.
139. Marson, pp. 45–46.
140. Marson, p. 46.
141. Marson, p. 46.
142. Una Marson, *News Chronicle*, August 6, 1935, n.p., repr. in Jarrett-Macauley, *Life of Una Marson*, p. 93.
143. Marson, in Jarrett-Macauley, pp. 94–95.
144. Jarrett-Macauley, *Life of Una Marson*, pp. 93–94.
145. "Race Enemy No. 1," *Wasu* 4, no. 2 (August 2, 1935), n.p., repr. in Jarrett-Macauley, *Life of Una Marson*, p. 94.
146. *The Keys*, 1, no. 1 (July 1933): p. 2.
147. For more on these groups, see Leila J. Rupp, *Worlds of Women: The Making of an International Women's Movement* (Princeton, NJ: Princeton University Press, 1997); Joyce Blackwell, *No Peace without Freedom: Race and the Women's International League for Peace and Freedom, 1915–1975* (Carbondale: Southern Illinois University Press, 2004); and Marie Sandell, *The Rise of Women's Transnational Activism: Identity and Sisterhood between the World Wars* (London: I. B. Tauris, 2015).
148. Sandell, *Rise of Women's Transnational Activism*, pp. 2–3.
149. BCL Conference reports, PC/04, Printed Collections, Saad Brown Library, The Women's Library, London School of Economics (hereafter TWL).
150. Jarrett-Macauley, *Life of Una Marson*, p. 74.

151. Jarrett-Macauley, pp. 74–75.

152. Unfortunately, no record of this speech remains. BCL Conference reports, PC/04; and Jarrett-Macauley, *Life of Una Marson*, p. 75.

153. Jarrett-Macauley, p. 72.

154. "Woman, Work and Pay within the British Commonwealth," Chair: Mrs. Corbett Ashby, Report of the Tenth Annual Conference Held on June 13th, 14th, & 15th 1934, at YWCA Central Club, Great Russell Street, London, n.p., PC/04, Printed Collections, Saad Brown Library, TWL; and Jarrett-Macauley, *Life of Una Marson*, p. 76.

155. Barbara Bush, "Gender and Empire: The Twentieth Century," in *Gender and Empire*, ed. Philippa Levine (Oxford: Oxford University Press, 2004), p. 82.

156. Jarrett-Macauley, *Life of Una Marson*, p. 77.

157. Una Marson, "Winifred Holtby," in *The Moth and The Star*, p. 79.

158. "Woman, Work and Pay within the British Commonwealth."

159. "Racial Prejudice in London Not Improving Says Miss Marson," *Daily Gleaner*, September 28, 1936, p. 5.

160. Jarrett-Macauley, *Life of Una Marson*, p. 87.

161. Jarrett-Macauley, p. 88.

162. Jarrett-Macauley, p. 87.

163. Una Marson, "East and West in Co-operation" (speech, International Alliance of Women for Suffrage and Equal Citizenship, Istanbul, April 1935), quoted in Jarrett-Macauley, *Life of Una Marson*, p. 89.

164. Marson, in Jarrett-Macauley, p. 90.

165. "Racial Prejudice in London," p. 5

166. Jarrett-Macauley, *Life of Una Marson*, p. 90.

167. Jarrett-Macauley, pp. 88–91.

168. Jarrett-Macauley, p. 91.

169. For more on Radziwill, see Carol Miller, "Geneva—The Key to Equality: Interwar Feminists and the League of Nations," *Women's History Review* 3, no. 2 (1994): pp. 219–45.

170. See Gabrielle Radziwill to Una Marson, May 29, 1935, R5162 13/13862/1008, United Nations Archives, Geneva.

171. See Una Marson to Gabrielle Radziwill June 5, 1935, R5162 13/13862/1008, United Nations Archives, Geneva.

172. Jarrett-Macauley, *Life of Una Marson*, p. 92. For more on the role of women in the LoN, see Glenda Sluga, "Women, Feminisms, and Twentieth-Century Internationalisms," in *Internationalisms: A Twentieth-Century History*, ed. Glenda Sluga and Patricia Clavin (Cambridge: Cambridge University Press, 2017), pp. 61–84.

173. Nancy Cunard, "Negroes in Britain 1941," for the Associated Negro Press, Cunard Papers, Chicago Historical Society, quoted in Jarrett-Macauley, *Life of Una Marson*, p. 92.

174. Jarrett-Macauley, pp. 92, 98.

175. Eslanda Goode Robeson, *Paul Robeson, Negro* (London: Victor Gollancz, 1930), p. 96.

176. "Hotel Colour Bar?," *Daily Mirror*, October 23, 1929, p. 2.

177. Ransby, *Eslanda*, pp. 62, 64.

178. Robeson, *African Journey*, p. 15.

179. Adi, *West Africans in Britain*, pp. 44, 60.

180. Ransby, *Eslanda*, p. 90; and Eslanda Robeson to Harold Moody, March 3, 1934, Correspondence, EGRP.
181. Ransby, *Eslanda*, pp. 74–75, 90.
182. Ransby, p. 52.
183. Sharpley-Whiting, *Bricktop's Paris*, p. 146; and Eslanda Robeson to Carl Van Vechten, November 16, 1925, Carl Van Vechten Papers, Beinecke Rare Book and Manuscript Library, Yale University, New Haven, CT.
184. Sharpley-Whiting, p. 146; and Robeson to Van Vechten.
185. Robeson, "Black Paris," p. 18.
186. Ransby, *Eslanda*, pp. 41–42.
187. Ransby, p. 71; Fabre, *From Harlem to Paris*, pp. 146–47.
188. Robeson, "Black Paris," pp. 12–18.
189. Sharpley-Whiting, *Bricktop's Paris*, pp. 148–49.
190. Dorothy West, "Dear Reader," *Challenge* 1, no. 1 (1934): p. 39.
191. Robeson, "Black Paris," p. 13.
192. Robeson, p. 12.
193. Robeson, pp. 12–13.
194. Ransby, *Eslanda*, pp. 59–80. She had previously taken classes in psychology, archaeology, and anthropology at University College London; see copy of University College of London coursework transcripts from 1933 to 1935, box 2, EGRP; and Sharpley-Whiting, *Bricktop's Paris*, p. 143.
195. On the links between anthropology and colonialism, see Henrika Kuklich, *The Savage Within: The Social History of British Anthropology, 1885–1945* (Cambridge: Cambridge University Press, 1991); and Bush, *Imperialism, Race, and Resistance*.
196. Ransby, *Eslanda*, p. 91.
197. For more on black colonials' study of anthropology at the LSE, see Matera, *Black London*, pp. 244–59.
198. Ransby, *Eslanda*, p. 89; Matera, p. 247.
199. Zora Neale Hurston to Eslanda Robeson, April 18, 1934, quoted in *Zora Neale Hurston: A Life in Letters*, ed. Carla Kaplan (New York: Doubleday, 2002), p. 299.
200. Eslanda Robeson, "Jomo Kenyatta," January 22, 1961, n.p., Writings, PERC, quoted in Ransby, *Eslanda*, p. 259.
201. Robeson, in Ransby, p. 259.
202. McDuffie, *Sojourning for Freedom*, pp. 71–72.
203. McDuffie, p. 62.
204. McDuffie, pp. 63, 53; and Joy Gleason Carew, *Blacks, Reds, and Russians: Sojourners in Search of the Soviet Promise* (New Brunswick, NJ: Rutgers University Press, 2008).
205. McDuffie, p. 53. The term "magic pilgrimage" was coined by Claude McKay in reference to blacks who travelled to the Soviet Union in the 1920s. See Claude McKay, *A Long Way From Home* (1937; repr., New York: Harcourt Brace Jovanovich, 1970), p. 15; and Kate A. Baldwin, *Beyond the Color Line and the Iron Curtain: Reading Encounters between Black and Red, 1922–1963* (Durham, NC: Duke University Press, 2002), p. 14.
206. Ransby, *Eslanda*, p. 92.
207. Ransby, p. 95.
208. Ransby, p. 94.

209. Ransby, p. 95.
210. McDuffie, *Sojourning for Freedom*, p. 70.
211. McDuffie, p. 72.

2. THE ITALIAN INVASION OF ETHIOPIA, THE SPANISH CIVIL WAR, AND ANTI-FASCIST INTERNATIONALISM, 1935-1939

1. Emily Musil, "La Marianne Noire: How Gender and Race in the Twentieth-Century Atlantic World Reshaped the Debate about Human Rights" (PhD diss., University of California Los Angeles, 2007), p. 158.

2. James H. Meriwether, *Proudly We Can Be Africans: Black Americans and Africa, 1935–1961* (Chapel Hill: University of North Carolina Press, 2002), p. 29.

3. Brenda Gayle Plummer, *Rising Wind: Black Americans and U.S. Foreign Affairs, 1935–1960* (Chapel Hill: University of North Carolina Press, 1996), p. 39.

4. Meriwether, *Proudly We Can Be Africans*, p. 29.

5. Meriwether, p. 29.

6. Plummer, *Rising Wind*, p. 51; Una Marson, "Racial Feelings?," *Public Opinion*, July 17, 1936, p. 3.

7. Harvey R. Neptune, *Caliban and the Yankees: Trinidad and the United States Occupation* (Chapel Hill: University of North Carolina Press, 2007), pp. 38–41.

8. Eric D. Duke, *Building a Nation: Caribbean Federation in the Black Diaspora* (Gainesville: University Press of Florida, 2016), p. 99; and "League of Coloured Peoples—Seventh Annual Report (Year 1937–38) as presented to the Seventh Annual General Meeting," March 11, 1938, Colonial Office Records, 3108/432/2, Public Record Office, National Archives, Kew, Richmond, Surrey (hereafter PRO).

9. Meriwether, *Proudly We Can Be Africans*, p. 49.

10. Meriwether, p. 49. For further information about these organizations, see William R. Scott, *The Sons of Sheba's Race: African-Americans and the Italo-Ethiopian War, 1935–1941* (Bloomington: Indiana University Press, 1993), pp. 105–20; Plummer, *Rising Wind*, pp. 47–52; and Joseph E. Harris, *African-American Reactions to War in Ethiopia* (Baton Rouge: Louisiana State University Press, 1994), pp. 63–75.

11. Clare Corbould, *Becoming African Americans: Black Public Life in Harlem* (Cambridge, MA: Harvard University Press, 2009), p. 15.

12. Psalms 68:31, King James Version; and Meriwether, *Proudly We Can Be Africans*, p. 30.

13. Penny M. Von Eschen, *Race against Empire: Black Americans and Anticolonialism, 1937–1957* (Ithaca, NY: Cornell University Press, 1997), p. 11.

14. Erik S. McDuffie, *Sojourning for Freedom: Black Women, American Communism, and the Making of Black Left Feminism* (Durham, NC: Duke University Press, 2011), p. 91.

15. Roi Ottley, *New World A-coming* (New York: Arno Press, 1968), p. 111.

16. Meriwether, *Proudly We Can Be Africans*, p. 55.

17. Langston Hughes, "The Ballad of Ethiopia," *Baltimore Afro-American*, September 28, 1935, n.p.

18. Meriwether, *Proudly We Can Be Africans*, p. 54.

19. McDuffie, *Sojourning for Freedom*, p. 95; Scott, *Sons of Sheba's Race*, pp. 3–37, 106–20; and Mark Naison, *Communists in Harlem during the Depression* (New York: Grove Press, 1983), pp. 138–40, 195–96.

20. Growling Tiger, accompanied by Gerald Clark and Caribbean Serenaders, "The Gold in Africa" (by Growling Tiger, Gerald Clark, Caribbean Serenaders, manufactured in USA: Decca Records, c. 1936).

21. For more on the Spanish Civil War, see Helen Graham, *The Spanish Republic at War, 1936–1939* (Cambridge: Cambridge University Press, 2002); and Helen Graham, *The War and Its Shadows: Spain's Civil War in Europe's Long Twentieth Century* (Brighton, UK: Sussex Academic, 2012).

22. Quoted in Robin D. G. Kelley, *Race Rebels: Culture, Politics, and the Black Working Class* (New York: Free Press, 1994), p. 124.

23. McDuffie, *Sojourning for Freedom*, p. 95; Joe Brandt, ed., *Black Americans in the Spanish People's War against Fascism, 1936–1939* (New York: Veterans of the Abraham Lincoln Battalion, 1980), pp. 4–5; Kelley, *Race Rebels*, pp. 124, 136–37.

24. McDuffie, pp. 95–96, citing *Daily Worker*, March 30, 1937; Brandt, pp. 8–12; and Naison, *Communists in Harlem*, pp. 193–197.

25. Jennifer Ann Boittin, *Colonial Metropolis: The Urban Grounds of Anti-Imperialism and Feminism in Interwar Paris* (Lincoln: University of Nebraska Press, 2010), p. 162.

26. Boittin, p. 162; Paulette Nardal, "Levée des races" (extrait de *Métromer*), *Le Périscope africain* 7, no. 318 (October 19, 1935), translated in Boittin, *Colonial Metropolis*, p. 162.

27. Boittin, *Colonial Metropolis*, p. 162.

28. Nardal, "Levée des races," in Boittin, p. 163.

29. Nardal, in Boittin, pp. 163–64.

30. Boittin, p. 161; and Comité international pour la défense du peuple éthiopien, September 4, 1935, sous-dossier, Ministère des Colonies, Service de liaison avec les originaires des territoires français d'outre-mer (hereafter SLOTFOM) III/73, Centre des archives d'outre-mer (hereafter CAOM).

31. Boittin, p. 161.

32. Musil, "La Marianne Noire," p. 159; and "A/S du 'Comité d'action ethiopienne,'" 17 août 1935, p. 1, file BA2177, Archives de la Préfecture de police, Paris (hereafter APP).

33. "A/S du 'Comité d'action éthiopienne,'" p. 1.

34. "A/S du 'Comité d'action éthiopienne,'" p. 3.

35. Boittin, *Colonial Metropolis*, p. 165; and "Éthiopie," n.d., n.p., file BA2177, APP.

36. Musil, "La Marianne Noire" p. 159; and "Comité d'action éthiopienne," 31 août 1935, file BA2177, APP.

37. "Activité du Comité de défense d'Éthiopie," *Africa* 1 (December 1, 1935): p. 3, translated in Brent Hayes Edwards, *The Practice of Diaspora: Literature, Translation and the Rise of Black Internationalism* (Cambridge, MA: Harvard University Press, 2003), p. 298.

38. Minkah Makalani, *In the Cause of Freedom: Radical Black Internationalism from Harlem to London, 1917–1939* (Chapel Hill: University of North Carolina Press, 2011), p. 204; and Edwards, *Practice of Diaspora*, p. 298.

39. Bill Schwarz, "George Padmore," in *West Indian Intellectuals in Britain*, ed. Bill Schwarz (Manchester: Manchester University Press, 2003), p. 140. For more on Ashwood Garvey's role in the IAFE and IASB, see Minkah Makalani, "An International African

Opinion: Amy Ashwood Garvey and C. L. R. James in Black Radical London," in *Escape from New York: The New Negro Renaissance Beyond Harlem*, ed. Davarian L. Baldwin and Minkah Makalani (Minneapolis: University of Minnesota Press, 2013), pp. 77–101; Daniel James Whittall, "Creolising London: Black West Indian Activism and the Politics of Race and Empire, 1931–1948" (PhD diss., Royal Holloway, University of London, 2012), p. 22; and George Padmore, *Pan-Africanism or Communism?: The Coming Struggle for Africa* (London: Dennis Dobson, 1956), p. 145. For more on James's time in Britain, see C. L. R. James, *Beyond a Boundary* (London: Stanley Paul, 1963).

40. Makalani, *In the Cause of Freedom*, p. 206, citing *Daily Herald*, August 26, 1935, p. 3; and Tony Martin, *Amy Ashwood Garvey: Pan-Africanist, Feminist, and Mrs. Marcus Garvey No. 1, or, A Tale of Two Amies* (Dover, MA: Majority Press, 2007), pp. 142–44.

41. Makalani, p. 206.

42. Makalani, p. 207.

43. Makalani, p. 204; Hakim Adi, *West Africans in Britain, 1900–1960: Nationalism, Pan-Africanism, and Communism* (London: Lawrence and Wishart, 1998), pp. 68–69; Padmore, *Pan-Africanism or Communism?*, pp. 144–45; Edwards, *Practice of Diaspora*, p. 298; and Barbara Bush, *Imperialism, Race, and Resistance: Africa and Britain, 1919–1945* (London: Routledge, 1999), p. 222.

44. Makalani, p. 210.

45. Boittin, *Colonial Metropolis*, pp. 160–61; Ligue anti-impérialiste, October 11, 1935, n.p., sous-dossier, dossier SRI, SLOTFOM III/73, CAOM.

46. Boittin, *Colonial Metropolis*, p. 138.

47. Boittin, pp. 160–61; and "On nous prie d'insérer," *Le Cri des nègres*, nouvelle serie 4, no. 17 (June 1935), p.1, 2M1A/242, CAOM.

48. "On nous prie d'insérer," p. 1.

49. Boittin, *Colonial Metropolis*, pp. 161–62; and "AG de l'UTN," October 5, 1935, SLOTFOM III/73, CAOM.

50. Boittin, p. 162; Comité international pour la défense du peuple éthiopien, October 25, 1935, sous-dossier, dossier SRI, SLOTFOM III/73, CAOM; and Ministry of the Interior to the Minister of the Colonies, "Note relative à une réunion organisée le 22 courant, par le Comité international pour la défense du peuple éthiopien," October 28, 1935, Archives nationales de l'Afrique occidentale française, Paris.

51. "Un manifeste des écrivains catholiques," *Le Journal*, October 18, 1935, n.p.

52. Kevin K. Gaines, *American Africans in Ghana: Black Expatriates and the Civil Rights Era* (Chapel Hill: University of North Carolina Press, 2006), p. 38.

53. Musil, "La Marianne Noire," p. 160. "Paulette Nardal, l'âme de la perfection," *Carib-Hebdo*, n.d., p. 24.

54. Musil, p. 160.

55. "Notes," *Journal of Negro History* 21, no. 4 (1936): p. 457, cited in Musil, "La Marianne Noire," p. 161.

56. Marson, "Racial Feelings?," p. 3.

57. Delia Jarrett-Macauley, *The Life of Una Marson, 1905–1965* (Manchester: Manchester University Press, 1998), p. 100; Marson, "Racial Feelings?," p. 3; and "Racial Prejudice in London Not Improving Says Miss Marson," *Daily Gleaner*, September 28, 1936, p. 5.

58. Jarrett-Macauley, p. 100.

59. Marson, "Racial Feelings?," p. 3.
60. Whittall, "Creolising London," p. 118. For more on Mosley, see Juliet Gardiner, *The Thirties: An Intimate History* (London: Harper Press, 2011), pp. 433–45; and Richard Overy, *The Morbid Age: Britain between the Wars* (London: Allen Lane, 2009), p. 267.
61. Jarrett-Macauley, *Life of Una Marson*, p. 100.
62. Helen McCarthy, *The British People and the League of Nations: Democracy, Citizenship, and Internationalism 1918–1945* (Manchester: Manchester University Press, 2011), p. 2.
63. Marson's speech at West Ealing Congregational Church on March 30, 1936, was reported in *Middlesex County Times*, April 4, 1936, quoted in Jarrett-Macauley, *Life of Una Marson*, p. 100.
64. Jarrett-Macauley, p. 100.
65. Corbould, *Becoming African Americans*, pp. 13, 57–128.
66. Plummer, *Rising Wind*, p. 53.
67. Jarrett-Macauley, *Life of Una Marson*, p. 101.
68. "Racial Prejudice in London," p. 5.
69. "Racial Prejudice in London," p. 5.
70. "Jamaican Girl Who Was Personal Secretary to Haile Selassie," *Daily Gleaner*, September 25, 1936, p. 17.
71. Una Marson, "To Joe and Ben," in *The Moth and the Star* (Kingston, Jam.: self-pub., 1937), pp. 81–83.
72. Plummer, *Rising Wind*, p. 54.
73. Boittin, *Colonial Metropolis*, p. 167.
74. Maureen Mahon, "Eslanda Goode Robeson's *African Journey*: The Politics of Identification and Representation in the African Diaspora," in *Transnational Blackness: Navigating the Global Color Line*, ed. Manning Marable and Vanessa Agard-Jones, pp. 120, 117 (New York: Palgrave Macmillan 2008).
75. Faye Venetia Harrison and Ira E. Harrison, "Introduction: Anthropology, African Americans, and the Emancipation of a Subjugated Knowledge," in *African-American Pioneers in Anthropology*, ed. Ira E. Harrison and Faye Venetia Harrison, p. 12 (Urbana: University of Illinois Press, 1999).
76. Mahon, "Eslanda Goode Robeson's *African Journey*," p. 120.
77. Eslanda Goode Robeson, *African Journey* (New York: John Day, 1945), p. 13.
78. Robeson, p. 17.
79. Plummer, *Rising Wind*, p. 57.
80. Barbara Ransby, *Eslanda: The Large and Unconventional Life of Mrs. Paul Robeson* (New Haven, CT: Yale University Press, 2013), p. 98.
81. Robeson, *African Journey*, p. 17.
82. Robeson, p. 14.
83. Robeson, p. 15.
84. Robeson, p. 16.
85. Robeson, p. 18.
86. Robeson, p. 17.
87. Robeson, pp. 17–18.
88. Robeson, p. 18.
89. Robeson, p. 18.

90. Robeson, p. 18.
91. Robeson, p. 19.
92. Robeson, p. 23.
93. Robeson, p. 31.
94. Robeson, p. 65.
95. Robeson, p. 50.
96. Robeson, p. 50.
97. Robeson, p. 66.
98. Mahon, "Eslanda Goode Robeson's *African Journey*," p. 116.
99. Robeson, *African Journey*, p. 47.
100. Robeson, p. 61.
101. Robeson, p. 89.
102. Robeson, p. 136.
103. Robeson, p. 108.
104. Robeson, p. 109.
105. Robeson, p. 138.
106. Robeson, p. 119.
107. Robeson, p. 138.
108. Robeson, p. 139.
109. Robeson, pp. 139–40.
110. Robeson, p. 140.
111. Robeson, p. 141.
112. Robeson, p. 150.
113. Robeson, p. 151.
114. Robeson, p. 152.
115. Mahon, "Eslanda Goode Robeson's *African Journey*," p. 116.
116. Von Eschen, *Race against Empire*, pp. 18–19.
117. Ransby, *Eslanda*, p. 134.
118. Paul Robeson, "A Message from the Chairman to Members and Friends of the Council on African Affairs," *New Africa*, July–August, 1949, in *Paul Robeson Speaks: Writings, Speeches, Interviews, 1918–1974*, ed. Philip S. Foner, p. 224 (London: Quartet Books, 1978).
119. Von Eschen, *Race against Empire*, pp. 19–20.
120. Ransby, *Eslanda*, p. 243.
121. Jarrett-Macauley, *Life of Una Marson*, p. 108. For more information about *Public Opinion*, see Raphael Dalleo, "The Public Sphere and Jamaican Anticolonial Politics: *Public Opinion*, *Focus*, and the Place of the Literary," *Small Axe* 14, no. 2 (2010): pp. 56–82.
122. "New Wine in New Bottles," *Public Opinion*, 20 February 1937, p. 1.
123. Ula Y. Taylor, *The Veiled Garvey: The Life and Times of Amy Jacques Garvey* (Chapel Hill: University of North Carolina Press, 2002), p. 196.
124. For more on the riots, see Kelvin Singh, *Race and Class Struggles in a Colonial State: Trinidad 1917–1945* (Calgary, AB: University of Calgary Press, 1994); O. N. Bolland, *On the March: Labour Rebellions in the British Caribbean, 1934–39* (Kingston, Jam.: Ian Randle, 1995); and O. N. Bolland, *The Politics of Labour in the British Caribbean: The Social Origins of Authoritarianism and Democracy in the Labour Movement* (Kingston, Jam.: Ian Randle, 2001).

125. Dalleo, "The Public Sphere and Jamaican Anticolonial Politics," pp. 58–59.
126. Dalleo, pp. 59–60.
127. Marson, "Racial Feelings?," p. 3.
128. Marson, p. 3.
129. Marson and Johnson's correspondence can be found in James Weldon Johnson and Grace Nail Johnson Papers, box 13, JWJ MSS 49, Beinecke Rare Book and Manuscript Library, Yale University (hereafter BRBM).
130. Marson, "Racial Feelings?," p. 3.
131. Lara Putnam, *Radical Moves: Caribbean Migrants and the Politics of Race in the Jazz Age* (Chapel Hill: University of North Carolina Press, 2013), p. 217; and R. A. Hill, *Dread History: Leonard P. Howell and Millenarian Visions in the Early Rastafarian Religion* (Chicago: Research Associates School Times Publications/Frontline Distribution Int'l; Kingston, Jam.: Miguel Lorne Publishers, 2001), p. 21.
132. Jason Parker, *Brother's Keeper: The United States, Race, and Empire in the British Caribbean 1937–1962* (New York: Oxford University Press, 2008), p. 18.
133. Meriwether, *Proudly We Can Be Africans*, p. 40.
134. "Helping Ethiopia," editorial, *Pittsburgh Courier*, July 20, 1935, p. 10.
135. Meriwether, *Proudly We Can Be Africans*, p. 41.
136. Jarrett-Macauley, *Life of Una Marson*, p. 130.
137. Fernando Ortiz, *Cuban Counterpoint: Tobacco and Sugar* (1940; repr., Durham, NC: Duke University Press, 1995), pp. 102–3.
138. Mary Lou Emery, *Modernism, the Visual, and Caribbean Literature* (New York: Cambridge University Press, 2007), pp. 137–38.
139. For a discussion of other Caribbean creolized religions, see Gordon K. Lewis, *Main Currents in Caribbean Thought: The Historical Evolution of Caribbean Society in Its Ideological Aspects, 1492–1900* (Baltimore: Johns Hopkins University Press, 1983), pp. 188–205.
140. Una Marson, "*Pocomania*: A New Three Act Play by Una Marson," in *Anglophone-Karibik-USA*, ed. H. Michael Hoenisch and Remco van Capelleveen, p. 136 (Hamburg: Redaktion Gulliver, 1991).
141. Musil, "La Marianne Noire," p. 163; "Paulette Nardal, l'âme de la perfection," p. 24.
142. Musil, pp. 163–64.
143. Musil, p. 164; Maïté Koda, "Portraits: Paulette Nardal," *Réseau France d'outre-mer* (April 25, 2006), n.p., http://martinique.rfo.fr/article114.html; and Philippe Tesseron, "Precurseur et apôtre feminine de la négritude et de l'émancipation de la femme noire: Qui est Paulette Nardal?," *Témoignages*, July 2006, p. 16.
144. Paulette Nardal, "The Family and Social Evolution of Black Women," translated from Paulette Nardal, "L'Évolution familiale et sociale des femmes noires," *Univers: Bulletin catholique international*, September 26, 1937, p. 120–21.
145. Paulette Nardal, "Les colonies françaises," *La femme dans la vie sociale*, no. 117 (February 1939): p. 1. Nardal may have published more articles in the 1930s, but as of now the articles included here are the ones that have been identified.
146. Musil, "La Marianne Noire," p. 178.
147. Paulette Nardal, "The Communists Are Using the Crisis to Cause Unrest in the Ancient Colonies/Les communistes profitent de la crise pour provoquer des troubles dans nos plus anciennes colonies," *Je suis partout* 347 (July 16, 1937): p. 5.

148. Eslanda Robeson, "We Go to Spain," p. 1, box 17, EGRP.
149. Ransby, *Eslanda*, pp. 126–27.
150. Robeson, "We Go to Spain," p. 15.
151. For more on their experiences, see McDuffie, *Sojourning for Freedom*, pp. 91–125.
152. Robeson, "We Go to Spain," p. 10.
153. Robeson, p. 22.
154. Robeson, p. 30; and Eslanda Goode Robeson, "Excerpts from a Diary: Journey into Spain," in *The Heart of Spain: Anthology of Fiction, Non-Fiction and Poetry*, ed. Alvah Bessie, pp. 245–46 (New York: Veterans of the Abraham Lincoln Brigade, 1952).
155. Kelley, *Race Rebels*, pp. 126–27.
156. Robeson, "Excerpts from a Diary," p. 248.
157. Robeson, "We Go to Spain," p. 58.
158. For more on women's peace activism in the postwar years, see Jacqueline Castledine, *Cold War Progressives: Women's Interracial Organizing for Peace and Freedom* (Urbana: University of Illinois Press, 2012).
159. Eslanda Robeson, "Spain, 1947," p. 2, box 12, EGRP.
160. Robeson, p. 1.
161. Robeson, "We Go to Spain," p. 74.
162. Kelley, *Race Rebels*, p. 146.

3. INTERNATIONALISMS DURING AND AFTER WORLD WAR II, 1939–1949

1. Barbara Ransby, *Eslanda: The Large and Unconventional Life of Mrs. Paul Robeson* (New Haven, CT: Yale University Press, 2013), p. 138.
2. Una Marson, "But My Own," *Public Opinion*, June 19, 1937, p. 3.
3. Delia Jarrett-Macauley, *The Life of Una Marson, 1905–1965* (Manchester: Manchester University Press, 1998), p. 141; and "Tax on Bachelors," *The Times*, October 1, 1938.
4. Jarrett-Macauley, pp. 141–45.
5. Emily Musil, "La Marianne Noire: How Gender and Race in the Twentieth-Century Atlantic World Reshaped the Debate about Human Rights" (PhD diss., University of California Los Angeles, 2007), p. 182.
6. Musil, p.182.
7. Musil, p. 182; Paulette Nardal to Governor of Martinique, November 7, 1943, 1M Côte 861/D, Archives departmentales de la Martinique, Fort-de-France (hereafter ADM).
8. Musil, pp. 23, 183; Annie Ramin (Cecyle Nardal's daughter), interview by Emily Musil, March 29, 2006, Fort-de-France.
9. Musil, pp. 32, 183; Nardal to Governor of Martinique, November 7, 1943.
10. Musil, p. 154.
11. "Wartime in Britain," n.d., n.p, box 1944, UMP, in Jarrett-Macauley, *Life of Una Marson*, p. 145.
12. Sonya O. Rose, *Which People's War?: National Identity and Citizenship in Wartime Britain, 1939–1945* (Oxford: Oxford University Press, 2003), p. 245. Figures from Ian Spencer, "World War Two and the Making of Multicultural Britain," in *War Culture: Social*

Change and Changing Experience in World War Two Britain, ed. Pat Kirkham and David Thom (London: Lawrence and Wishart, 1995), p. 212.

13. Jarrett-Macauley, *Life of Una Marson*, p. 146; James, "The Black Experience in Twentieth-Century Britain," pp. 366–367; Rose, *Which People's War?* p. 245, Spencer, "World War Two and the Making of Multicultural Britain," p. 212.

14. Rose, *Which People's War?*, p. 246; Spencer, "World War Two and the Making of Multicultural Britain," p. 212.

15. Stephen Tuck, *We Ain't What We Ought To Be: The Black Freedom Struggle from Emancipation to Obama* (Cambridge, MA: Harvard University Press, 2010), p. 219.

16. Rose, *Which People's War?*, pp. 249–50.

17. Rose, p. 252.

18. Glenda Sluga, *Internationalism in the Age of Nationalism* (Philadelphia: University of Pennsylvania Press, 2013), pp. 79–117.

19. "Calling the West Indies," talk by Una Marson, Thursday, September 3, 1942, pp. 2–3, file E2/584, folder WI21, BBC Written Archives Centre, Caversham, Reading (hereafter BBC).

20. Rose, *Which People's War?*, p. 247.

21. See Una Marson to Mr. Gilliam, n.d., file L1/290/1, BBC; and James Procter, "Una Marson at the BBC," *Small Axe* 48, November 2015, p. 28.

22. Jarrett-Macauley, *Life of Una Marson*, p. 147.

23. Ulric Cross, "Coming Visitor," *West Indian*, October 24, 1945, quoted in Jarrett-Macauley, *Life of Una Marson*, p. 171.

24. Jarrett-Macauley, p. 148.

25. Richards, *Maida Springer*, p 77.

26. Richards, p. 85.

27. Maida Springer-Kemp, interview by Yevette Richards, quoted in Richards, pp. 85–86.

28. *Daily Gleaner*, May 11, 1965, p. 12, quoted in Jarrett-Macauley, *Life of Una Marson*, p. 148.

29. Jarrett-Macauley, pp. 162–63.

30. Interview with Una Marson, memo by J. L. Keith, February 14, 1941, Colonial Office, 859/76/1, National Archives, Kew, Richmond, Surrey; Daniel James Whittall, "Creolising London: Black West Indian Activism and the Politics of Race and Empire, 1931–1948" (PhD diss., Royal Holloway, University of London, 2012), p. 179; and Jarrett-Macauley, p. 146.

31. For more on Marson's experiences at the BBC, see Procter, "Una Marson at the BBC," pp. 1–28.

32. Jarrett-Macauley, *Life of Una Marson*, p. 158. According to Procter, *Caribbean Voices* first aired in October 1944; see Procter, "Una Marson at the BBC," pp. 23–28.

33. Jarrett-Macauley, p. 158.

34. Anne Spry Rush, *Bonds of Empire: West Indians and Britishness from Victoria to Decolonization* (Oxford: Oxford University Press, 2011), p. 197.

35. Letters between Marson and Orwell are located in the George Orwell Archive, University College London.

36. Whittall, "Creolising London," p. 106. For more on the West Indies Committee, see Douglas Hall, *A Brief History of the West India Committee* (St. Lawrence, Barbados:

Caribbean Universities Press, 1971); and Ken Post, *Arise Ye Starvelings: The Jamaican Labour Rebellion of 1938 and Its Aftermath* (London: Nijoff, 1978), p. 91.

37. Una Marson to John Grenfall Williams, memo, October 15, 1941, file E2/584, BBC.

38. Jarrett-Macauley, *Life of Una Marson*, pp. 153, 152. Dr. H. B. Morgan MP, Assistant Controller (Overseas Services), to C (N.C.), copy to C (O.S.), subject: West Indian Programmes, BBC Internal Circulating Memo, January 7, 1942, file E2/584, BBC.

39. See Internal Circulating Memo from Joan Hilbert to Mr. Grenfall Williams, May 1, 1941, file L1/290/1, BBC; Rush, *Bonds of Empire*, p. 175.

40. Procter, "Una Marson at the BBC," p. 2.

41. Dr. H. B. Morgan to C (N.C.), January 7, 1942, pp. 2–3, file E2/584, BBC.

42. Amy Bell, "Landscapes of Fear: Wartime London, 1939–1945," *Journal of British Studies* 48, no. 1 (January 2009): p. 153.

43. Jarrett-Macauley, *Life of Una Marson*, p. 164. Statistics show that between September 1940 and May 1941 more than 40,000 civilians lost their lives; see Malcolm Smith, *Britain and 1940: History, Myth, and Popular Memory* (London: Routledge, 2000), p. 70.

44. Una Marson, "London Revisited," *Sunday Gleaner*, February 28, 1965, p. 21.

45. Jarrett-Macauley, *Life of Una Marson*, p. 167.

46. Claus Füllberg-Stolberg, "The Caribbean in the Second World War" in *General History of the Caribbean*, vol. 5, *The Caribbean in the Twentieth Century*, ed. Bridget Brereton (London: UNESCO, 2004), p. 136.

47. Füllberg-Stolberg, pp. 113–14.

48. Füllberg-Stolberg, p. 114; Sir John MacPherson, Comptroller, *Development and Welfare in the West Indies 1945–46*, Colonial no. 212 (London: HMSO, 1947); and Herward Sieberg, *Colonial Development: Die Grundlegung moderner Entwicklungspolitik durch Großbritannien, 1919–1949* (Stuttgart: Franz Steiner, 1985), p. 238.

49. Jarrett-Macauley, *Life of Una Marson*, pp. 168–73.

50. Jarrett-Macauley, p. 168.

51. Jarrett-Macauley, p. 172.

52. Jarrett-Macauley, p. 173.

53. A. F. Whyte, Medical Adviser, May 3, 1946, file L1/290/2, BBC.

54. Marson to Gilliam.

55. Procter, "Una Marson at the BBC," p. 22.

56. Jarrett-Macauley, *Life of Una Marson*, p. 173.

57. Peter Fryer, *Staying Power: The History of Black People in Britain* (London: Pluto Press, 1984), p. 350; and Hakim Adi and Marika Sherwood, *The 1945 Manchester Pan-African Congress Revisited with Colonial and . . . Coloured Unity*, ed. George Padmore (London: New Beacon Books, 1995), p. 98.

58. Jarrett-Macauley, *Life of Una Marson*, p. 84; and Alison Donnell, "Una Marson: Feminism, Anti-Colonialism, and a Forgotten Fight for Freedom," in *West Indian Intellectuals in Britain*, ed. Bill Schwarz (Manchester: Manchester University Press, 2003), p. 116.

59. Kristen Stromberg Childers, *Seeking Imperialism's Embrace: National Identity, Decolonization, and Assimilation in the French Caribbean* (New York: Oxford University Press, 2016), p. 16.

60. Keith L. Walker, "Translator's Introduction: Suzanne Césaire and the Great Camouflages," in *The Great Camouflage: Writings of Dissent (1941–1945) Suzanne Césaire*, ed.

Daniel Maximin, trans. Keith L. Walker (Middletown, CT: Wesleyan University Press, 2012), p. ix.

61. Eric T. Jennings, *Vichy in the Tropics: Pétain's National Revolution in Madagascar, Guadeloupe, and Indochina 1940-1944* (Stanford, CA: Stanford University Press, 2001), p. 2; and Musil, "La Marianne Noire," p. 68.

62. Childers, *Seeking Imperialism's Embrace*, p. 34.

63. Kristen Stromberg Childers, "The Second World War as Watershed in the French Caribbean," *Atlantic Studies* 9, no. 4 (2012), p. 420; and Carrie Gibson, *Empire's Crossroads: A History of the Caribbean from Columbus to the Present Day* (New York: Atlantic Monthly Press, 2014), p. 261.

64. Childers, *Seeking Imperialism's Embrace*, p. 34.

65. Daniel Maximin, "Editor's Introduction: Suzanne Césaire Sun-Filled Fountain," in *The Great Camouflage*, p. xxv.

66. Musil, "La Marianne Noire," p. 189; and Tony Chafer, *The End of Empire in French West Africa: France's Successful Decolonization?* (New York: Berg, 2002), p. 47.

67. Ransby, *Eslanda*, pp. 139, 141, 143.

68. Ransby, p. 141.

69. Eslanda Robeson, "An Open Letter to the Students of Fisk University from Mrs. Paul Robeson," September 1943, p. 1, box 10, Eslanda Goode Robeson Papers, Moorland-Spingarn Research Center, Howard University, Washington, DC (hereafter EGRP).

70. Roi Ottley, *New World A-coming* (New York: Arno Press, 1968), p. v; and James H. Meriwether, *Proudly We Can Be Africans: Black Americans and Africa, 1935-1961* (Chapel Hill: University of North Carolina Press, 2002), p. 60.

71. James L. Roark, "American Black Leaders: The Response to Colonialism and the Cold War, 1943-1953," *African Historical Studies* 4, no. 2 (1971), p. 255; and A. Philip Randolph, "March on Washington Movement Presents Program for the Negro," in *What the Negro Wants*, ed. Rayford W. Logan (Chapel Hill: University of North Carolina Press, 1944), p. 152.

72. Erik S. McDuffie, *Sojourning for Freedom: Black Women, American Communism, and the Making of Black Left Feminism* (Durham, NC: Duke University Press, 2011), p. 128.

73. Nico Slate, *Colored Cosmopolitanism: The Shared Struggle for Freedom in the United States and India* (Cambridge, MA: Harvard University Press, 2012), p. 126.

74. Eslanda Goode Robeson, *African Journey* (New York: John Day, 1945), p. 14.

75. Ransby, *Eslanda*, p. 144.

76. Childers, *Seeking Imperialism's Embrace*, p. 1.

77. Nick Nesbitt, "Departmentalization and the Logic of Decolonization," *L'Ésprit créateur* 47, no. 1 (2007), p. 33.

78. Edouard Glissant, *Caribbean Discourse: Selected Essays*, trans. and introduction by J. Michael Dash (Charlottesville: University Press of Virginia, 1989), p. 88.

79. Nesbitt, "Departmentalization and the Logic of Decolonization," p. 33.

80. Childers, *Seeking Imperialism's Embrace*, p. 48.

81. Childers, "Second World War in the French Caribbean," p. 410. For more on the US occupation of Haiti, see Mary A. Renda, *Taking Haiti: Military Occupation and the Culture of US Imperialism, 1915-1940* (Chapel Hill: University of North Carolina Press, 2001).

82. Eric Jennings, "Last Exit from Vichy France: The Martinique Escape Route and the Ambiguities of Emigration," *Journal of Modern History* 74, no. 2 (2002): p. 303.

83. Paulette Nardal to Jacques Louis Hymans, November 17, 1963, quoted in R. P. Smith Jr., "Black Like That: Paulette Nardal and the Negritude Salon," *CLA Journal* 45, no. 1 (2001): p. 59; and Musil, "La Marianne Noire," p. 150.

84. Musil, pp. 23, 206.

85. Paulette Nardal, "Rassemblement féminin," *La Femme dans la cité*, January 15, 1945, p. 1; and Musil, p. 203.

86. Paulette Nardal, "From an Electoral Point of View," *La Femme dans la cité*, March 1945, quoted in Paulette Nardal, *Beyond Negritude: Essays from Woman in the City*, trans., introduction, and notes by T. Denean Sharpley-Whiting (New York: State University of New York Press, 2009), p. 35.

87. Paulette Nardal, "Martinican Women and Social Action," *La Femme dans la cité*, October 1945, quoted in Nardal, *Beyond Negritude*, p. 47.

88. Childers, *Seeking Imperialism's Embrace*, pp. 164–65.

89. Musil, "La Marianne Noire," pp. 210–11, 10.

90. Childers, *Seeking Imperialism's Embrace*, p. 162.

91. Childers, p. 166.

92. T. Denean Sharpley-Whiting, "Introduction: On Race, Rights, and Women," in Nardal, *Beyond Negritude*, p. 6.

93. Paulette Nardal, "Realisations," *La Femme dans la cité*, December 1945, p. 3.

94. Sharpley-Whiting, "Introduction," in Nardal, *Beyond Negritude*, p. 10.

95. Paulette Nardal, "Woman in the City," *La Femme dans la cité*, January 1945, in Nardal, *Beyond Negritude*, p. 21.

96. Karen Offen, "Defining Feminism: A Comparative Historical Approach," *Signs: Journal of Women in Culture and Society* 14, no. 1 (Autumn 1988): pp. 138–39.

97. Nardal, "Woman in the City," p. 21.

98. Nardal, p. 23.

99. Musil, "La Marianne Noire," p. 215.

100. Nardal, "Woman in the City," p. 23.

101. Childers, *Seeking Imperialism's Embrace*, p. 53.

102. Nardal, "From an Electoral Point of View," p. 35.

103. Nardal, p. 33.

104. Nardal, p. 33.

105. Nardal, p. 35.

106. Paulette Nardal, "Abstention: A Social Crime," *La Femme dans la cité*, November 1946, in Nardal, *Beyond Negritude*, p. 75.

107. Paulette Nardal, "Facing History," *La Femme dans la cité*, October 1946, in Nardal, p. 69, 71.

108. Nardal, "Abstention: A Social Crime," p. 75.

109. Paulette Nardal, "Editorial," *La Femme dans la cité*, July 1951, in Nardal, *Beyond Negritude*, p. 97.

110. Childers, *Seeking Imperialism's Embrace*, p. 146.

111. Gary Wilder, *Freedom Time: Negritude, Decolonization, and the Future of the World* (Durham, NC: Duke University Press, 2015), p. 123; and Armand Nicolas, *Histoire de la Martinique*, tome 3, *De 1939 à 1971* (Paris: L'Harmattan, 1998), pp. 139–41.

112. Paulette Nardal, "Poverty Does Not Wait," *La Femme dans la cité*, May 1945, in Nardal, *Beyond Negritude*, p. 39.

113. Nardal, p. 41.

114. Paulette Nardal, "And Now, What Are Our Objectives?," *La Femme dans la cité*, November 1945, in Nardal, *Beyond Negritude*, p. 51.

115. Nardal, p. 53.

116. Nardal, p. 53.

117. Paulette Nardal, "On Intellectual Laziness," *La Femme dans la cité*, November 1948, in Nardal, *Beyond Negritude*, p. 91.

118. Nardal, "Facing History," p. 69.

119. Mark Mazower, *No Enchanted Palace: The End of Empire and the Ideological Origins of the United Nations* (Princeton, NJ: Princeton University Press, 2009), p. 6; and Mark Mazower, *Governing the World: The Making of an Idea* (New York: Penguin, 2012)

120. Mazower, *No Enchanted Palace*, p. 7.

121. Paulette Nardal, "United Nations," *La Femme dans la cité*, January 1947, in Nardal, *Beyond Negritude*, p. 81.

122. Sluga, *Internationalism in the Age of Nationalism*, p. 94; and United Nations Charter, chap. 1, art. 1.3, http://www.un.org/en/sections/un-charter/chapter-i/index.html.

123. Nardal, "United Nations," in Nardal, *Beyond Negritude*, p. 81.

124. Sluga, *Internationalism in the Age of Nationalism*, p. 90.

125. Musil, "La Marianne Noire," p. 217.

126. Sluga, *Internationalism in the Age of Nationalism*, p. 94.

127. Sluga, p. 93.

128. "Le départ de notre directrice," *La Femme dans la cité*, December 25, 1946, p. 3; Musil, "La Marianne Noire," p. 223; and Sharpley-Whiting, "Introduction," in Nardal, *Beyond Negritude*, p. 7.

129. Musil, p. 223; and Christiane Eda-Pierre, interview by Emily Musil, January 27, 2006.

130. Paulette Nardal, "Lettre d'Amérique/Letter from America," *La Femme dans la cité*, July-August 1947, p. 4.

131. Sluga, *Internationalism in the Age of Nationalism*, p. 102.

132. Sluga, pp. 102-3; and Laura Reanda, "Human Rights and Women's Rights: The United Nations Approach," *Human Rights Quarterly* 3, no. 2 (1981): p. 18.

133. Annie Devenish, "Being, Belonging and Becoming: A Study of Gender in the Making of Post-colonial Citizenship in India 1946-1961" (DPhil thesis, 2014, University of Oxford), p. 210; United Nations, *The United Nations and the Advancement of Women 1945-1995*, Blue Book Series, vol. 6 (New York: United Nations, 1996); Arnold Whittick, *Woman into Citizen* (London: Athenaeum, distributed by Muller, 1979); and Allida Black, "Are Women 'Human'? The UN and the Struggle to Recognize Women's Rights as Human Rights," in *The Human Rights Revolution: An International History*, ed. Akira Iriye, Petra Goedde, and William I. Hitchcock (New York: Oxford University Press, 2012), pp. 133-55.

134. Vijay Prashad, *The Darker Nations: A People's History of the Third World* (New York: New Press, 2007), p. 56; and Margaret E. Galey, "Promoting Nondiscrimination against Women: The UN Commission on the Status of Women," *International Studies Quarterly* 23, no. 2 (1979): p. 276.

135. Musil, "La Marianne Noire," pp. 223–24.
136. Nardal, "Lettre d'Amérique/Letter from America," p. 4.
137. Paulette Nardal, "Le Congrès de l'U.F.C.S./The UFCS Congress," *La Femme dans la cité*, May-June 1946, p. 4.
138. Nardal, "Martinican Women and Social Action," p. 47.
139. Shireen K. Lewis, *Race, Culture, and Identity: Francophone West African and Caribbean Literature and Theory from Négritude to Créolité* (Oxford: Lexington Books, 2006), p. 64.
140. Eslanda Robeson, "Congo Diary Transcriptions," 1946, p. 6, box 11, EGRP.
141. Robeson, p. 7.
142. Ransby, *Eslanda*, p. 287.
143. For an extensive study of Africans during World War II, see Judith A. Byfield, Carolyn A. Brown, Timothy Parsons, and Ahmad Alawad Sikainga, eds., *Africa and World War II* (New York: Cambridge University Press, 2015); and David Killingray, *Fighting for Britain: African Soldiers in the Second World War* (Suffolk: James Currey, 2010).
144. Timothy Parsons, "The Military Experiences of Ordinary Africans in World War II," in Byfield, Brown, Parsons, and Sikainga, p. 4.
145. Judith A. Byfield, "Preface," in Byfield, Brown, Parsons, and Sikainga, p. xx.
146. Prashad, *The Darker Nations*, p. 24.
147. Eslanda Robeson, "Congo III," 1951, p.1, series E: Writings by Eslanda Goode Robeson, box 13, EGRP.
148. For more on MI5's surveillance of Robeson, see Ransby, *Eslanda*, pp. 164–65.
149. Ransby, *Eslanda*, p. 162.
150. See Eslanda Robeson, "Congo Jim Crow Hits a Captain," *New York Amsterdam News*, March 31, 1951; and Eslanda Robeson, "Story of a Battle for Dignity," *New York Amsterdam News*, April 14, 1951.
151. Eslanda Robeson, "Days with a Deputy" (Gabriel D'Arboussier, French Congo), June 1946, p. 1, series E, box 11, EGRP.
152. Ransby, *Eslanda*, p. 167; and Robeson, p. 1.
153. Robeson, p. 3.
154. Robeson, p. 4.
155. Robeson, p. 5.
156. Robeson, p. 6.
157. Robeson, p. 9.
158. Ransby, *Eslanda*, pp. 167–68.
159. Eslanda Robeson, "African Women," 1946, p. 1, series E, box 11, EGRP.
160. Robeson, p. 2.
161. Robeson, p. 2.
162. Robeson, p. 3.
163. Robeson, p. 5.
164. Eslanda Robeson, "Congo Diary," 1946, n.p., series E, box 17, EGRP.
165. Ransby, *Eslanda*, p. 172.
166. Ransby, pp. 196–97.
167. Eslanda Robeson, "140,000 Women Can't Be Wrong," *New World Review*, June 1954, p. 18. For more on the WIDF, see Francisca de Haan, "Continuing Cold War Paradigms in Western Historiography of Transnational Women's Organsations: The Case of the

Women's International Democratic Federation (WIDF)," *Women's History Review* 19, no. 4 (2010): pp. 547–73.

168. Eslanda Robeson, "Trip to China," 1950, pp. 1–2, series E, box 12, EGRP. For more on the CAW, see Jacqueline Castledine, *Cold War Progressives: Women's Interracial Organizing for Peace and Freedom* (Urbana: University of Illinois Press, 2012), pp. 45–52.

169. Ransby, *Eslanda*, pp. 197, 194. For more on Ada Jackson, see Castledine, pp. 110–31.

170. "Ada Jackson to 'Reveal' All at Boro ALP Rally," *New York Amsterdam News*, January 28, 1950, p. 21, quoted in Ransby, *Eslanda*, p. 198.

171. Ransby, p. 198, 200.

172. On Afro-Asian solidarity, see Gallichio, *The African American Encounter with China and Japan: Black Internationalism in Asia* (Chapel Hill: University of North Carolina Press, 2000); Vijay Prashad, *Everybody Was Kung Fu Fighting: Afro-Asian Connections and the Myth of Cultural Purity* (Boston: Beacon Press, 2001); Heike Raphael-Hernandez and Shannon Steen, eds., *AfroAsian Encounters: Culture, History, Politics* (New York: New York University Press, 2006); Fred Ho and Bill V. Mullen, eds., *Afro-Asia: Revolutionary Political and Cultural Connections between African Americans and Asian Americans* (Durham, NC: Duke University Press, 2008); Slate, *Colored Cosmopolitanism;* Yuichiro Onishi, *Transpacific Antiracism: Afro-Asian Solidarity in 20th-Century Black America, Japan, and Okinawa* (New York: New York University Press, 2013); and Robeson Taj Frazier, *The East Is Black: Cold War China in the Black Radical Imagination* (Durham, NC: Duke University Press, 2015).

173. See Eslanda Robeson, "China I," for *Freedom,* May 9–12, 1951, p. 1, series E, box 13, EGRP.

174. Ransby, *Eslanda*, p. 206.

175. Kevin K. Gaines, *American Africans in Ghana: Black Expatriates and the Civil Rights Era* (Chapel Hill: University of North Carolina Press, 2006), p. 162.

176. Robeson, "China I," p. 4.

177. Robeson, p. 7.

178. Robeson, p. 1.

179. Eslanda Robeson, "World Woman Number One," *New World Review,* July 1951, p. 20.

180. Robeson, p. 21.

181. Ransby, *Eslanda*, p. 200.

182. Ransby, p. 201.

183. Ransby, p. 202.

184. Jarrett-Macauley, *Life of Una Marson,* p. 177.

185. Jarrett-Macauley, pp. 177–78. Una Marson to Langston Hughes, November 20, 1948, JWJ MSS 26, folder 2073, box 110, Series I: Personal Correspondence, Langston Hughes Papers, Beinecke Rare Book and Manuscript Library, Yale University, New Haven, CT (hereafter BRBM).

186. Hughes's letters to Marson have not been located. Instead, researchers have gleaned his responses from the letters that Marson sent Hughes.

187. Marson to Hughes, November 20, 1948, p. 2.

188. Marson to Hughes, p. 3.

189. Marson to Hughes, p. 3.

190. Jarrett-Macauley, *Life of Una Marson,* p. 182.

191. Jarrett-Macauley, p. 189.

192. See Una Marson, "I Can Tell You What's Wrong with Jamaica," *Public Opinion*, February 17, 1951, p. 4; and Una Marson, "The Cinema and Our Youth," *Public Opinion*, March 10, 1951, p. 6.

193. Una Marson to John Grenfall Williams, January 6, 1951, file E1/1303, BBC; and Rush, *Bonds of Empire*, p. 179.

194. Una Marson to Claude A. Barnett, September 25, 1952, Claude Barnett Papers, Chicago Historical Society, quoted in Jarrett-Macauley, *Life of Una Marson*, p. 196.

195. Gaines, *American Africans in Ghana*, p. 47.

196. Claude A. Barnett to Una Marson, October 4, 1952, Claude Barnett Papers, Chicago Historical Society, quoted in Jarrett-Macauley, *Life of Una Marson*, p. 197.

197. Jarrett-Macauley, p. 199.

4. CONTINUITIES AND CHANGES, 1950–1966

1. For more, see Mary L. Dudziak, *Cold War Civil Rights: Race and the Image of American Democracy* (Princeton, NJ: Princeton University Press, 2000); and Thomas Borstelmann, *The Cold War and the Color Line: American Race Relations in the Global Arena* (Cambridge, MA: Harvard University Press, 2001).

2. For more on the NAACP's politics during the Cold War, see Carol Anderson, *Eyes Off the Prize: The United Nations and the African American Struggle for Human Rights, 1944–1955* (New York: Cambridge University Press, 2003).

3. Erik S. McDuffie, *Sojourning for Freedom: Black Women, American Communism, and the Making of Black Left Feminism* (Durham, NC: Duke University Press, 2011); and Dayo F. Gore, *Radicalism at the Crossroads: African American Women Activists in the Cold War* (New York: New York University Press, 2011).

4. Emily Musil, "La Marianne Noire: How Gender and Race in the Twentieth-Century Atlantic World Reshaped the Debate about Human Rights" (PhD diss., University of California Los Angeles, 2007), pp. 23–24; and "Paulette Nardal, l'âme de la perfection," *Carib-Hebdo*, n.d., p. 24.

5. Musil, p. 24.

6. "La chorale Joie de chanter, ou l'amour du chant choral à la Martinique," *Télé 7 jours Martinique*, no. 92 (March 30–April 5, 1981): p. 8; and "Paulette Nardal, l'âme de la perfection," p. 24.

7. "La chorale Joie de chanter," p. 8.

8. "Paulette Nardal, l'âme de la perfection," p. 24.

9. Musil, "La Marianne Noire," p. 24.

10. Una Marson, "The America I have discovered—Miami and Washington," n.d., p. 2, folder 12, MS 1944B, UMP.

11. Marson, p. 3.

12. Marson, p. 5.

13. Marson, p. 6.

14. Marson, p. 5.

15. Marson, p. 6.

16. Marson, p. 7.

17. Marson, p. 7.
18. Marson, p. 8.
19. Marson, p. 10.
20. Una Marson, "Discovering America," n.d., p. 9, folder 12, MS 1944B, UMP.
21. For more on these figures, see Treva Lindsey, "Climbing the Hilltop: In Search of New Negro Womanhood at Howard University," in *Escape from New York: The New Negro Renaissance beyond Harlem*, ed. Davarian L. Baldwin and Minkah Makalani (Minneapolis: University of Minnesota Press, 2013), pp. 271–90; Barbara D, Savage, "Professor Merze Tate: Diplomatic Historian, Cosmopolitan Woman" in *Toward an Intellectual History of Black Women*, ed. Mia Bay, Farah Jasmine Griffin, Martha S. Jones, and Barbara D. Savage (Chapel Hill: University of North Carolina Press, 2015), pp. 252–69; and Treva B. Lindsey, *Colored No More: Reinventing Black Womanhood in Washington, DC* (Urbana: University of Illinois Press, 2017).
22. Marson, "The America I have discovered," p. 6.
23. Marson, p. 7.
24. Delia Jarrett-Macauley, *The Life of Una Marson, 1905–1965* (Manchester: Manchester University Press, 1998), p. 203.
25. Una Marson to Mr. Gilliam, n.d., file L1/290/1, BBC Written Archives Centre, Caversham, Reading (hereafter BBC); here Marson states that she got married in 1955.
26. Jarrett-Macauley, *Life of Una Marson*, p. 204.
27. Una Marson, "What I have discovered in America—New York," n.d., p. 2, folder 12, MS 1944B, UMP.
28. Marson, p. 6.
29. "The Rehabilitation of Western Kingston," *Daily Gleaner*, n.d., n.p., c. 1962, quoted in Jarrett-Macauley, *Life of Una Marson*, p. 202.
30. Marson to Gilliam.
31. Eric D. Duke, *Building a Nation: Caribbean Federation in the Black Diaspora* (Gainesville: University Press of Florida, 2016), p. 21.
32. Duke, p. 219; Zachery R. Williams, *In Search of the Talented Tenth: Howard University Public Intellectuals and the Dilemmas of Race, 1926–1970* (Columbia: University of Missouri Press, 2009), p. 131; "Friends of West Indies Federation Set in D.C.," *Afro-American*, April 12, 1958, p. 9; "Form WIF Chapter," *Pittsburgh Courier*, April 12, 1958, p. 17; H. Con. Res. 298, March 25, 1958; Rayford Logan to Frederick Stanton, April 23, 1958, folder 3, box 166-7, Rayford Logan Papers, Moorland-Spingarn Research Center, Howard University, Washington, DC. Duke and Williams give her name as Mrs. Una Morrison Staples. For more on the work of AFWIF, see Williams, *In Search of the Talented Tenth*, p. 131.
33. Duke, *Building a Nation*, p. 219.
34. Williams, *In Search of the Talented Tenth*, p. 131; "Friends of West Indies Federation Set in D.C.," *Baltimore African American*, April 12, 1958, p. 9.
35. Marson to Gilliam. The *Washington Star* articles could not be located.
36. Jarrett-Macauley, *Life of Una Marson*, p. 203.
37. Jarrett-Macauley, pp. 204–5.
38. Martin Bauml Duberman, *Paul Robeson* (London: Bodley Head, 1988), pp. 336–62; Paul Robeson quoted, p. 342.
39. Duberman, p. 342; James H. Meriwether, *Proudly We Can Be Africans: Black Americans and Africa, 1935–1961* (Chapel Hill: University of North Carolina Press, 2002), p. 81.

40. Barbara Ransby, *Eslanda: The Large and Unconventional Life of Mrs. Paul Robeson* (New Haven, CT: Yale University Press, 2013), p. 232.

41. Ransby, p. 231.

42. Meriwether, *Proudly We Can Be Africans,* p. 82.

43. Pearl Buck and Eslanda Robeson, *American Argument* (London: Methuen, 1950), p. 3.

44. Buck and Robeson, p. 125.

45. Buck and Robeson, p. 133.

46. Buck and Robeson, p. 203.

47. Ransby, *Eslanda,* p. 224; and "Mrs. Robeson tells McCarthy about the 15th Amendment," *Amsterdam News,* July 20, 1953, p. 6.

48. Gore, *Radicalism at the Crossroads,* p. 155

49. Gore, p. 156. For more on African Americans and Communism, see Robin D. G. Kelley, *Hammer and Hoe: Alabama Communists during the Great Depression* (Chapel Hill: University of North Carolina Press, 1990); Bill V. Mullen and James Edward Smethurst, eds., *Left of the Color Line: Race, Radicalism and Twentieth-Century Literature of the United States* (Chapel Hill: University of North Carolina Press, 2003); Kate A. Baldwin, *Beyond the Color Line and the Iron Curtain: Reading Encounters between Black and Red, 1922–1963* (Durham, NC: Duke University Press, 2002); Carol Boyce Davies, *Left of Karl Marx: The Political Life of Black Communist Claudia Jones* (Durham, NC: Duke University Press, 2008); Joy Gleason Carew, *Blacks, Reds, and Russians: Sojourners in Search of the Soviet Promise* (New Brunswick, NJ: Rutgers University Press, 2008); and McDuffie, *Sojourning for Freedom.*

50. Ransby, *Eslanda,* p. 206.

51. Jeremi Suri, "Non-governmental Organizations and Non-state Actors," in *Palgrave Advances in International History,* ed. Patrick Finney (New York: Palgrave Macmillan, 2005), p. 238; Jacqueline L. Castledine, *Cold War Progressives: Women's Interracial Organizing for Peace and Freedom* (Urbana: University of Illinois Press, 2012), p. 96; and Ransby, *Eslanda,* p. 146.

52. Eslanda Robeson, "Unofficial America Goes to the Conference," n.d, p. 2, series E: Writings by Eslanda G. Robeson, box 9, Eslanda Goode Robeson Papers, Moorland-Spingarn Research Center, Howard University, Washington, DC (hereafter EGRP).

53. Robeson, p. 11.

54. Derek Heater, *World Citizenship: Cosmopolitan Thinking and Its Opponents* (London: Continuum, 2002), pp. 5–7.

55. Heater, p. 5. See also Derek Heater, *What Is Citizenship?* (Cambridge: Polity, 1999); Gerard Delanty, *Citizenship in a Global Age: Society, Culture, Politics* (Buckingham: Open University Press, 2000); and Derek Heater, *World Citizenship and Government: Cosmopolitan Ideas in the History of Western Political Thought* (Basingstoke, UK: Macmillan, 1996).

56. Eslanda Robeson, "Women in the United Nations," *New World Review,* July 1954, p. 7.

57. Robeson, p. 8.

58. Robeson, p. 10.

59. Eslanda Robeson, "Some Women at the United Nations," draft for *New World Review,* February 1958, p. 1, series E, box 14, EGRP.

60. Robeson, p. 2.

61. Karen Offen, "Defining Feminism: A Comparative Historical Approach," *Signs: Journal of Women in Culture and Society* 14, no. 1 (Autumn 1988), pp. 138–39.

62. Nico Slate, *Colored Cosmopolitanism: The Shared Struggle for Freedom in the United States and India* (Cambridge, MA: Harvard University Press, 2012), p. 142; Ransby, *Eslanda*, p. 218.

63. Slate, p. 181; Ransby, *Eslanda*, p. 219.

64. Annie Devenish, "Performing the Political Self: A Study of Identity Making in the Autobiographies of India's First Generation of Parliamentary Women," *Women's History Review* 22. no. 2 (2013): pp. 280–94.

65. Eslanda Robeson, "Last Stand of Colonialism in the UN," *New World Review,* October 1955, p. 1, series E, box 14, EGRP.

66. Ransby, *Eslanda*, p. 210; Eslanda Robeson, "Krishna Menon: A New Type of Diplomat," *New World Review,* June 1956, p. 10.

67. Robeson, p. 10.

68. Robeson, p. 11.

69. Richard Wright, *The Color Curtain: A Report on the Bandung Conference* (London: Dobson, 1956), p. 117.

70. Thomas Borstelmann, *The Cold War and the Color Line: American Race Relations in the Global Arena* (Cambridge MA: Harvard University Press, 2001), p. 95.

71. Kevin K. Gaines, *American Africans in Ghana: Black Expatriates and the Civil Rights Era* (Chapel Hill: University of North Carolina Press, 2006), p. 71.

72. Eslanda Robeson, "President Sukarno: Brother, Father, Son of the Indonesian People," *New World Review,* August 1956, p. 8.

73. Eslanda Robeson, "Race Conflict in South Africa," for *The Afro-American,* February 12, 1957, p. 1, series E, box 14, EGRP.

74. Robeson, pp. 1–2.

75. Robeson, p. 3.

76. Castledine, *Cold War Progressives*, p. 86; and Borstelmann, *The Cold War and the Color Line*, p. 66.

77. Ransby, *Eslanda*, p. 185.

78. Castledine, *Cold War Progressives*, p. 97.

79. Ransby, *Eslanda*, p. 186; and Castledine, p. 13.

80. Ransby, pp. 185–86.

81. Borstelmann, *The Cold War and the Color Line*, p. 66.

82. Ransby, *Eslanda*, p. 186; and Henry Wallace, "Where I Was Wrong," *New York Herald Tribune,* September 1952, n.p.

83. Ransby, *Eslanda*, p. 186.

84. Castledine, *Cold War Progressives*, p. 39. Figures from *The Crisis* quoted in Curtis D. MacDougall, *Gideon's Army* (New York: Marzani and Munsell, 1965), p. 664.

85. Castledine, p. 85.

86. Castledine, p. 86; Gore, *Radicalism at the Crossroads*, p. 3.

87. Castledine, pp. 99–102.

88. McDuffie, *Sojourning for Freedom*, p. 19.

89. McDuffie, p. 164; Committee to Free the Trenton Six, *Lynching Northern Style,* n.d., Mass Organizations subject files, box 6, folder 62, Communist Party of the United States of

America Records, Tamiment Library and Robert F. Wagner Labor Archives, Bobst Library, New York University; Gerald Horne, *Communist Front?: The Civil Rights Congress* (London: Associated University Presses, 1988), pp. 131–54; and Castledine, *Cold War Progressives*, p. 100.

90. Castledine, p. 104.

91. Ransby, *Eslanda*, pp. 188–89; Charlotta Bass and Louise T. Patterson to Miss Ray Alexander, Food and Canning Workers Union, South Africa, April 5, 1952, "Sojourners for Truth and Justice" folder, Louise Thompson Patterson Papers, Emory University Library, Atlanta.

92. Ransby, pp. 188–89; Bass and Patterson to Alexander; Castledine, *Cold War Progressives*, p. 104.

93. McDuffie, *Sojourning for Freedom*, p. 174. For more on the TWWA, see Stephen Ward, "The Third World Women's Alliance: Black Feminist Radicalism and Black Power Politics," in *The Black Power Movement: Rethinking the Civil Rights-Black Power Era*, ed. Peniel Joseph (New York: Routledge, 2006), pp. 119–44.

94. Castledine, *Cold War Progressives*, p. 108.

95. Duke, *Building a Nation*, p. 224. "Carver Bank Shows WI-American Unity," *New York Amsterdam News*, April 26, 1958, p. 18; and Carver Federal Savings and Loan Association ad, *New York Amsterdam News*, April 26, 1958, p. 18.

96. Duke, *Building a Nation*, p. 28.

97. Eslanda Robeson, "The West Indies: A New Nation," April 20, 1958, p. 1, series E, box 14, EGRP.

98. Eslanda Robeson, "History Is Made," April 25, 1958, p. 1, box 25, EGRP.

99. Robeson, p. 3.

100. Ransby, *Eslanda*, p. 237.

101. Alice Colón and Rhoda Reddock, "The Changing Status of Women in the Contemporary Caribbean," in *General History of the Caribbean*, vol. 5, *The Caribbean in the Twentieth Century*, ed. Bridget Brereton (London: UNESCO, 2004), p. 480.

102. Ransby, *Eslanda*, p. 237.

103. Eslanda Robeson, "Women in a New Nation," April 28, 1958, p. 2, box 25, EGRP.

104. Ransby, *Eslanda*, p. 221.

105. Carrie Gibson, *Empire's Crossroads: A History of the Caribbean from Columbus to the Present Day* (New York: Atlantic Monthly Press, 2014), p. 268.

106. Una Marson, "Building National Culture," n.d., p. 1, folder 12, MS 1944B, UMP.

107. Marson, p. 1.

108. Marson, p. 2.

109. Marson, p. 2.

110. Marson, p. 2.

111. See C. L. R. James, *The Black Jacobins: Toussaint L'Ouverture and the San Domingo Revolution* (London: Secker and Warburg, 1938).

112. Marson, "Building National Culture," p. 2.

113. Jarrett-Macauley, *Life of Una Marson*, p. 211. For more on independence, see Gordon K. Lewis, *The Growth of the Modern West Indies* (London: MacGibbon & Kee, 1968).

114. Jarrett-Macauley, p. 211.

115. Ula Y. Taylor, *The Veiled Garvey: The Life and Times of Amy Jacques Garvey* (Chapel Hill: University of North Carolina Press, 2002), p. 199.

116. Una Marson, "The Foundations of Independence," *Daily Gleaner*, August 1, 1964, p. 3.
117. Una Marson, "Have married women taken the wrong turning?," n.d., p. 5, folder 12, MS 1944B, UMP.
118. Marson, p. 7.
119. Marson, p. 8.
120. Una Marson, "Serving Each Other with Love," *Sunday Gleaner*, February 12, 1961, p. 15.
121. Una Marson, "Save The Children Fund Needs You," *Sunday Gleaner*, June 25, 1961, p. 5.
122. Jarrett-Macauley, *Life of Una Marson*, p. 209.
123. Una Marson, "The Rehabilitation of Western Kingston," *Daily Gleaner*, c. 1962, n.p., quoted in Jarrett-Macauley, *Life of Una Marson*, p. 209.
124. Marson, in Jarrett-Macauley, p. 210.
125. Jarrett-Macauley, p. 214.
126. Ransby, *Eslanda*, p. 239.
127. Stephen Tuck, *The Night Malcolm X Spoke at the Oxford Union: A Transatlantic Story of Antiracist Protest* (Berkeley: University of California Press, 2014), p. 69.
128. Tuck, p. 69; and "Migration Plan in Caribbean," *Times*, November 3, 1948, p. 3.
129. Tuck, p. 69.
130. Donald Hinds, "The *West Indian Gazette*: Claudia Jones and the Black Press in Britain," *Race and Class* 50, no. 1 (2008): p. 93.
131. Kennetta Hammond Perry, *London Is the Place for Me: Black Britons, Citizenship, and the Politics of Race* (New York: Oxford University Press, 2015), p. 6.
132. Eslanda Robeson, "Summary of the Accra Conference," December 1958, p. 2, series E, box 14, EGRP; and Ransby, *Eslanda*, p. 242.
133. Robeson, p. 2
134. Gaines, *American Africans in Ghana*, pp. 77–78.
135. Ransby, *Eslanda*, p. 242; Eslanda Robeson, "Learning How to Live Together," *Seamen's Journal*, November 1960, supp., pp. 378–79, 383.
136. Eslanda Robeson, "The Accra Conference," *New World Review*, February 1959, p. 13.
137. Gaines, *American Africans in Ghana*, p. 92.
138. Robeson, "The Accra Conference," p. 14.
139. Robeson, p. 14.
140. Gaines, *American Africans in Ghana*, p. 16.
141. Ransby, *Eslanda*, pp. 243–44.
142. Ransby, p. 246.
143. Ransby, p. 248.
144. Ransby, p. 249.
145. Eslanda Robeson, "Kelso Cochrane Memorial Meeting, St. Pancras Town Hall," May 28, 1959, p. 1, series E, box 14, EGRP.
146. Eslanda Robeson, "Anti-Apartheid Meeting, Trafalgar Square," March 19, 1961, p. 1, series E, box 15, EGRP.
147. Robeson, p. 1.
148. Robeson, p. 2.

149. Ransby, *Eslanda*, p. 258; UPI, "So. African Woe Brings Clash in London at Rally," *Atlanta Daily World*, March 23, 1961, p. 8.

150. Bill Schwarz, "Introduction: Crossing the Seas," in *West Indian Intellectuals in Britain*, ed. Bill Schwarz (Manchester: Manchester University Press, 2003), p. 15.

151. For more on black British anti-apartheid activism, see Elizabeth Williams, *The Politics of Race in Britain and South Africa: Black British Solidarity and the Anti-apartheid Struggle* (London: I. B. Tauris, 2015).

152. Ransby, *Eslanda*, pp. 252–53.

153. Ransby, pp. 254–55.

154. Ransby, p. 263.

155. Ransby, p. 263; "Africa Women's Day" flyer, series B: Personal Papers, "Programs" 1960–1961 folder, box 2, EGRP.

156. Ransby, p. 263.

157. Ransby, p. 264.

158. Eslanda Robeson, "Collection Speech, Africa Day Meeting, Festival Hall, London, April 8, 1962," p. 1, series E, box 15, EGRP.

159. Robeson, p. 1.

160. Ransby, *Eslanda*, p. 267.

161. Ransby, p. 269.

162. Ransby, p. 271; "Eslanda Robeson Receives GDR Peace Medal," *New World Review*, October 1963, p. 37.

163. Ransby, p. 271.

164. Eslanda Robeson, "The March on Washington (From a Distance)," Berlin, October 4, 1963, p. 1, series E, box 15, EGRP.

165. Eslanda Robeson, "Eslanda Robeson Visits East Germany," *New World Review*, April 1964, p. 14.

166. Robeson, p. 15.

167. Robeson, pp. 15–16.

168. Robeson, p. 15.

169. Robeson, p. 16.

170. Robeson, p. 16.

171. Robeson, p. 17.

172. Ransby, *Eslanda*, p. 270.

173. See Eslanda Robeson, "No Communication between Blacks and 'The Enemy,'" *Sun-Reporter*, June 20, 1964, p. 14, series E, box 15, EGRP; and Eslanda Robeson, "The Time Is Now," *Sun-Reporter*, November 28, 1964, p. 26, series E, box 15, EGRP.

174. Ransby, *Eslanda*, p. 274.

175. Ransby, p. 275.

176. Jarrett-Macauley, *Life of Una Marson*, p. 214.

177. Mount Carmel Training Centre, 1981 brochure, quoted in Jarrett-Macauley, *Life of Una Marson*, p. 216.

178. Jarrett-Macauley, *Life of Una Marson*, p. 216.

179. "Una Marson Tells of an Unusual Visit to the Holy Land," BBC Home Service, December 1964, quoted in Jarrett-Macauley, *Life of Una Marson*, p. 216.

180. Jarrett-Macauley, *Life of Una Marson*, p. 216.

181. Jarrett-Macauley, p. 217.
182. Jarrett-Macauley, p. 217.
183. Una Marson, "London Revisited," *Sunday Gleaner*, February 28, 1965, p. 25.
184. Marson, p. 21.
185. Marson, p. 21.
186. Jarrett-Macauley, *Life of Una Marson*, pp. 218–20.
187. Marson, "London Revisited," p. 21.
188. Marson, p. 25.
189. Jarrett-Macauley, *Life of Una Marson*, p. 219.
190. Marson, "London Revisited," p. 25.
191. Jarrett-Macauley, *Life of Una Marson*, p. 218.
192. Marson, "London Revisited," p. 21.
193. Marson, p. 25.
194. Perry, *London Is the Place for Me*, p. 191.
195. Una Marson, "After thoughts on London," unpublished article, box 1944C, UMP, quoted in Jarrett-Macauley, *Life of Una Marson*, p. 220.
196. Perry, *London Is the Place for Me*, pp. 229, 242.
197. Marson, "London Revisited," p. 25; and Jarrett-Macauley, *Life of Una Marson*, pp. 221–22.
198. Una Marson to Mina Ben-Zwi, Marson file, Mount Carmel Training Centre papers, Haifa, Israel, quoted in Jarrett-Macauley, p. 222.
199. Jarrett-Macauley, p. 223.
200. Jarrett-Macauley, p. 224.
201. Jarrett-Macauley, p. 226.
202. Jarrett-Macauley, pp. 226–27.
203. Musil, "La Marianne Noire," p. 24; "Paulette Nardal, l'âme de la perfection," p. 24; and Jean-Jacques Eda-Pierre, interview by Emily Musil, July 11, 2002.
204. Musil, "La Marianne Noire," p. 43.
205. Musil, p. 24; and Eda-Pierre interview.

CONCLUSION

1. For more on black feminist organizations, see Kimberly Springer, *Living for the Revolution: Black Feminist Organizations 1968–1980* (Durham, NC: Duke University Press, 2005).
2. Rhoda Reddock, "Women's Organizations and Movements in the Commonwealth Caribbean: The Response to Global Economic Crisis in the 1980s," *Feminist Review* no. 59 (1998): p. 63.
3. Alice Colón and Rhoda Reddock, "The Changing Status of Women in the Contemporary Caribbean," in *General History of the Caribbean*, vol. 5, *The Caribbean in the Twentieth Century*, ed. Bridget Brereton (London: UNESCO, 2004), p. 491; and Rhoda Reddock, address to the Planning Meeting (First Caribbean Feminist Encounter, Port-of-Spain, December 12–3, 1998).
4. Reddock, "Women's Organizations and Movements," p. 63.
5. Reddock, p. 64.

BIBLIOGRAPHY

MANUSCRIPT AND ARCHIVAL SOURCES

Archives de la Préfecture de police, Paris.
Archives departementales de la Martinique, Fort-de-France, Martinique.
Archives nationales de l'Afrique occidentale française, Paris.
Barnett, Claude. Papers. Chicago Historical Society.
Bibliothèque nationale de France, François Mitterrand, Paris.
Centre des archives d'outre-mer, Aix-en-Provence.
Colonial Office: Social Services Department. Public Record Office. National Archives, Kew, Richmond, Surrey.
Colonial Office: West India Royal Commission (1938–1940). Public Record Office. National Archives, Kew, Richmond, Surrey.
Communist Party of the United States of America Records. Mass Organizations Subject Files. Tamiment Library and Robert F. Wagner Labor Archives. Bobst Library, New York University.
Cunard, Nancy. Papers. Chicago Historical Society.
Hughes, Langston. Papers. Beinecke Rare Book and Manuscript Library, Yale University.
Johnson, James Weldon. Memorial Collection. Beinecke Rare Book and Manuscript Library, Yale University.
Johnson, James Weldon, and Grace Nail Johnson. Papers. Beinecke Rare Book and Manuscript Library, Yale University.
League of Coloured Peoples, The. Colonial Office Records, Public Record Office. National Archives, Kew, Richmond, Surrey.
Letters from Blacks. Beinecke Rare Book and Manuscript Library, Yale University.
Locke, Alain. Papers. Moorland-Spingarn Research Center, Howard University, Washington, DC.

Logan, Rayford. Papers. Moorland-Spingarn Research Center, Howard University, Washington, DC.
Marson, Una. "At What a Price?," unpublished playscript, n.d. LCP1933/47, Lord Chamberlain's Plays. Manuscript Collections, The British Library, London.
———. Files. BBC Written Archives Centre, Caversham, Reading.
———. "London Calling," unpublished playscript, 1937. MD1944A-D, Una Marson Papers. National Library of Jamaica, Kingston.
———. Papers. National Library of Jamaica, Kingston.
Patterson, Louise Thompson. Papers. Emory University Library, Atlanta.
Printed Collections. Saad Brown Library. The Women's Library, London School of Economics.
Public Record Office. National Archives, Kew, Richmond, Surrey.
Robeson, Eslanda Goode. Collection. Moorland-Spingarn Research Center, Howard University, Washington, DC.
Robeson, Paul, and Eslanda Robeson. Collection. Moorland-Spingarn Research Center, Howard University, Washington, DC.
United Nations Archives, Geneva.
Van Vechten, Carl. Papers. Beinecke Rare Book and Manuscript Library, Yale University.

PRIMARY SOURCES

Journal Articles, Book Chapters, and Books

Achille, Louis T. "Préface." In *La revue du monde noir/The Review of the Black World 1931–1932: Collection complete nos. 1 á 6*, pp. xv–xvii. 1932. Reprint, Paris: Jean-Michel Place, 1992.
Buck, Pearl, S., and Eslanda Goode Robeson. *American Argument*. London: Methuen, 1950.
"La chorale Joie de chanter ou l'amour du chant choral à la Martinique." *Télé 7 jours Martinique*, no. 92, March 30–April 5, 1981, pp. 8–9.
Cooper, Anna Julia. *A Voice from the South*. 1892. Reprint, New York: Oxford University Press, 1988.
Du Bois, W. E. B. *The World and Africa*. 1946. Republication, New York: International Publishers, 1978.
Foner, Philip S., ed. *Paul Robeson Speaks: Writings, Speeches, Interviews, 1918–1974*. London: Quartet Books, 1978.
Johnson, James Weldon. "Harlem: The Culture Capital." In *The New Negro: Voices of the Harlem Renaissance*, edited by Alain Locke, pp. 301–11. 1925. Reprint, New York: Atheneum, 1992.
Jones, Claudia. "An End to the Neglect of the Problems of Negro Women." *Political Affairs*, June 1949, p. 53.
Locke, Alain, ed. *The New Negro: Voices of the Harlem Renaissance*. 1925. Reprint, New York: Atheneum, 1992.
Marson, Una. *The Moth and the Star*. Kingston, Jam.: self-published, 1937.
———. "*Pocomania*: A New Three-Act Play by Una Marson." In *Anglophone-Karibik-USA*, edited by H. Michael Hoenisch and Remco van Capelleveen, pp. 117–47. Hamburg: Redaktion Gulliver, 1991.

———. *Towards the Stars*. London: University of London Press, 1945.
McKay, Claude. *A Long Way From Home*. 1937. Reprint, New York: Harcourt Brace Jovanovich, 1970.
Nardal, Paulette. *Beyond Negritude: Essays from Woman in the City*. Translated, with introduction and notes, by T. Denean Sharpley-Whiting. New York: State University of New York Press, 2009.
Ottley, Roi. *New World A-Coming*. New York: Arno Press, 1968.
Padmore, George. *Pan-Africanism or Communism?: The Coming Struggle for Africa*. London: Dennis Dobson, 1956.
"Paulette Nardal: L'âme de la perfection." *Carib-Hebdo*, n.d., p. 24.
Randolph, A. Philip. "March on Washington Movement Presents Program for the Negro." In *What the Negro Wants*, edited by Rayford W. Logan, pp. 133–62. Chapel Hill: University of North Carolina Press, 1944.
Reid, Ira De A. *The Negro Immigrant: His Background, Characteristics, and Social Adjustment, 1899–1937*. 1939. Reprint, New York: Arno Press, 1969.
Roark, James L. "American Black Leaders: The Response to Colonialism and the Cold War." *African Historical Studies* 4, no. 2 (1971): pp. 253–62.
Robeson, Eslanda Goode. *African Journey*. New York: John Day, 1945.
———. "Excerpts From A Diary: Journey Into Spain." In *The Heart of Spain: Anthology of Fiction, Non-Fiction, and Poetry*, edited by Alvah Bessie. New York: Veterans of the Abraham Lincoln Brigade, 1952.
———. *Paul Robeson, Negro*. London: Victor Gollancz, 1930.
Robeson, Paul. "A Message from the Chairman to Members and Friends of the Council on African Affairs," *New Africa*, July–August, 1949. In *Paul Robeson Speaks: Writings, Speeches, Interviews, 1918–1974*, edited by Philip S. Foner. London: Quartet, 1978.
Thurman, Wallace, and William Jourdan Rapp. "Few Know Real Harlem, the City of Surprises: Quarter Million Negroes Form a Moving, Colorful Pageant of Life." In *The Collected Writings of Wallace Thurman: A Harlem Renaissance Reader*, edited by Amritjit Singh and Daniel M. Scott III. New Brunswick, NJ: Rutgers University Press, 2003.
United Nations. Charter. Chapter 1: "Purposes and Principles," article 1.3. San Francisco, signed June 26, 1945. http://www.un.org/en/sections/un-charter/chapter-i/index.html.
Walters, Alexander. *My Life and Work*. New York: Fleming H. Revell, 1917.
Wright, Richard. *The Color Curtain: A Report on the Bandung Conference*. London: Dennis Dobson, 1956.
US Bureau of the Census. *Census of the United States 1930*, vol. 2, pp. 33, 70–71, 250. Washington, DC: Government Printing Office, 1933. http://www2.census.gov/prod2/decennial/documents/16440598v2.zip.

Newspapers and Journals

Atlanta Daily World (Georgia, US; 1928–)
Baltimore Afro-American (1892–)
Birmingham Daily Post (UK; 1857–)
Carib-Hebdo (Martinique)
Challenge (Boston, ed. Dorothy West; 1934–1937)
The Chicago Defender (1905–)

The Cosmopolitan (Kingston, Jamaica, ed. Una Marson; 1928–1931; renamed *New Cosmopolitan* in 1931)
Le Cri des nègres: Organe mensuel de l'Union des travailleurs nègres (Paris; 1931–1936)
Daily Gleaner (Kingston, Jamaica; 1902–1992)
Daily Herald (London; 1912–1964)
Daily Mirror (London; 1903–)
Daily Worker (New York; 1924–1958)
La Dépêche africaine (Paris; 1928–1956)
L'Étudiant noir: Journal mensuel de l'Association des étudiants martiniquais en France (1935)
La Femme dans la cité: Revue mensuelle du Rassemblement féminin (Martinique; 1945–1951)
La Femme dans la vie sociale (France, Mouvement mondial des mères; 1927–1959)
Freedom (New York City, 1950–1955)
Je suis partout (France; 1930–1944)
Le Journal (France; 1892–1944)
Journal of Negro History (US, Association for the Study of African American Life; 1916– ; renamed *Journal of African American History* in 2002)
The Keys (London, League of Coloured People; 1933–1939)
The Liberator (New York; 1918–1924)
Manchester Guardian (UK; 1821– ; renamed *The Guardian* in 1959)
The National Guardian (New York; 1948–1992)
Negro Digest (Chicago; 1942–1976)
New Cosmopolitan (Kingston, Jamaica; 1931; originally named *The Cosmopolitan*)
News Chronicle (London; 1872–1960)
New World Review (New York; 1951–1985)
New York Amsterdam News (1909–)
New York Herald Tribune (1924–1966)
Le Périscope africain: Journal hebdomadaire indépendant défendant les intérêts de l'Afrique occidentale française et l'Afrique équatoriale française (Dakar; 1929–1936)
Pittsburgh Courier (1907–1966)
Political Affairs (New York; 1944–2016)
Public Opinion (Jamaica; 1937–1974)
La Revue du monde noir/The Review of the Black World (Paris, ed. Paulette Nardal; 1931–1932)
Seamen's Journal
Le Soir colonial
Sunday Express (London; 1918–)
Sunday Gleaner (Kingston, Jamaica; 1939–)
The Sun-Reporter (San Francisco; 1943–)
Télé 7 jours Martinique (TV magazine)
The Times (London; 1788–)
Univers: Bulletin catholique international (France, Comité français pour la justice et la paix; 1935–194?)
The Washington Post (Washington, DC; 1877–)
Wasu (London, West African Students Union; 1926–1932)

Musical Recordings

Growling Tiger, accompanied by Gerald Clark and his Caribbean Serenaders. "The Gold in Africa." Manufactured in USA: Decca Records, c. 1936. https://youtu.be/z7XuESilexM.

SECONDARY SOURCES

Articles and Book Chapters

Anderson, Clare. "Global Mobilities." In *World Histories from Below: Disruption and Dissent, 1750 to the Present*, edited by Antoinette Burton and Tony Ballantyne, pp. 169–95. New York: Bloomsbury, 2016.

Arsan, Andrew, Su Lin-Lewis, and Anne-Isabelle Richards. "Editorial—The Roots of Global Civil Society and the Interwar Moment." *Journal of Global History* 7, no. 2 (2012): pp. 157–65.

Bell, Amy. "Landscapes of Fear: Wartime London 1939–1945." *Journal of British Studies* 48. no. 1 (January 2009): pp. 153–75.

Black, Allida. "Are Women 'Human?' The UN and the Struggle to Recognize Women's Rights as Human Rights." In *The Human Rights Revolution: An International Perspective*, edited by Akira Iriye, Petra Goedde, and William I. Hitchcock, pp. 133–55. New York: Oxford University Press, 2012.

Blain, Keisha N. "'Confraternity among All Dark Races': Mittie Maude Lena Gordon and the Practice of Black (Inter)nationalism in Chicago, 1932–1942." *Palimpsest: A Journal on Women, Gender, and the Black International* 5, no. 2 (Fall 2016): pp. 151–81.

———. "For the Rights of Dark People in Every Part of the World: Pearl Sherrod, Black Internationalist Feminism, and Afro-Asian Politics during the 1930s." *Souls: A Critical Journal of Black Politics, Culture and Society* 17, no. 1–2 (2015): pp. 90–112.

———. "'We Want to Set the World on Fire': Black Nationalist Women and Diasporic Politics in the New Negro World, 1940–1944." *Journal of Social History* 49, no. 1 (2015): pp. 194–212.

Britton, Sarah. "'Come and See the Empire by the All Red Route!': Anti-Imperialism and Exhibitions in Interwar Britain." *History Workshop Journal* 69, no. 1 (2010): pp. 68–89.

Bush, Barbara. "Gender and Empire: The Twentieth Century." In *Gender and Empire*, edited by Philippa Levine, pp. 77–111. Oxford: Oxford University Press, 2004.

Byfield, Judith A. "From Ladies to Women: Funmilayo Ransome-Kuti and Women's Political Activism in Post–World War II Nigeria." In *Toward an Intellectual History of Black Women*, edited by Mia Bay, Farah Jasmine Griffin, Martha S. Jones, and Barbara D. Savage, pp. 197–213. Chapel Hill: University of North Carolina Press, 2015.

———. "Preface." In *Africa and World War Two*, edited by Judith A. Byfield, Carolyn A. Brown, Timothy Parsons, and Ahmad Alawad Sikainga, pp. xvii–xxiii. New York: Cambridge University Press, 2015.

Campbell, Elaine. "The Unpublished Plays of Una Marson." In *Anglophone-Karibik-USA*, edited by H. Michael Hoenisch and Remco van Capelleveen, pp. 110–16. Hamburg: Redaktion Gulliver, 1991.

Childers, Kristen Stromberg. "The Second World War as Watershed in the French Caribbean." *Atlantic Studies* 9, no. 4 (2012): pp. 409–30.

Church, Emily Musil. "In Search of Seven Sisters: A Biography of the Nardal Sisters of Martinique." *Callaloo: A Journal of African Diaspora Arts and Letters* 36, no. 2 (2013): pp. 375–90.

Colón, Alice, and Rhoda Reddock. "The Changing Status of Women in the Contemporary Caribbean." In *The Caribbean in the Twentieth Century*, edited by Bridget Brereton, pp. 465–505. Vol. 5 of *General History of the Caribbean*. London: UNESCO, 2004.

Crenshaw, Kimberlé. "Demarginalizing the Intersection of Race and Sex: A Black Feminist Critique of Antidiscrimination Doctrine, Feminist Theory, and Antiracist Politics." *University of Chicago Legal Forum* 14 (1989): pp. 538–54.

Dalleo, Raphael. "The Public Sphere and Jamaican Anticolonial Politics: *Public Opinion, Focus,* and the Place of the Literary." *Small Axe* 14, no. 2 (2010): pp. 56–82.

Devenish, Annie. "Performing the Political Self: A Study of Identity Making in the Autobiographies of India's First Generation of Parliamentary Women." *Women's History Review* 22, no. 2 (2013): pp. 280–94.

Donnell, Alison. "Una Marson: Feminism, Anti-colonialism and a Forgotten Fight for Freedom." In *West Indian Intellectuals in Britain*, edited by Bill Schwarz, pp. 114–131. Manchester: Manchester University Press, 2003.

Edwards, Brent Hayes, "The Uses of Diaspora." *Social Text* 66, 19, no. 1 (Spring 2001): pp. 45–73.

Füllberg-Stolberg, Claus. "The Caribbean in the Second World War." In *The Caribbean in the Twentieth Century*, edited by Bridget Brereton, pp. 82–140. Vol. 5 of *General History of the Caribbean*. London: UNESCO, 2004.

Galey, Margaret E. "Promoting Nondiscrimination against Women: The UN Commission on the Status of Women." *International Studies Quarterly* 23, no. 2 (1979): pp. 273–302.

Garcia, Claire Oberon. "Black Women Writers, Modernism, and Paris." *International Journal of Francophone Studies* 14, no. 1–2 (2011): pp. 27–42.

Gillet, Rachel. "Jazz Women, Gender Politics, and the Francophone Atlantic." *Atlantic Studies: Global Currents* 10., no. 1 (2013): pp. 109–30.

Grant, Nicholas. "The National Council of Negro Women and South Africa: Black Internationalism, Motherhood and the Cold War." *Palimpsest: A Journal of Women, Gender, and the Black International* 5, no. 1 (2016): pp. 59–87.

Haan, Francisca de. "Continuing Cold War Paradigms in Western Historiography of Transnational Women's Organisations: The Case of the Women's International Democratic Federation (WIDF)." *Women's History Review* 19, no. 4 (2010): pp. 547–73.

Harrison, Faye Venetia, and Ira E. Harrison. "Introduction: Anthropology, African Americans, and the Emancipation of a Subjugated Knowledge." In *African-American Pioneers in Anthropology*, edited by Ira E. Harrison and Faye Venetia Harrison, pp. 1–36. Urbana: University of Illinois Press, 1999.

Hinds, Donald. "The *West Indian Gazette*: Claudia Jones and the Black Press in Britain." *Race and Class* 50, no. 1 (2008): pp. 88–97.

Hine, Darlene Clark. "Rape and the Inner Lives of Black Women in the Middle West: Preliminary Thoughts on the Culture of Dissemblance." *Signs: Journal of Women in Culture and Society* 14, no. 4 (1989): pp. 912–20.

James, Winston. "The Black Experience in Twentieth-Century Britain." In *Black Experience and The Empire*, edited by Phillip D. Morgan and Sean Hawkins, pp. 347–86. Oxford: Oxford University Press, 2004.

Jennings, Eric. "Last Exit from Vichy France: The Martinique Escape Route and the Ambiguities of Emigration." *Journal of Modern History* 74, no. 2 (2002): pp. 289–324.
Kelley, Robin D. G. "'But a Local Phase of a World Problem': Black History's Global Vision, 1883–1950." *Journal of American History* 86 (1999): pp. 1045–77.
Killingray, David. "'To Do Something for the Race': Harold Moody and the League of Coloured Peoples." In *West Indian Intellectuals in Britain*, edited by Bill Schwarz, pp. 51–70. Manchester: Manchester University Press, 2003.
King, Deborah K. "Multiple Jeopardy, Multiple Consciousness: The Context of a Black Feminist Ideology." *Signs: Journal of Women in Culture and Society* 14, no. 1 (1988): pp. 42–72.
Koda, Maïté. "Portraits: Paulette Nardal." *Réseau France d'Outre-Mer*, April 25, 2006, n.p. http://martinique.rfo.fr/article114.html.
Lewis, Earl. "To Turn as on a Pivot: Writing African Americans into a History of Overlapping Diasporas." *American Historical Review* 100, no. 3 (1995): pp. 765–87.
Lindsey, Treva. "Climbing the Hilltop: In Search of New Negro Womanhood at Howard University." In *Escape from New York: The New Negro Renaissance beyond Harlem*, edited by Davarian L. Baldwin and Minkah Makalani, pp. 271–90. Minneapolis: University of Minnesota Press, 2013.
"Louis Achille." In *Biographies of Speakers from the 1956 1st Congress of Black Writers*. Cambridge, MA: W. E. B. Du Bois Institute for African and African American Research, 2006, p. 1.
Mahon, Maureen. "Eslanda Goode Robeson's *African Journey*: The Politics of Identification and Representation in the African Diaspora." In *Transnational Blackness: Navigating the Global Color Line*, edited by Manning Marable and Vanessa Agard-Jones, pp. 115–33. New York: Palgrave Macmillan, 2008.
Makalani, Minkah. "An International African Opinion: Amy Ashwood Garvey and C. L. R. James in Black Radical London." In *Escape from New York: The New Negro Renaissance Beyond Harlem*, edited by Davarian L. Baldwin and Minkah Makalani, pp. 77–101. Minneapolis: University of Minnesota Press, 2013.
Materson, Lisa G. "African American Women's Global Journeys and the Construction of Cross-ethnic Racial Identity." *Women's Studies International Forum* 32 (2009): pp. 35–42.
Maximin, Daniel. "Editor's Introduction: Suzanne Césaire, Sun-Filled Fountain." In *The Great Camouflage: Writings of Dissent (1941–1945)*, by Suzanne Césaire, edited by Daniel Maximin, translated by Keith L. Walker, pp. xxv–xxxvi. Middletown, CT: Wesleyan University Press, 2012.
McKeown, Adam. "A World Made Many: Integration and Segregation in Global Migration, 1840–1940." In *Connecting Seas and Connected Ocean Rims: Indian, Atlantic, and Pacific Oceans and China Seas Migrations from the 1830s to the 1930s*, edited by Donna R. Gabaccia and Dirk Hoerder, pp. 42–64. Leiden: Brill, 2011.
Miller, Carol. "Geneva—The Key to Equality: Interwar Feminists and the League of Nations." *Women's History Review* 3, no. 2 (1994): pp. 219–45.
Nesbitt, Nick. "Departmentalization and the Logic of Decolonization." *L'Ésprit créateur* 47, no. 1 (2007): pp. 32–43.
Offen, Karen. "Defining Feminism: A Comparative Historical Approach." *Signs: Journal of Women in Culture and Society* 14, no. 1 (Autumn 1988): pp. 119–57.

Paravisini-Gebert, Lizabeth, and Ivette Romero-Cesareo. "Introduction: Traveling the Margins of Caribbean Discourse." In *Women at Sea: Travel Writing and the Margins of Caribbean Discourse*, edited by Lizabeth Paravisini-Gebert and Ivette Romero-Cesareo, pp. 1–7. New York: Palgrave Macmillan, 2001.

Parsons, Timothy. "The Military Experiences of Ordinary Africans in World War II." In *Africa and World War Two*, edited by Judith A. Byfield, Carolyn A. Brown, Timothy Parsons, and Ahmad Alawad Sikainga, pp. 3–23. New York: Cambridge University Press, 2015.

Patterson, Tiffany Ruby, and Robin D. G. Kelley. "Unfinished Migrations: Reflections on the African Diaspora and the Making of the Modern World." *African Studies Review* 43, no. 1 (April 2000): pp 11–45.

Procter, James. "Una Marson at the BBC." *Small Axe* 48 (November 2015): pp. 1–28.

Putnam, Lara. "Contact Zones: Heterogeneity and Boundaries in Caribbean Central America at the Start of the Twentieth Century." *Iboamericana* (IberoAmerikanisches Institut, Berlin) 6, no. 23 (2006): pp. 113–25.

———. "Undone by Desire: Migration, Sex Across Boundaries, and Collective Destinies in the Greater Caribbean, 1840–1940." In *Connecting Seas and Connected Ocean Rims: Indian, Atlantic, and Pacific Oceans and China Seas Migrations from the 1830s to the 1930s*, edited by Donna R. Gabaccia and Dirk Hoerder, pp. 302–37. Leiden: Brill, 2011.

Reanda, Laura. "Human Rights and Women's Rights: The United Nations Approach." *Human Rights Quarterly* 3, no. 2 (1981): pp. 11–31.

Reddock, Rhoda. "Diversity, Difference, and Caribbean Feminism: The Challenge of Anti-Racism." *Caribbean Review of Gender Studies: A Journal of Caribbean Perspectives on Gender and Feminism*, no. 1 (April 2007): pp. 1–24.

———. "Women's Organizations and Movements in the Commonwealth Caribbean: The Response to Global Economic Crisis in the 1980s." *Feminist Review*, no. 59 (1998): pp. 57–73.

Rexer, Raisa. "Black and White and Re(a)d All Over: *L'Étudiant noir*, Communism, and the Birth of Negritude." *Research in African Literatures* 44, no. 4 (2013): pp. 1–14.

Rief, Michelle. "Thinking Locally, Acting Globally: The International Agenda of African American Clubwomen 1880–1940." *Journal of African American History* 89, no. 3 (Summer 2004): pp. 203–22.

Rosenberg, Leah. "Modern Romances: The Short Stories in Una Marson's 'The Cosmopolitan' (1928–1931)." *Journal of West Indian Literature* 12, no. 1–2 (2004): pp. 170–83.

———. "The New Woman and 'The Dusky Strand': The Place of Feminism and Women's Literature in Early Jamaican Nationalism." *Feminist Review* 95, no. 1 (2010): pp. 45–63.

Savage, Barbara D. "Professor Merze Tate: Diplomatic Historian, Cosmopolitan Woman." In *Toward an Intellectual History of Black Women*, edited by Mia Bay, Farah Jasmine Griffin, Martha S. Jones, and Barbara D. Savage, pp. 252–69. Chapel Hill: University of North Carolina Press, 2015.

Schwarz, Bill. "George Padmore." In *West Indian Intellectuals in Britain*, edited by Bill Schwarz, pp. 132–52. Manchester: Manchester University Press, 2003.

———. "Introduction: Crossing the Seas." In *West Indian Intellectuals in Britain*, edited by Bill Schwarz, pp. 1–30. Manchester: Manchester University Press, 2003.

Sharpley-Whiting, T. Denean. "Introduction: On Race, Rights, and Women." In *Beyond Negritude: Essays from Woman in the City*, by Paulette Nardal, pp. 1–14. Translated, with introduction and notes, by T. Denean Sharpley-Whiting. New York: State University of New York Press, 2009.

Sinha, Mrinalini, Donna J. Guy, and Angela Woollacott. "Introduction: Why Feminisms and Internationalism?" *Gender and History* 10, no. 3 (November 1998): pp. 345–57.

Sluga, Glenda. "Women, Feminisms and Twentieth-Century Internationalisms." In *Internationalisms: A Twentieth-Century History*, edited by Glenda Sluga and Patricia Clavin, pp. 61–84. Cambridge: Cambridge University Press, 2017.

Smith, R. P., Jr. "Black Like That: Paulette Nardal and the Negritude Salon." *CLA Journal* 45, no. 1 (2001): pp. 53–68.

Spencer, Ian. "World War Two and the Making of Multicultural Britain." In *War Culture: Social Change and Changing Experience in World War Two Britain*, edited by Pat Kirkham and David Thoms, pp. 209–18. London: Lawrence and Wishart, 1995.

Squires, Catherine. "Rethinking the Black Public Sphere: An Alternative Vocabulary for Multiple Public Spheres." *Communication Theory* 12, no. 4 (2002): pp. 440–67.

Suri, Jeremi. "Non-governmental Organizations and Non-state Actors." In *Palgrave Advances in International History*, edited by Patrick Finney, pp. 223–46. New York: Palgrave Macmillan, 2005.

Taylor, Ula Y. "Street Scholars: Grounding the Theory of Black Women Intellectuals." *Afro-Americans in New York Life and History* 30. no. 2 (July 2006), pp. 153–171.

Tesseron, Philippe. "Précurseur et apôtre féminin de la négritude et de l'émancipation de la femme noire: Qui est Paulette Nardal?" *Temoignages*, July 2006, p. 16.

Umoren, Imaobong D. "This Is the Age of Woman: Black Feminism and Black Internationalism in the Works of Una Marson 1928–1938." *History of Women in the Americas* 1, no. 1 (2013): pp. 50–72.

Walker, Keith L. "Translator's Introduction: Suzanne Césaire and the Great Camouflages." In *The Great Camouflage: Writings of Dissent (1941–1945)*, by Suzanne Césaire, edited by Daniel Maximin, translated by Keith L. Walker, pp. vii–xix. Middletown, CT: Wesleyan University Press, 2012.

Ward, Stephen. "The Third World Women's Alliance: Black Feminist Radicalism and Black Power Politics." In *The Black Power Movement: Rethinking the Civil Rights-Black Power Era*, edited by Peniel Joseph, pp. 119–44. New York: Routledge, 2006.

Warren, Kenneth W. "Appeals for (Mis)recognition: Theorizing the Diaspora." In *Cultures of United States Imperialism*, edited by Amy Kaplan and Donald E. Pease, pp. 392–406. Durham, NC: Duke University Press, 1993.

West, Michael O., William G. Martin, and Fanon Che Wilkins. "Preface." In *From Toussaint to Tupac: The Black International since the Age of Revolution*, edited by Michael O. West, William G. Martin, and Fanon Che Wilkins, pp. xi–xiii. Chapel Hill: University of North Carolina Press, 2009.

Wilks, Jennifer M. "Black Modernist Women at the Parisian Crossroads." In *Escape from New York: The New Negro Renaissance beyond Harlem*, edited by Davarian L. Baldwin and Minkah Makalani, pp. 227–45. Minneapolis: University of Minnesota Press, 2013.

Books

Adi, Hakim. *West Africans in Britain 1900–1960: Nationalism, Pan-Africanism and Communism*. London: Lawrence and Wishart, 1998.

Adi, Hakim, and Marika Sherwood. *The 1945 Manchester Pan-African Congress Revisited, with Colonial and . . . Coloured Unity (the Report of the 5th Pan-African Congress)*. Edited by George Padmore. London: New Beacon Books, 1995.

Altink, Henrice. *Destined for a Life of Service: Defining African-Jamaican Womanhood, 1865–1938*. Manchester: Manchester University Press, 2011.

Anderson, Benedict. *Imagined Communities: Reflections on the Origin and Spread of Nationalism*. London: Verso, 1983.

Anderson, Carol. *Eyes off the Prize: The United Nations and the African American Struggle for Human Rights, 1944–1955*. New York: Cambridge University Press, 2003.

Andrews, Gregg. *Thyra J. Edwards: Black Activist in the Global Freedom Struggle*. Columbia: University of Missouri Press, 2011.

Anzaldúa, Gloria. *Borderlands/La Frontera: The New Mestiza*. San Francisco: Aunt Lute, 1987.

Archer-Straw, Petrine. *Negrophilia: Avant-Garde Paris and Black Culture in the 1920s*. London: Thames and Hudson, 2000.

Azakansky, Sarah. *This Worldwide Struggle: Religion and the International Roots of the Civil Rights Movement*. New York: Oxford University Press, 2017.

Baldwin, Davarian L., and Minkah Makalani, eds. *Escape from New York: The New Negro Renaissance beyond Harlem*. Minneapolis: University of Minnesota Press, 2013.

Baldwin, Kate A. *Beyond the Color Line and the Iron Curtain: Reading Encounters between Black and Red, 1922–1963*. Durham, NC: Duke University Press, 2002.

Baptiste, Fitzroy and Rupert Lewis, eds. *George Padmore: Pan-African Revolutions*. Kingston, Jamaica. Ian Randle, 2009.

Bay, Mia, Farah Jasmine Griffin, Martha S. Jones, and Barbara D. Savage, eds. *Toward an Intellectual History of Black Women*. Chapel Hill: University of North Carolina Press, 2015.

Berliner, Brett A. *Ambivalent Desires: The Exotic Black Other in Jazz-Age France*. Amherst: University of Massachusetts Press, 2002.

Bessie, Alvah, ed. *The Heart of Spain: Anthology of Fiction, Non-Fiction, and Poetry*. New York: Veterans of the Abraham Lincoln Brigade, 1952.

Blackwell, Joyce. *No Peace without Freedom: Race and the Women's International League for Peace and Freedom, 1915–1975*. Carbondale: Southern Illinois University Press, 2004.

Blain, Keisha N. *Set the World on Fire: Black Nationalist Women and the Global Struggle for Freedom*. Philadelphia: University of Pennsylvania Press, 2018.

Blake, Jody. *Le tumulte noir: Modernist Art and Popular Entertainment in Jazz-Age Paris, 1900–1930*. University Park: Pennsylvania State University Press, 1999.

Blower, Brooke L. *Becoming Americans in Paris: Transatlantic Politics and Culture between the World Wars*. New York: Oxford University Press, 2011.

Boehmer, Elleke. *Indian Arrivals 1870–1915: Networks of British Empire*. Oxford: Oxford University Press, 2015.

Bogues, Anthony. *Caliban's Freedom: The Early Political Thought of C. L. R. James*. London: Pluto Press, 1997.

Boittin, Jennifer Anne. *Colonial Metropolis: The Urban Grounds of Anti-Imperialism and Feminism in Interwar Paris*. Lincoln: University of Nebraska Press, 2010.

Bolland, O. N. *On the March: Labour Rebellions in the British Caribbean 1934–1939*. Kingston, Jam.: Ian Randle, 1995.

———. *The Politics of Labour in the British Caribbean: The Social Origins of Authoritarianism and Democracy in the Labour Movement.* Kingston, Jam.: Ian Randle, 2001.

Borstelmann, Thomas. *The Cold War and the Color Line: American Race Relations in the Global Arena.* Cambridge, MA: Harvard University Press, 2001.

Brandt, Joe, ed. *Black Americans in the Spanish People's War against Fascism, 1936–1939.* New York: Veterans of the Abraham Lincoln Battalion, 1980.

Brereton, Bridget, ed. *The Caribbean in the Twentieth Century.* Vol. 5 of *General History of the Caribbean.* London: UNESCO, 2004.

Bressey, Caroline. *Empire, Race, and the Politics of Anti-Caste.* London: Bloomsbury, 2013.

Brown, Jayna. *Babylon Girls: Black Women Performers and the Shaping of the Modern.* Durham, NC: Duke University Press, 2008.

Buhle, Paul. *C. L. R. James: His Life and Work.* London: Allison and Busby, 1986.

Burton, Antoinette, and Tony Ballantyne, eds. *World Histories from Below: Disruption and Dissent, 1750 to the Present.* New York: Bloomsbury, 2016.

Bush, Barbara. *Imperialism, Race, and Resistance: Africa and Britain, 1919–1945.* London: Routledge, 1999.

Byfield, Judith A., Carolyn A. Brown, Timothy Parsons, and Ahmad Alawad Sikainga, eds. *Africa and World War Two.* New York: Cambridge University Press, 2015.

Calhoun, Craig, ed. *Habermas and the Public Sphere.* Cambridge, MA: MIT Press, 1992.

Campt, Tina M. *Other Germans: Black Germans and the Politics of Race, Gender, and Memory in the Third Reich.* Ann Arbor: University of Michigan Press, 2005.

Carby, Hazel V. *Race Men.* Cambridge, MA: Harvard University Press, 1998.

Carew, Joy Gleason. *Blacks, Reds, and Russians: Sojourners in Search of the Soviet Promise.* New Brunswick, NJ: Rutgers University Press, 2008.

Castledine, Jacqueline L. *Cold War Progressives: Women's Interracial Organizing for Peace and Freedom.* Urbana: University of Illinois Press, 2012.

Chafer, Tony. *The End of Empire in French West Africa: France's Successful Decolonization?* New York: Berg, 2002.

Chancy, Myriam J. A. *Searching for Safe Spaces: Afro-Caribbean Women Writers in Exile.* Philadelphia: Temple University Press, 1997.

Chapman, Erin D. *Prove It on Me: New Negroes, Sex, and Popular Culture in the 1920s.* New York: Oxford University Press, 2012.

Chater, Kathleen. *Untold Histories: Black People in England and Wales during the Period of the British Slave Trade, 1660–1807.* Manchester: Manchester University Press, 2009.

Childers, Kristen Stromberg. *Seeking Imperialism's Embrace: National Identity, Decolonization, and Assimilation in the French Caribbean.* New York: Oxford University Press, 2016.

Clifford, James. *Routes: Travel and Translation in the Late Twentieth Century.* Cambridge, MA: Harvard University Press, 1997.

Collins, Patricia Hill. *Black Feminist Thought: Knowledge, Consciousness, and the Politics of Empowerment.* Boston: Unwin Hyman, 1990.

Cooper, Brittney C. *Beyond Respectability: The Intellectual Thought of Race Women.* Urbana: University of Illinois Press, 2017.

Corbould, Clare. *Becoming African Americans: Black Public Life in Harlem, 1919–1939.* Cambridge, MA: Harvard University Press, 2009.

Cromwell, Adelaide M. *An African Victorian Feminist: The Life and Times of Adelaide Smith Casely Hayford, 1868–1960.* London: Frank Cass, 1986.

Cudjoe, Selwyn, and William E. Cain, eds. *C. L. R. James: His Intellectual Legacies.* Amherst: University of Massachusetts Press, 1995.

Cummings-John, Constance Agatha. *Memoirs of a Krio Leader.* Edited, with introduction and annotation, by La Ray Denzer. Ibadan: Nigeria, Humanities Research Centre, 1995.

Davies, Carole Boyce. *Black Women, Writing and Identity: Migrations of the Subject.* London: Routledge 1994.

———. *Claudia Jones: Beyond Containment: Autobiographical Reflections, Essays, and Poems.* Banbury, Oxfordshire: Ayebia Clarke, 2011.

———. *Left of Karl Marx: The Political Life of Black Communist Claudia Jones.* Durham, NC: Duke University Press, 2008.

Delanty, Gerard. *Citizenship in a Global Age: Society, Culture, Politics.* Buckingham: Open University Press, 2000.

Dewitte, Philippe. *Les mouvements nègres en France, 1919–1939.* Paris: L'Harmattan, 1985.

Donnell, Alison, ed. *Una Marson: Selected Poems.* Leeds: Peepal Tree Press, 2011.

Dossett, Kate. *Bridging Race Divides: Black Nationalism, Feminism, and Integration in the United States, 1896–1935.* Gainesville: University Press of Florida, 2008.

Duberman, Martin Bauml. *Paul Robeson.* London: Bodley Head, 1988.

Dudziak, Mary L. *Cold War Civil Rights: Race and the Image of American Democracy.* Princeton, NJ: Princeton University Press, 2000.

Duke, Eric D. *Building a Nation: Caribbean Federation in the Black Diaspora.* Gainesville: University Press of Florida, 2016.

Edmondson, Belinda. *Caribbean Middlebrow: Leisure Culture and the Middle Class.* Ithaca, NY: Cornell University Press, 2009.

Edwards, Brent Hayes. *The Practice of Diaspora: Literature, Translation, and the Rise of Black Internationalism.* Cambridge, MA: Harvard University Press, 2003.

Emery, Mary Lou. *Modernism, the Visual, and Caribbean Literature.* New York: Cambridge University Press, 2007.

Ewing, Ada. *The Age of Garvey: How a Jamaican Activist Created a Mass Movement and Changed Global Black Politics.* Princeton, NJ: Princeton University Press, 2014.

Ezra, Elizabeth. *The Colonial Unconscious: Race and Culture in Interwar France.* Ithaca, NY: Cornell University Press, 2000.

Fabre, Michel. *From Harlem to Paris: Black American Writers in France, 1840–1980.* Urbana: University of Illinois Press, 1991.

Finney, Patrick, ed. *Palgrave Advances in International History.* New York: Palgrave Macmillan, 2005.

Fish, Cheryl J. *Black and White Women's Travel Narratives: Antebellum Explorations.* Gainesville: University Press of Florida, 2004.

Ford, Tanisha. *Liberated Threads: Black Women, Style, and the Global Politics of Soul.* Chapel Hill: University of North Carolina Press, 2015.

Frazier, Robeson Taj. *The East Is Black: Cold War China in the Black Radical Imagination.* Durham, NC: Duke University Press, 2015.

Fryer, Peter. *Staying Power: The History of Black People in Britain.* London: Pluto Press, 1984.

Gabaccia, Donna R., and Dirk Hoerder, eds. *Connecting Seas and Connected Ocean Rims: Indian, Atlantic, and Pacific Oceans and China Seas Migrations from the 1830s to the 1930s*. Leiden: Brill, 2011.

Gaines, Kevin K. *American Africans in Ghana: Black Expatriates and the Civil Rights Era*. Chapel Hill: University of North Carolina Press, 2006.

———. *Uplifting the Race: Black Leadership, Politics, and Culture in the Twentieth Century*. Chapel Hill: University of North Carolina Press, 1996.

Gallichio, Marc S. *The African American Encounter with China and Japan: Black Internationalism in Asia*. Chapel Hill: University of North Carolina Press, 2000.

Gandhi, Leela. *Affective Communities: Anticolonial Thought, Fin-de-Siècle Radicalism, and the Politics of Friendship*. Durham, NC: Duke University Press, 2006.

Gardiner, Juliet. *The Thirties: An Intimate History*. London: Harper Press, 2011.

Gerzina, Gretchen. *Black London: Life before Emancipation*. New Brunswick, NJ: Rutgers University Press, 1995.

———, ed. *Black Victorians, Black Victoriana*. New Brunswick, NJ: Rutgers University Press, 2003.

Gibson, Carrie. *Empire's Crossroads: A History of the Caribbean from Columbus to the Present Day*. New York: Atlantic Monthly Press, 2014.

Gilroy, Paul. *The Black Atlantic: Modernity and Double Consciousness*. London: Verso, 1993.

Glissant, Edouard. *Caribbean Discourse: Selected Essays*. Translated, with introduction, by J. Michael Dash. Charlottesville: University Press of Virginia, 1989.

Goebel, Michael. *Anti-Imperial Metropolis: Interwar Paris and the Seeds of Third World Nationalism*. New York: Cambridge University Press, 2015.

Gore, Dayo F. *Radicalism at the Crossroads: African American Women Activists in the Cold War*. New York: New York University Press, 2011.

Gore, Dayo F., Jeanne Theoharis, and Komozi Woodward, eds. *Want to Start a Revolution? Radical Women in the Black Freedom Struggle*. New York: New York University Press, 2009.

Graham, Helen. *The Spanish Republic at War, 1936–1939*. Cambridge: Cambridge University Press, 2002.

———. *The War and Its Shadows: Spain's Civil War in Europe's Long Twentieth Century*. Brighton: Sussex Academic, 2012.

Grant, Nicholas. *We Shall Win Our Freedoms Together: African Americans and Apartheid, 1945–1960*. Chapel Hill: University of North Carolina Press, 2017.

Green, Jeffrey. *Black Edwardians: Black People in Britain, 1900–1914*. New York: Frank Cass, 1998.

Gregg, Veronica Marie. *Caribbean Women: An Anthology of Non-Fiction Writing, 1890–1980*. Notre Dame, IN: University of Notre Dame Press, 2005.

Griffin, Farah Jasmine. *Harlem Nocturne: Women Artists and Progressive Politics during World War II*. New York: Basic Civitas, 2013.

———. *"Who Set You Flowing?": The African American Migration Narrative*. New York: Oxford University Press, 1995.

Griffin, Farah Jasmine, and Cheryl J. Fish, eds. *A Stranger in the Village: Two Centuries of African-American Travel Writing*. Boston: Beacon Press, 1998.

Grimshaw, Anna, ed. *The C. L. R. James Reader*. Oxford: Blackwell, 1992.

Guridy, Frank Andre. *Forging Diaspora: Afro-Cubans and African Americans in a World of Empire and Jim Crow*. Chapel Hill: University of North Carolina Press, 2010.

Habermas, Jürgen. *The Structural Transformation of the Public Sphere: An Inquiry into a Category of Bourgeois Society.* Translated by Thomas Burger. Cambridge, MA: MIT Press, 1989.

Hall, Douglas. *A Brief History of the West India Committee.* St. Lawrence, Barb.: Caribbean Universities Press, 1971.

Hanson, Joyce A. *Mary McLeod Bethune and Black Women's Political Activism.* Columbia: University of Missouri Press, 2003.

Harris, Joseph E. *African-American Reactions to War in Ethiopia.* Baton Rouge: Louisiana State University Press, 1994.

Harrison, Ira E., and Faye Venetia Harrison, eds. *African-American Pioneers in Anthropology.* Urbana: University of Illinois Press, 1999.

Heater, Derek. *What Is Citizenship?* Cambridge: Polity, 1999.

———. *World Citizenship: Cosmopolitan Thinking and Its Opponents.* London: Continuum, 2002.

———. *World Citizenship and Government: Cosmopolitan Ideas in the History of Western Political Thought.* Basingstoke, UK: Macmillan, 1996.

Higashida, Cheryl. *Black Internationalist Feminism: Women Writers of the Black Left 1945–1995.* Urbana: University of Illinois Press, 2011.

Higginbotham, Evelyn Brooks. *Righteous Discontent: The Women's Movement in the Black Baptist Church.* Cambridge, MA: Harvard University Press, 1993.

Hill, Robert A. *Dread History: Leonard P. Howell and Millenarian Visions in the Early Rastafarian Religion.* Chicago: Research Associates School Times Publications/Frontline Distribution Int'l; Kingston, Jam.: Miguel Lorne Publishers, 2001.

Hine, Darlene Clark, Trica Danielle Keaton and Stephen Small, eds. *Black Europe and the African Diaspora.* Urbana: University of Illinois Press, 2009.

Ho, Fred, and Bill V. Mullen, eds. *Afro-Asia: Revolutionary Political and Cultural Connections between African Americans and Asian Americans.* Durham, NC: Duke University Press, 2008.

Høgsbjerg, Christian. *C. L. R. James in Imperial Britain.* Durham, NC: Duke University Press, 2014.

Holub, Renate. *Antonio Gramsci: Beyond Marxism and Postmodernism.* New York: Routledge, 1992.

Hooker, James. *Black Revolutionary: George Padmore's Path from Communism to Pan-Africanism.* New York: Praeger, 1967.

Horne, Gerald. *Communist Front?: The Civil Rights Congress.* London: Associated University Presses, 1988.

———. *Race Woman: The Lives of Shirley Graham Du Bois.* New York: New York University Press, 2000.

Hull, Gloria T., Patricia Bell-Scott, and Barbara Smith, eds. *All the Women Are White, All the Men Are Black but Some of Us Are Brave: Black Women's Studies.* New York: Feminist Press, 1982.

Hymans, Jacques Louis. *Léopold Sédar Senghor: An Intellectual Biography.* Edinburgh: Edinburgh University Press, 1971.

Innes, C. L. *A History of Black and Asian Writing in Britain, 1700–2000.* Cambridge: Cambridge University Press, 2002.

Iriye, Akira, Petra Goedde, and William I. Hitchcock, eds. *The Human Rights Revolution: An International Perspective*. New York: Oxford University Press, 2012.
James, C. L. R. *Beyond a Boundary*. London: Stanley Paul, 1963.
———. *The Black Jacobins: Toussaint L'Ouverture and the San Domingo Revolution*. London: Secker and Warburg, 1938.
James, Leslie. *George Padmore and Decolonization from Below: Pan-Africanism, the Cold War, and the End of Empire*. Basingstoke, UK: Palgrave Macmillan, 2015.
James, Stanlie M., Frances Smith Foster, and Beverly Guy-Sheftall, eds. *Still Brave: The Evolution of Black Women's Studies*. New York: Feminist Press, 2009.
James, Winston. *Holding Aloft the Banner of Ethiopia: Caribbean Radicalism in Early Twentieth-Century America*. London: Verso, 1998.
Jarrett-Macauley, Delia. *The Life of Una Marson, 1905–65*. Manchester: Manchester University Press, 1998.
Jenkinson, Jacqueline. *Black 1919: Riots, Racism, and Resistance in Imperial Britain*. Liverpool: Liverpool University Press, 2009.
Jennings, Eric T. *Vichy in the Tropics: Pétain's National Revolution in Madagascar, Guadeloupe, and Indochina 1940–1944*. Stanford, CA: Stanford University Press, 2001.
Johnson-Odim, Cheryl, and Nina Emma Mba. *For Women and the Nation: Funmilayo Ransome-Kuti of Nigeria*. Urbana: University of Illinois Press, 1997.
Kaldor, Mary. *Global Civil Society: An Answer to War*. Cambridge, UK: Polity Press, 2003.
Kaplan, Amy, and Donald E. Pease, eds. *Cultures of United States Imperialism*. Durham, NC: Duke University Press, 1993.
Kaplan, Carla, ed. *Zora Neale Hurston: A Life in Letters*. New York: Doubleday, 2002.
Keane, John. *Global Civil Society*. Cambridge: Cambridge University Press, 2001.
Keaton, Tricia Danielle, T. Denean Sharpley-Whiting, and Tyler Stovall, eds. *Black France/France Noire: The History and Politics of Blackness*. Durham, NC: Duke University Press, 2012.
Kelley, Robin D. G. *Hammer and Hoe: Alabama Communists during the Great Depression*. Chapel Hill: University of North Carolina Press, 1990.
———. *Race Rebels: Culture, Politics and the Black Working Class* New York: Free Press, 1994.
Kelley, Robin D. G., and Stephen Tuck, eds. *The Other Special Relationship: Race, Rights, and Riots in Britain and the United States*. New York: Routledge, 2015.
Killingray, David. *Fighting for Britain: African Soldiers in the Second World War*. Suffolk: James Currey, 2010.
Kirkham, Pat, and David Thoms, eds. *War Culture: Social Change and Changing Experience in World War Two Britain*. London: Lawrence and Wishart, 1995.
Kuklich, Henrika. *The Savage Within: The Social History of British Anthropology, 1885–1945*. Cambridge: Cambridge University Press, 1991.
Lake, Marilyn, and Henry Reynolds. *Drawing the Global Colour Line: White Men's Countries and the International Challenge of Racial Equality*. Cambridge: Cambridge University Press, 2008.
Landes, Joan B. *Women and the Public Sphere in the Age of the French Revolution*. Ithaca, NY: Cornell University Press, 1988.

Laxer, Gordon, and Sandra Halperin, eds. *Global Civil Society and Its Limits*. Basingstoke, UK: Palgrave Macmillan, 2003.

Lemelle, Sidney J., and Robin D. G. Kelley, eds. *Imagining Home: Class, Culture, and Nationalism in the African Diaspora*. London: Verso, 2004.

Levine, Philippa, ed. *Gender and Empire*. Oxford: Oxford University Press, 2004.

Lewis, Gordon K. *The Growth of the Modern West Indies*. London: MacGibbon and Kee, 1968.

———. *Main Currents in Caribbean Thought: The Historical Evolution of Caribbean Society in Its Ideological Aspects, 1492–1900*. Baltimore: Johns Hopkins University Press, 1983.

Lewis, Shireen K. *Race, Culture, and Identity: Francophone West African and Caribbean Literature and Theory from Négritude to Créolité*. Oxford: Lexington Books, 2006.

Lindsey, Treva B. *Colored No More: Reinventing Black Womanhood in Washington, DC*. Urbana: University of Illinois Press, 2017.

MacDougall, Curtis D. *Gideon's Army*. 3 vols. New York: Marzani and Munsell, 1965.

MacKenzie, J. M. *Propaganda and Empire: The Manipulation of British Public Opinion, 1880–1960*. Manchester: Manchester University Press, 1984.

MacPherson, Sir John, Comptroller. *Development and Welfare in the West Indies 1945–46*. Colonial no. 212. London: HMSO, 1947.

Makalani, Minkah. *In the Cause of Freedom: Radical Black Internationalism from Harlem to London, 1917–1939*. Chapel Hill: University of North Carolina Press, 2011.

Marable, Manning, and Vanessa Agard-Jones, eds. *Transnational Blackness: Navigating the Global Color Line*. New York: Palgrave Macmillan, 2008.

Martin, Tony. *Amy Ashwood Garvey: Pan-Africanist, Feminist, and Mrs. Marcus Garvey No. 1, Or, A Tale of Two Amies*. Dover, MA: Majority Press, 2007.

Matera, Marc. *Black London: The Imperial Metropolis and Decolonization in the Twentieth Century*. Berkeley: University of California Press, 2015.

May, Vivian M. *Anna Julia Cooper, Visionary Black Feminist: A Critical Introduction*. New York: Routledge, 2007.

Mazower, Mark. *Governing the World: The Making of an Idea*. New York: Penguin, 2012.

———. *No Enchanted Palace: The End of Empire and the Ideological Origins of the United Nations*. Princeton, NJ: Princeton University Press, 2009.

McCarthy, Helen. *The British People and the League of Nations: Democracy, Citizenship, and Internationalism, 1918–1945*. Manchester: Manchester University Press, 2011.

McDuffie, Erik S. *Sojourning for Freedom: Black Women, American Communism, and the Making of Black Left Feminism*. Durham, NC: Duke University Press, 2011.

McKittrick, Katherine. *Demonic Grounds: Black Women and the Cartographies of Struggle*. Minneapolis: University of Minnesota Press, 2006.

McMurry, Linda O. *To Keep the Waters Troubled: The Life of Ida B. Wells*. New York: Oxford University Press, 1998.

Meriwether, James H. *Proudly We Can Be Africans: Black Americans and Africa, 1935–1961*. Chapel Hill: University of North Carolina Press, 2002.

Miller, James. *Remembering Scottsboro: The Legacy of an Infamous Trial*. Princeton, NJ: Princeton University Press, 2009.

Mitchell, Michelle. *Righteous Propagation: African Americans and the Politics of Racial Destiny after Reconstruction*. Chapel Hill: University of North Carolina Press, 2004.

Morgan, Philip D., and Sean Hawkins, eds. *Black Experience and the Empire*. Oxford: Oxford University Press, 2004.
Morton, Patricia A. *Hybrid Modernities: Architecture and Representation at the 1931 Colonial Exposition, Paris*. Cambridge, MA: MIT Press, 2009.
Moyn, Samuel, and Andrew Sartori, eds. *Global Intellectual History*. New York: Columbia University Press, 2013.
Mullen, Bill V., and James Edward Smethurst, eds. *Left of the Color Line: Race, Radicalism, and Twentieth-Century Literature of the United States*. Chapel Hill: University of North Carolina Press, 2003.
Naison, Mark. *Communists in Harlem during the Depression*. New York: Grove Press, 1983.
Neptune, Harvey, R. *Caliban and the Yankees: Trinidad and the United States Occupation*. Chapel Hill: University of North Carolina Press, 2007.
Ngô, Fiona I. B. *Imperial Blues: Geographies of Race and Sex in Jazz Age New York*. Durham, NC: Duke University Press, 2014.
Nicolas, Armand. *Histoire de la Martinique*. Tome 3: *De 1939 à 1971*. Paris: L'Harmattan, 1998.
Onishi, Yuichiro. *Transpacific Antiracism: Afro-Asian Solidarity in 20th-Century Black America, Japan, and Okinawa*. New York: New York University Press, 2013.
Ortiz, Fernando. *Cuban Counterpoint: Tobacco and Sugar*. 1940. Reprint, Durham, NC: Duke University Press, 1995.
Overy, Richard. *The Morbid Age: Britain between the Wars*. London: Allen Lane, 2009.
Paravisini-Gebert, Lizabeth, and Ivette Romero-Cesareo, eds. *Women at Sea: Travel Writing and the Margins of Caribbean Discourse*. New York: Palgrave, 2000.
Parker, Jason. *Brother's Keeper: The United States, Race, and Empire in the British Caribbean, 1937–1962*. New York: Oxford University Press, 2008.
Peabody, Sue, and Tyler Stovall, eds. *The Color of Liberty: Histories of Race in France*. Durham, NC: Duke University Press, 2003.
Pennybacker, Susan D. *From Scottsboro to Munich: Race and Political Culture in 1930s Britain*. Princeton, NJ: Princeton University Press, 2009.
Perry, Kennetta Hammond. *London Is the Place for Me: Black Britons, Citizenship, and the Politics of Race*. New York: Oxford University Press, 2015.
Plummer, Brenda Gayle. *In Search of Power: African Americans in the Era of Decolonization, 1956–1974*. New York: Cambridge University Press, 2013.
———. *Rising Wind: Black Americans and U.S. Foreign Affairs, 1935–1960*. Chapel Hill: University of North Carolina Press, 1996.
———, ed. *Window on Freedom: Race, Civil Rights, and Foreign Affairs, 1945–1988*. Chapel Hill: University of North Carolina Press, 2003.
Post, Ken. *Arise Ye Starvelings: The Jamaican Labour Rebellion of 1938 and Its Aftermath*. London: Nijoff, 1978.
Prashad, Vijay. *The Darker Nations: A People's History of the Third World*. New York: New Press, 2007.
———. *Everybody Was Kung Fu Fighting: Afro-Asian Connections and the Myth of Cultural Purity*. Boston: Beacon Press, 2001.
Pratt, Mary Louise. *Imperial Eyes: Travel Writing and Transculturation*. 2nd ed. New York: Routledge, 2008.

Putnam, Lara. *Radical Moves: Caribbean Migrants and the Politics of Race in the Jazz Age*. Chapel Hill: University of North Carolina Press, 2013.

Quigley, Joan. *Just Another Southern Town: Mary Church Terrell and the Struggle for Racial Justice in the Nation's Capital*. New York: Oxford University Press, 2016.

Racine, Daniel. *Léon-Gontran Damas: L'homme et l'oeuvre*. Paris: Présence Africaine, 1983.

Ransby, Barbara. *Eslanda: The Large and Unconventional Life of Mrs. Paul Robeson*. New Haven: Yale University Press, 2013.

Raphael-Hernandez, Heike, and Shannon Steen, eds. *AfroAsian Encounters: Culture, History, Politics*. New York: New York University Press, 2006.

Renda, Mary A. *Taking Haiti: Military Occupation and the Culture of U.S. Imperialism, 1915–1940*. Chapel Hill: University of North Carolina Press, 2001.

Richards, Yevette. *Conversations with Maida Springer: A Personal History of Labor, Race, and International Relations*. Pittsburgh: University of Pittsburgh Press, 2004.

———. *Maida Springer: Pan-Africanist and International Labor Leader*. Pittsburgh: University of Pittsburgh Press, 2000.

Robinson-Tomsett, Emma. *Women, Travel, and Identity: Journeys by Rail and Sea, 1870–1940*. Manchester: Manchester University Press 2013.

Rose, Sonya O. *Which People's War?: National Identity and Citizenship in Wartime Britain, 1939–1945*. Oxford: Oxford University Press, 2003.

Rosenberg, Clifford D. *Policing Paris: The Origins of Modern Immigration Control between the Wars*. Ithaca, NY: Cornell University Press, 2006.

Rupp, Leila J. *Worlds of Women: The Making of an International Women's Movement*. Princeton: Princeton University Press, 1997.

Rush, Anne Spry. *Bonds of Empire: West Indians and Britishness from Victoria to Decolonization*. Oxford: Oxford University Press, 2011.

Sandell, Marie. *The Rise of Women's Transnational Activism: Identity and Sisterhood between the World Wars*. London: I. B. Tauris, 2015.

Sandhu, Sukhdev. *London Calling: How Black and Asian Writers Imagined a City*. London: Harper Collins, 2003.

Schechter, Patricia A. *Exploring the Decolonial Imaginary: Four Transnational Lives*. New York: Palgrave Macmillan, 2012.

Schwarz, Bill, ed. *West Indian Intellectuals in Britain*. Manchester: Manchester University Press, 2003.

Scott, William R. *The Sons of Sheba's Race: African-Americans and the Italo-Ethiopian War, 1935–1941*. Bloomington: Indiana University Press, 1993.

Sharpley-Whiting, T. Denean. *Bricktop's Paris: African American Women in Paris between the Two World Wars*. Albany: State University of New York Press, 2015.

———. *Negritude Women*. Minneapolis: University of Minnesota Press, 2002.

Sherrard-Johnson, Cherene. *Portraits of New Negro Women: Visual and Literary Culture in the Harlem Renaissance*. New Brunswick, NJ: Rutgers University Press, 2007.

Sieberg, Herward. *Colonial Development: Die Grundlegung moderner Entwicklungspolitik durch Großbritannien, 1919–49*. Stuttgart: Franz Steiner, 1985.

Singh, Amritjit, and Daniel M. Scott III, eds. *The Collected Writings of Wallace Thurman: A Harlem Renaissance Reader*. New Brunswick, NJ: Rutgers University Press, 2003.

Singh, Kelvin. *Race and Class Struggles in a Colonial State: Trinidad 1917–1945*. Calgary: University of Calgary Press, 1994.
Singh, Nikhil Pal. *Black Is a Country: Race and the Unfinished Struggle for Democracy*. Cambridge, MA: Harvard University Press, 2005.
Slate, Nico. *Colored Cosmopolitanism: The Shared Struggle for Freedom in the United States and India*. Cambridge, MA: Harvard University Press, 2012.
Sluga, Glenda. *Internationalism in the Age of Nationalism*. Philadelphia: University of Pennsylvania Press, 2013.
Sluga, Glenda, and Patricia Clavin, eds. *Internationalisms: A Twentieth-Century History*. Cambridge: Cambridge University Press, 2017.
Smith, Malcolm. *Britain and 1940: History, Myth, and Popular Memory*. London: Routledge, 2000.
Snaith, Anna. *Modernist Voyages: Colonial Women Writers in London 1890–1945*. Cambridge: Cambridge University Press, 2014.
Springer, Kimberly. *Living for the Revolution: Black Feminist Organizations 1968–1980*. Durham, NC: Duke University Press, 2005.
Stephen, Daniel Mark. *The Empire of Progress: West Africans, Indians, and Britons at the British Empire Exhibition, 1924–25*. Basingstoke, UK: Palgrave Macmillan, 2013.
Stephens, Michelle Ann. *Black Empire: The Masculine Global Imaginary of Caribbean Intellectuals in the United States 1914–1962*. Durham, NC: Duke University Press, 2005.
Stovall, Tyler E. *Paris Noir: African Americans in the City of Light*. New York: Houghton Mifflin, 1996.
Tabili, Laura. *"We Ask for British Justice": Workers and Racial Difference in Late Imperial Britain*. Ithaca, NY: Cornell University Press, 1994.
Taylor, Ula Y. *The Veiled Garvey: The Life and Times of Amy Jacques Garvey*. Chapel Hill: University of North Carolina Press, 2002.
Terrell, Mary Church. *A Colored Woman in a White World*. Amherst, NY: Humanity Books, 2005. First published 1940.
Thompson, Robert Farris. *Flash of the Spirit: African and Afro-American Art and Philosophy*. New York: Vintage Books, 1983.
Tuck, Stephen. *The Night Malcolm X Spoke at the Oxford Union: A Transatlantic Story of Antiracist Protest*. Berkeley: University of California Press, 2014.
———. *We Ain't What We Ought to Be: The Black Freedom Struggle from Emancipation to Obama*. Cambridge, MA: Harvard University Press, 2010.
United Nations. *The United Nations and the Advancement of Women 1945–1995*. Blue Book Series, vol. 6. New York: Department of Public Information, UN, 1996.
Von Eschen, Penny M. *Race against Empire: Black Americans and Anticolonialism, 1937–1957*. Ithaca, NY: Cornell University Press, 1997.
Walkowitz, Judith R. *Nights Out: Life in Cosmopolitan London*. New Haven, CT: Yale University Press, 2012.
Waters, Kristen, and Carol B. Conaway, eds. *Black Women's Intellectual Traditions: Speaking Their Minds*. Hanover, NH: University Press of New England, 2007.
West, Michael O., W. G. Martin, and Fanon Che Wilkins, eds. *From Toussaint to Tupac: The Black International since the Age of Revolution*. Chapel Hill: University of North Carolina Press, 2011.

White, Deborah Gray. *Too Heavy a Load: Black Women in Defense of Themselves, 1894–1994.* New York: Norton, 1999.
Whittick, Arnold. *Woman into Citizen: The World Movement Towards the Emancipation of Women in the Twentieth Century.* London: Athenaeum, distributed by Muller, 1979.
Wilder, Gary. *Freedom Time: Negritude, Decolonization, and the Future of the World.* Durham, NC: Duke University Press, 2015.
———. *The French Imperial Nation-State: Negritude and Colonial Humanism between the Two World Wars.* Chicago: University of Chicago Press, 2005.
Wilks, Jennifer M. *Race, Gender, and Comparative Black Modernism: Suzanne Lacascade, Marita Bonner, Suzanne Césaire, Dorothy West.* Baton Rouge: Louisiana State University, 2008.
Williams, Elizabeth. *The Politics of Race in Britain and South Africa: Black British Solidarity and the Anti-Apartheid Struggle.* London: I. B. Tauris, 2015.
Williams, Zachery R. *In Search of the Talented Tenth: Howard University Public Intellectuals and the Dilemmas of Race, 1926–1970.* Columbia: University of Missouri Press, 2009.
Wolcott, Victoria W. *Remaking Respectability: African American Women in Interwar Detroit.* Chapel Hill: University of North Carolina Press, 2001.

Unpublished Theses, Speeches, and Manuscripts

Blain, Keisha N., and Tiffany Gill, eds. *To Turn This Whole World Over: Black Women's Internationalism in Historical Perspective*, under review.
Devenish, Annie. "Being, Belonging and Becoming: A Study of Gender in the Making of Post-colonial Citizenship in India, 1946–1961." DPhil thesis, University of Oxford, 2014.
Joseph-Gabriel, Annette. *Decolonial Citizenship: Black Women's Resistance in the Francophone World*, forthcoming.
Musil, Emily K. M. "'La Marianne Noire': How Gender and Race in the Twentieth Century Atlantic World Reshaped the Debate about Human Rights." PhD diss., University of California Los Angeles, 2007.
Reddock, Rhoda. "Address to the Planning Meeting of the First Caribbean Feminist Encounter." Port of Spain, Trinidad, December 12–13, 1998.
Spiegler, James. "Aspects of Nationalist Thought among French-Speaking West Africans, 1921–1939." DPhil thesis, University of Oxford, 1968.
Whittall, Daniel James. "Creolising London: Black West Indian Activism and the Politics of Race and Empire, 1931–1948." PhD thesis, Royal Holloway, University of London, 2012.

Interviews

Eda-Pierre, Jean-Jacques (nephew of Paulette Nardal), interview by Emily Musil, July 11, 2002, Schoelcher, Martinique.
Ramin, Annie (Cecyle Nardal's daughter), interview by Emily Musil, March 29, 2006, Fort-de-France, Martinique.
Springer-Kemp, Madia, interview by Yevette Richards. In *Maida Springer: Pan-Africanist and International Labor Leader,* pp. 85–86. Pittsburgh: University of Pittsburgh Press, 2000.

INDEX

Umoren, Race Women Internationalists
Do Mi Stauber Indexing Service
AAWFM (All African Women's Freedom Movement), 113
Ablack, Kenny, 70
Abraham, Emmanuel, 44
Abraham Lincoln Battalion, 39
Abyssinian Association (Britain), 42
Acheson, Dean, 89
Achille, Louis, 17, 67–68, 134n54
Achille, Louise, 4
Adams, Grantley, 73
Addae, Gloria, 101
Africa and the World (IASB), 42
African Americans: diasporic black views of, 34; and Ethiopian crisis, 38, 39, 54; Harlem, 3–4, 38, 97; Marson on, 53; and respectability, 16; and *La Revue du monde noir*, 18–19; Robeson's speeches to, 75; and Spanish Civil War, 57, 58; and World War II, 75. *See also* U.S. racism; *specific people and organizations*
African Journey (Robeson), 32, 46, 49, 51, 55, 100
African National Congress (ANC), 49, 105
African National Congress Women's League, 105
African Progress Union (APU), 24
African Races Association of Glasgow, 24
African Sentinel (IASB), 42
African Students' Union, 24
African Telegraph, 24

African Times and Orient Review, 13
Afro-American, 57
Afro-Asian solidarity, 26, 87–89, 102
AFWIF (American Friends of the West Indies Federation), 98
Aggrey, James E. Kwegyir, 24
Aggrey House (London), 24, 71
Ali, Dusé Mohammed, 13
All-African Conference (Accra) (1958), 110–11
All-African National Convention, 49
All African Women's Freedom Movement (AAWFM), 113
Allfrey, Phyllis, 106
ALP (American Labor Party), 87
American Argument (Robeson), 99–100
American Committee for the Defense of Ethiopia, 38
American Committee on the Ethiopian Crisis/American Aid for Ethiopia and the Committee for Ethiopia, 38
American Continental Congress for Peace (1949), 87
American Friends of the West Indies Federation (AFWIF), 98
American Labor Party (ALP), 87
ANC (African National Congress), 49, 105
Anderson, Marian, 17, 35
Angelou, Maya, 121
anthropology, 34–35, 46, 47, 49–50, 74

INDEX

anti-communism, 92, 98–99, 100, 104
anti-fascist internationalism, 40–43, 69. *See also* Ethiopian crisis; Spanish Civil War
Antillean culture, 16
Anzaldua, Gloria, 6
APU (African Progress Union), 24
Ashby, Margery Corbett, 30
Ashwood Garvey, Amy, 2, 3, 24, 42, 73
Asian Women's Federation, 87, 88
assimilation, 17–18, 20–21
Associated Negro Press (ANP), 90, 110
Association des étudiants martiniquais en France, 17
Association for Ethiopia (Britain), 45
Association for the Protection of Children and Adolescents (Martinique), 94
Atatürk, Kemal, 31
Atta, Ofori, 25
At What a Price? (Marson), 5, 14, 25–26
autonomy, 6
Avenol, Joseph, 31
"Awakening of Race Consciousness" (Nardal), 19, 20–21
Azango, Augustin, 41
Azikiwe, Nnamdi, 96

Bailey, Amy, 52
Baker, Josephine, 12, 16, 20, 33, 34
"The Ballad of Ethiopia" (Hughes), 38
Banda, Hastings, 111
Bandung Conference, 103, 104
Bankole-Bright, Herbert, 24
Barnes, Leonard, 33
Barnett, Claude, 90
Bass, Charlotta, 52, 104, 105
Batouala (Maran), 15
BBC, 68–69, 71–72
BCL (British Commonwealth League), 29–30, 67
Beach, Sylvia, 14
Bean, Marjorie, 106
Bell, Amy, 72
Benglia, Habib, 16, 34
Bennett, Gwendolyn, 16
Bennett, Louise, 93, 106
Ben-Zwi, Mina, 117
Bernardino, Minerva, 82
Bethune, Mary McLeod, 2, 52
Beton, Issac, 34
"Black Burden" (Marson), 23
black feminist organizations, 104–5, 121
"Black Internationalism" (Nardal), 15, 20
"Black Is Fancy" (Marson), 23

"Black Paris" (Robeson), 34
"A Black Woman Sculptor" (Nardal), 15
Blain, Keisha N., 8
Boas, Franz, 46
Boittin, Jennifer Anne, 15, 46
Bokwe, Rosebery, 47
borderlands, 6
Bricktop Smith, Ada, 16–17, 20, 34
Bright, Nellie, 19
Britain: black feminist organizations, 121; Blitz, 72, 148n43; Marson's London visit (1964), 115–16; postwar West Indian migration to, 110; World War II-era West Indian community, 68, 69–72. *See also* interwar Britain
British Commonwealth League (BCL), 29–30, 67
British Empire Exhibition (1924–25), 13–14
British Guiana Association, 45
British Nationality Act, 110
British Union of Fascists, 44
Brooks, Angie, 101
Brown, Larry, 32
Brown v. Board of Education, 92
Buck, Pearl, 99–100
Buckle, Desmond, 25
Buell, Raymond, 51
"Building National Culture" (Marson), 107
Bunche, Ralph, 17, 51, 83
Burnham, Louis, 88
Burroughs, Williana, 35
Bustamante, Alexander, 52, 108

CAA (Council on African Affairs), 51–52, 75, 87, 88, 92, 100
CAE (Ethiopian Action Committee/Comité d'action éthiopienne), 41
CAI (Center for Native Affairs/Centre des affaires indigènes) (France), 18
Calling the West Indies, 68, 71
Campaign Against Racial Discrimination (CARD) (Britain), 116–17
Campbell, Elaine, 27
Candace, Gratien, 34
Canudo, Jeanne, 84
CAO (Committee of African Organisations), 113
CARD (Campaign Against Racial Discrimination) (Britain), 116–17
Caribbean: departmentalization, 75–76, 80; and Ethiopian crisis, 37, 39, 53–54; feminist internationalism, 84, 121–22; and World War II, 69, 72–73, 74. *See also* Caribbean nationalism; Jamaica; Martinique

INDEX 185

Caribbean Association for Feminist Research and Action (CAFRA), 121
Caribbean nationalism: and departmentalization, 76; Marson on, 70, 71, 107–8; and Vichy regime, 74; West Indies Federation, 70, 93, 97–98, 105–6, 107
Caribbean Voices, 71
Castillo, Fernando, 56–57, 58
Catholic University Association of Secular Missionaries/Association universitaire catholique des laïques missionnaires (France), 43
CDIRN (Comité de défense des intérêts de la ra(France), 15, 18
CDRN (Comité de défense de la racre), 18
Center for Native Affairs/Centre des affaires indigènes (CAI) (France), 18
Le Cerf, 21
Césaire, Aimé, 16, 17, 74, 79
Césaire, Suzanne Roussi, 16, 74, 86
Challenge, 34
Childers, Kristen Stromberg, 74, 76
Childress, Alice, 88, 100, 104
China, Robeson visit (1949), 87–89
la Chorale de la jeunesse étudiante chrétienne (la Chorale de Paulette Nardal), 94
"Christmas on Poinsettia Island" (Marson), 98
Church, Emily Musil, 8
"Cinema Eyes" (Marson), 23
Ciselet, Georgette, 101
civil rights movement (United States), 92, 113–14
Clamart salon, 17–18, 20, 21, 83, 134n52
class: and feminism, 7, 78; and League of Coloured Peoples, 25, 28; and Nardal, 21, 43, 44, 55–56; and race women internationalists, 3, 5–6; sub-Saharan Africa, 50
clubwomen, 1–2
Cochrane, Kelso, 112
Cold War: and anti-communism, 92, 98–99, 100, 104; nonaligned movement, 103; and U.S. racism, 96
Colón, Alice, 106
Colonial Development Act, 72–73
Colonial Exhibition (Paris, 1931), 12, 19
colonialism/imperialism: and black migration to Britain, 13; and black visits to Africa, 47–48; and Colonial Exhibition (Paris, 1931), 12, 19; departmentalization, 75–76, 80; and *La Dépêche africaine*, 15, 18; and Ethiopian crisis, 39, 40; and League of Coloured Peoples, 25, 30; Marson on, 22, 29–30, 31; Nardal on, 74; and racism, 12, 13; and *La Revue du monde noir*, 21; Robeson on, 33, 48, 50–51, 84; and Soviet Union, 36; and travelling, 6. See also decolonization

colored cosmopolitanism, 2
Combahee River Collective, 121
Comité de défense de la race nègre (CDRN), 18
Comité de défense des intérêts de la race noire (CDIRN) (France), 15, 18
Commission on the Status of Women (United Nations), 83, 101
Committee for Ethiopia, 38
Committee of African Organisations (CAO), 113
Committee to Restore Paul Robeson's Passport, 99
Commonwealth Immigration Act (1962), 116
Communication Services and General Workers Union, 106
communism: and Ethiopian crisis, 38, 40; Nardal on, 56; Robeson on, 36, 99; and Spanish Civil War, 39. See also anti-communism; Soviet Union
Communist Party of Great Britain (CPGB), 33
Communist Party of the United States of America (CPUSA), 38
Conaway, Carol B., 8
Congo, 50, 85, 87
Congress of American Women (CAW), 87
Congress of the World Partisans of Peace, 98
Constantine, Learie, 24, 71, 116
Les Continents, 33
Cook, Mercer, 17
Cooper, Anna Julie, 1–2, 12, 16
The Cosmopolitan (Jamaica), 5, 7
Council on African Affairs (CAA), 51–52, 75, 87, 88, 92, 100
CPUSA (Communist Party of the United States of America), 38
Le Cri des nègres, 15, 42
The Crisis, 13
Cross, Ulric, 70
Cullen, Countee, 17
Cummings-John, Constance, 2

Daily Gleaner (Jamaica), 90, 108, 109
Damas, Léon-Gontran, 17, 21
dance, 16
Danquah, Joseph Boakye, 24
Danse de sauvage, 12
D'Arboussier, Gabriel, 85–86
Davies, Carole Boyce, 6, 8
Davis, Angela, 121

decolonization, 92–93; and All-African Conference (1958), 111; Marson on, 107; Robeson on, 100, 102; and World War II, 84. *See also* Caribbean nationalism
de Gaulle, Charles, 82
Delany, Hubert T., 51
de Miribel, Elisabeth, 82
La Dépêche africaine, 15–16, 18
Diagne, Blaise, 11
Dickinson, Anita Thompson, 16
Diggs, Charles C., 98
Diouf, Galandou, 55
dissemblance, 9–10
Domingo, Eulalie, 52–53
Domingo, W. A., 52–53
Donnell, Alison, 8
Dossett, Kate, 7
Double Victory campaign, 75
Douglas, Aaron, 34
Du Bois, Shirley Graham, 2, 16, 100, 104, 111
Du Bois, W. E. B., 11, 35, 52, 92, 111
Dubouillé, Gisèle, 16
Duke, Eric, 97–98
Dunbar, Rudolph, 72

Eastman, Max, 14
Ebony, 89
Éboué, Félix, 18, 84, 87
Edwards, Brent Hayes, 21
Edwards, Linda, 69
Edwards, Thyra, 2, 35, 57
Egyptian Feminist Union/Union féministe egyptienne, 40
Eisenhower, Dwight D., 103
Eisenstein, Sergei, 35
Eliot, T. S., 116
Ellington, Duke, 12
Emperor Jones, 13, 14, 16
Eshete, Workeneh (Charles Martin), 42, 44, 45
Ethiopian Action Committee/Comité d'action éthiopienne (CAE), 41
Ethiopian crisis, 40–46; African diaspora reactions, 37–39, 54; and Marson, 39, 44–45, 46, 53–54; and Nardal, 39, 40–44, 46
Ethiopian Defense Committee/Comité de défense d'Éthiopie, 41–42
Ethiopian Research Council, 38
L'Étudiant noir, 17, 21

Fairclough, O. T., 52
"The Family and Social Evolution of Black Women" (Nardal), 55–56

Fauset, Jessie, 12–13, 16, 132n10
FBI (Federal Bureau of Investigation), 75, 87, 105
feminism: and class, 7, 78; and colonialism/imperialism, 30; and Marson, 7, 29–31; and Nardal, 7, 21–22, 76–80, 101; relational, 78, 101; and Robeson, 7, 101, 106. *See also* feminist internationalism
feminist internationalism: and All-African Conference (1958), 111; and black feminist organizations, 104–5, 121; Caribbean, 84, 121–22; and Ethiopian crisis, 40; interwar Britain, 29–31; interwar France, 21–22; and Robeson's China visit, 88–89; and "The Role of Women in the Struggle for Peace and Development" conference, 115; Sojourners for Truth and Justice, 104–5; sub-Saharan Africa, 86; and United Nations, 101; Women's Civic and Social Union, 21–22, 55–56, 76, 83–84
La femme dans la cité/Woman in the City, 63fig., 76–77, 78–83
La femme dans la vie sociale, 56
Field, Edith, 51
Field, Fred, 51
Finot, Louis-Jean, 18
First World War. *See* World War I
Firth, Raymond, 35
Fisk University, 75
Fitte-Duval, Solange, 77
Ford, Tanisha, 8
France: women's franchise, 75, 76, 79–80; World War II-era black community, 68. *See also* interwar France
Franco, Francisco, 39
Frazier, E. Franklin, 52
Freedom, 88
Freedomways, 88
French Equatorial Africa, 85
Friends of Ethiopia, 38
Friends of the Ethiopian People/Les amis du peuple éthiopien, 41
"From an Electoral Point of View" (Nardal), 79
Fujita, Taki, 101
Füllberg-Stolberg, Claus, 72

Gaines, Kevin, 18
Gambo, Mallama, 111
Garvey, Amy Jacques, 2, 108
Garvey, Marcus, 3
Garvin, Vicki, 88, 100, 121
gender: and Clamart salon, 17, 20; Nardal on, 19, 20, 21; and United Nations, 101. *See*

also feminism; feminist internationalism; interracial relationships
Germany, 114
Gildersleeve, Virginia, 82
Gill, Tiffany, 8
Gillet, Rachel, 16
Giuseppe, Neville, 71
Glissant, Edouard, 76
global cities, 6. *See also* interwar Britain; interwar France
global citizenship, 68
Goebel, Michael, 11
Gold Coast Students Association, 45
"The Gold in Africa" (Growling Tiger), 39
Goldman, Emma, 14
Goode, Frank, 35
Gore, Dayo, 8
Grant, Nicholas, 8
Graves, Anna Melissa, 33
Gregory, Yvonne, 104
Growling Tiger, 39
Guillén, Nicolás, 17
Guyana, 106

Haldane, Charlotte, 56
Hall, Adelaide, 12
Hands Off Ethiopia campaign, 57
Hansberry, Lorraine, 88
Harlem, 3–4, 38, 97
Harris, William, 73
Harrison, Faye V., 46
Harrison, Ira E., 46
"Harvest Thanksgiving Festival" (Marson), 98
Hawariate, Teele, 44
Hayes, Roland, 17
Hayford, Adelaide Casely, 2
Heater, Derek, 100
Heights and Depths (Marson), 14
Hemingway, Ernest, 14
Hercules, Felix E. M., 24
Herskovits, Melville, 46
Higashida, Cheryl, 8
Hilbert, Joan, 72
Hill, Frank, 52
Hine, Darlene Clark, 9
Holtby, Winifred, 29
Horner, Ruth, 71
Houénou, Kojo Touvalou, 33, 34
Howard University, 95, 96
Hughes, Langston, 18, 35, 38, 57, 89, 90
Huiswoud, Hermina Dumont, 35
Hunton, Alphaeus, 52, 104

Hunton, Oscar, 39
Hurston, Zora Neale, 35, 46, 96

IAFE (International African Friends of Ethiopia), 41–42, 45
IASB (International African Service Bureau), 42
IAWSEC (International Alliance of Women for Suffrage and Equal Citizenship), 30–31
ICAA. *See* Council on African Affairs; International Committee on African Affairs
I Know Why the Caged Bird Sings (Angelou), 121
imperialism. *See* colonialism/imperialism
independence struggles. *See* decolonization
"In Exile" (Nardal), 16
Ingledew, Margaret, 30
Ingram, Rosa Lee, 104
International African Friends of Ethiopia (IAFE), 41–42, 45
International African Opinion (IASB), 42
International African Service Bureau (IASB), 42
International Alliance of Women, 29
International Alliance of Women for Suffrage and Equal Citizenship (IAWSEC), 30–31
International Bank for Reconstruction and Development (World Bank), 68
International Committee for the Defense of the Ethiopian People/Comité international pour la défense du peuple éthiopien, 40, 41, 43
International Committee on African Affairs (ICAA), 51. *See also* Council on African Affairs
International Convention on the Political Rights of Women, 101
International Council of Women, 29
International League of Women, 40
International Monetary Fund, 68
interracial cooperation: Caribbean, 106; and Ethiopian crisis, 38, 40; and feminism, 29; interwar Britain, 24; Nardal on, 55–56; and *La Revue du monde noir*, 18
interracial relationships: and colonialism/imperialism, 85–86; interwar Britain, 13; interwar France, 19–20; World War II-era Britain, 68
interwar Britain: anti-fascist internationalism, 42; black internationalist organizations, 23–24; black migration to, 13; British Empire Exhibition, 13–14; and Ethiopian crisis, 45; fascism, 44; feminist internationalism, 29–31; interracial cooperation, 24; interracial relationships, 13; London as contact zone, 14–15, 34; London School of Economics, 34–35; Marson's move to London (1932), 14, 22;

interwar Britain *(continued)*
  racism, 13, 22–23, 26–27, 32–33; Robeson's move to London (1925), 13, 14. *See also* League of Coloured Peoples
interwar Europe: Soviet Union, 35–36, 139n205. *See also* interwar Britain; interwar France
interwar France, 15–22; anti-fascist internationalism in, 40–42; assimilation vs. Afrocentrism, 17–18, 20–21; black migration to, 11–12, 34; Clamart salon, 17–18, 20, 21, 83, 134n52; *La Dépêche africaine*, 15–16, 18; feminist internationalism, 21–22; interracial relationships, 19–20; *Negritude*, 17–18; notable black women in, 16–17; Paris as contact zone, 14–15; racism, 12, 17, 19, 33; *La Revue du monde noir*, 18–19, 21; Robeson's impressions, 33; *vogue noire*, 12; Women's Civic and Social Union, 21–22. *See also* Nardal, Paulette
Israel, 115, 117
"The Italo-Ethiopian Conflict and Colonization/Le conflit italo-éthiopien et la colonisation" (Nardal), 43

Jabavu, D. D. T., 51
Jackson, Ada, 87
Jackson, Lily, 71
Jackson, Yolande, 34
Jacobs, H. P., 52
Jagan, Janet, 106
Jamaica: feminism, 7; Marson's background, 4–5; and Marson's plays, 54–55; Pioneer Press, 90; *Public Opinion*, 52–54; Robeson's conservative journalism, 107–9; and West Indies Federation, 106, 107; and World War II, 72–73. *See also* Caribbean
Jamaica Critic, 5
Jamaica Labour Party (JLP), 72, 108
James, C. L. R., 24, 33, 42, 108
Jamsave, 53, 67, 109
Jarrett-Macauley, Delia, 8, 109
Jazz Age, 12
Jeffers, Audrey, 25, 29, 73, 106
Jennings, Eric, 74
Je suis partout, 56
Jet, 89
Jim Crow. *See* U.S. racism
JLP (Jamaica Labour Party), 72, 108
John H. Johnson, 89
Johnson, James Weldon, 3, 53
Johnson, Mordecai, 51
la Joie de chanter, 94

Joint Council to Promote Understanding between White and Coloured People in Great Britain, 24, 29
Jones, Chris, 42
Jones, Claudia, 2, 92, 110, 112
Jones, Loïs Mailou, 16
Le Journal, 43
Joyce, James, 14

Kee, Salaria, 57
Keep England White, 112
Kenyatta, Jomo, 25, 29, 35, 42, 47
The Keys, 24, 26
Khama, Tshekedi, 47
Kikuyu Association of Kenya, 45
King, Martin Luther, Jr., 110, 116
"Kinky Hair Blues" (Marson), 23
Koch, Erica, 116
Kouyaté, Tiémoko Garan, 41, 43
Kung Pu Shen, 89

Lacascade, Suzanne, 16
Lagrosillière, Joseph, 13, 41
LAI (League Against Imperialism), 33, 42
Lamming, George, 71, 116
Larsen, Nella, 16
Law, Oliver, 57
LCP. *See* League of Coloured Peoples
LDRN (Ligue de défense de la race nègre), 18
League Against Imperialism (LAI), 33, 42
League against Imperialism and Colonial Oppression/Ligue française contre l'impérialisme et l'oppression coloniale, 41
League of Coloured Peoples (LCP): and colonialism/imperialism, 25, 30; and Ethiopian crisis, 38, 45; ideology of, 24; and interracial organizing, 29; *The Keys*, 24, 26, 27–28; Marson's role in, 23, 25, 26, 27–28, 67, 70; and Robeson, 25, 33; and WASU, 24, 28
League of Nations (LoN): and Ethiopian crisis, 37, 41, 43, 44, 45; and Marson, 31–32, 44, 82
League of Nations Union (LNU), 44–45
Légitime défense, 21
Léro, Étienne, 17, 21
lesbianism, 20, 25
Lewis, W. Arthur, 24
Ligue de défense de la race nègre (LDRN), 18
Lindsey, Treva B., 2
Lindstrom, Ulla, 101
"Little Brown Girl" (Marson), 22–23
Little Rock Nine, 103
LNU (League of Nations Union), 44–45

Locke, Alain, 17, 18–19, 96
Logan, Rayford, 96, 98
LoN. *See* League of Nations
London. *See* interwar Britain
London Calling (Marson), 27
London School of Economics (LSE), 34–35, 47, 50
Lorde, Audre, 121
LSE (London School of Economics), 34–35, 47, 50
LUDRN (Universal League for the Defense of the Black Race/Ligue universelle pour la défense de la race noire), 33
Lumumba, Patrice, 87, 111
Lutete, Samuel, 85
Lutz, Bertha, 82

Mahon, Maureen, 46
Makeba, Miriam, 121
Malinowski, Bronislaw, 24, 35, 46
Mandel, Georges, 67
Mandela, Nelson, 112
Manley, Edna, 52
Manley, Norman, 52, 110
Manning, Sam, 42
Maran, René, 15, 17, 33, 34, 41, 51
March on Washington (1963), 113–14
marriage imperative, 5
Marryshow, Theophilus Albert, 42, 106
Marson, Una, 59*fig.*, 60*fig.*, 119–20; and autonomy, 6; background of, 4–5; BBC employment, 68–69, 71–72; and black identity, 22–23; and British Commonwealth League, 29–30, 67; Caribbean trip (1945), 72–73; conservative journalism, 5, 107–9; death of, 117; and Ethiopian crisis, 39, 44–45, 46, 53–54; and feminism, 7, 29–31; and Howard University, 96–97; Israel visits (1964 and 1965), 115, 117; and League of Coloured Peoples, 23, 25, 26, 27–28, 67, 70; and League of Nations, 31–32, 44, 82; London visit (1964), 115–16; marriage of, 97, 108, 155n25; mental illness, 73, 89; move to London (1932), 14, 22; move to United States (1952), 90, 94; and Pioneer Press, 90; as playwright, 5, 14, 25–26, 54–55; political development of, 7; and *Public Opinion*, 52–54; and racism, 22–23, 26–27, 72, 93, 94–96, 97; and religion, 7, 26, 95–96; return to Jamaica (1936), 45; return to London (1938), 67; single status, 5; sources for, 9; and West Indies Federation, 70, 97–98, 107; and World War II–era West Indian community, 69–72
Martin, Charles (Workeneh Eshete), 42, 44, 45

Martin, William G., 14
Martin Cissé, Jeanne, 114
Martinique: departmentalization, 76, 80; *La femme dans la cité*, 76–83; Nardal's background, 4; Nardal's musical projects, 94; and World War II, 69, 74. *See also* Caribbean
Martinsville Seven, 105
Marxism, 21
Matera, Marc, 14
Maugée, Aristide, 74
Mazower, Mark, 82
Mbanefo, Louis, 25
Mboya, Tom, 111
McCarthy, Joseph, 100
McDuffie, Erik S., 7, 8, 104
McFarlane, Clare, 73
McGee, Willie, 104–5
McGhee, Bert, 33
McKay, Claude, 5, 14, 17, 18, 139n205
McKittrick, Katherine, 6
Mead, Stella, 116
Meikle, Rupert, 53
Meir, Golda, 101, 115
Ménil, René, 17, 21, 74
Menon, Krishna, 102–3
migratory subjectivity, 6
Milliard, Peter, 42
Mills, Florence, 12
Mironova, Z. V., 101
Mitchell, Michelle, 3, 126n12
Monnerot, Jules, 17, 21
Monolulu, Ras (Peter McKay), 42
Moody, Harold, 22, 71, 95
Moody, Ronald, 71
Moorhead, Halois, 100
Moos, Elizabeth, 100
Morgan, H. B., 72
Mosley, Oswald, 44
The Moth and the Star (Marson), 22–23, 53, 72
motherhood, and respectability, 5
Mount Carmel International Training Centre for Community Services (Haifa), 115, 116, 117
Movement for Colonial Freedom (MCF), 113
Moyne Commission, 52, 67
Mukherjee, Geeta, 111
Murphy, George, Jr., 100
music, 3, 16, 94, 121
Mussolini, Benito, 37, 39

NAACP (National Association for the Advancement of Colored People), 13, 38, 92
Nabarawi, Saiza, 111

INDEX

NACW (National Association of Colored Women), 1
Naipaul, V. S., 71
Nardal, Alice, 17, 134n52
Nardal, Andrée, 17, 43
Nardal, Cécile, 134n52
Nardal, Jane: and Clamart salon, 17; and Cooper, 12; and *La Dépêche africaine*, 15; and *La Revue du monde noir*, 18–19, 20, 135n68
Nardal, Lucie, 134n52
Nardal, Paul, 4
Nardal, Paulette, 120; on assimilation, 20–21; background of, 4; and Clamart salon, 17–18, 20, 21, 83; commemoration of, 66*fig.*, 117; death of, 117; and *La Dépêche africaine*, 15–16; and Ethiopian crisis, 39, 40–44, 46; and feminism, 7, 21–22, 76–80, 101; and *La femme dans la cité*, 76–83; and French African politics, 55–56; on gender, 19, 20, 21; on interracial relationships, 19–20; migration to France, 11; and music, 94; obituaries, 64*fig.*, 65*fig.*; political development of, 7; and religion, 7–8, 43, 44, 77; and *La Revue du monde noir*, 18–19, 21; and Robeson, 19–20, 34; single status, 5; Sorbonne contacts, 12–13, 132n10; sources for, 9; and Spanish Civil War, 56; and SS *Bretagne* attack, 67–68; and United Nations, 68, 82–83; and Vichy regime, 74; and Women's Assembly, 76, 93–94; and World War II, 67–68, 69
National Association for the Advancement of Colored People (NAACP), 13, 38, 92
National Association of Colored Women (NACW), 1
National Council of American-Soviet Friendship (NCASF), 100
National Urban League, 19
NCASF (National Council of American-Soviet Friendship), 100
Negritude, 17–18
"The Negro and Drama" (Nardal), 16
"The Negro Problem: An Approach to the Problem of Race Relations in the U.S.A. and a Suggested Solution" (Robeson), 74
Negro Welfare Association, 33, 45
Negro Workers Union/Union des travailleurs nègres (UTN) (France), 41, 42
Nehru, Jawaharlal, 33, 102, 103
Nesbitt, Nick, 76
New Negro, 2
The New Negro (Locke), 18–19
New Times and Ethiopia News, 42

New World Review, 100–103, 111
Nigerian Progress Union, 24
"Nigger" (Marson), 26
Nkrumah, Kwame, 52
nonaligned movement, 103, 104
"Notebook of a Return to My Native Land/Cahier d'un retour au pays natal" (Césaire), 17
Nuegebauer, Frieda, 51
Nyabongo, Akiki, 47, 49

Offen, Karen, 78
Opportunity (National Urban League), 19
Organisation of Women of Asian and African Descent, 121
Ortiz, Fernando, 54
Orwell, George, 71
Ottley, Roi, 38, 75
Ouandie, Martha, 111

pacifism, 57, 77
Padmore, George, 33, 36, 42, 70, 111
Palimpsest: A Journal of Women, Gender, and the Black International, 8
Pan-African congresses, 1, 11, 73
Pan-African Federation, 45
Pandit, Vijaya, 101–2
Pankhurst, Sylvia, 42
Paris. *See* interwar France
Patel, Rajni, 33
Patterson, Louise Thompson, 2; and China, 89; and *Freedom*, 88; and Sojourners for Truth and Justice, 104, 105; Soviet Union visits, 35; and Spanish Civil War, 57
Patterson, William, 35
Paul Robeson: Negro (Robeson), 100
People's National Movement (Trinidad), 106
People's National Party (PNP) (Jamaica), 52, 72, 107
Perham, Margery, 24
Perkins, Thelma Dale, 100
Perry, Kennetta Hammond, 110
Pioneer Press (Jamaica), 90
PNP (People's National Party) (Jamaica), 52, 72, 107
Pocomania (Marson), 54–55
political development, 6–7
Popular Front, 38
postwar era: global citizenship, 68; Martinique, 93–94; U.S. racism, 94–96, 97; West Indian migration to Britain, 110. *See also* Cold War; decolonization
Powell, Adam Clayton, 98, 105

Pratt, Mary Louise, 6
Prix du roman des D.O.M., 94
Procter, James, 72
Progressive Party (United States), 87, 104
Provisional Committee for the Defense of Ethiopia, 38
Public Opinion, 52–54
Pukkumina, 54–55

La Race nègre, 15
race women, defined, 1
race women internationalists: ongoing impact, 121–22; overview, 2–3; scholarship on, 8–9; sources for, 9
racial destiny, 3, 126n12
"Racial Feelings?" (Marson), 53–54
racism: Congo, 50; interwar Britain, 13, 22–23, 26–27, 32–33; interwar France, 12, 17, 19, 33; postwar Britain, 112, 116–17; South Africa, 48, 49; South African apartheid, 93, 103, 112; and Soviet Union, 36; and Spanish Civil War, 57–58; and Vichy regime, 74; World War II–era Britain, 68, 71–72. *See also* U.S. racism
Radziwill, Gabrielle, 31
Ramkeeson, J. D., 106
Randolph, A. Philip, 75
Ransby, Barbara, 8, 86
Ransome-Kuti, Funmilayo, 2
Rastafarian movement, 54, 109
Ratisimamango, Albert Raakoto, 41
Reddock, Rhoda, 7, 106
Reid, Gladys, 75
Reid, Ira, 75
relational feminism, 78, 101
religion: Jamaica, 54–55; and Marson, 7, 26, 95–96; and Moody, 22; and Nardal, 7–8, 43, 44, 77; and Robeson, 8; and U.S. racism, 95–96
respectability, 5, 16, 25, 109
La Revue du monde noir/The Review of the Black World, 18–19, 21
Rich, Ruby, 29
Richardson, Beulah, 104
Robert, Georges, 74
Robeson, Eslanda, 61*fig.*, 62*fig.*, 120; and All African Women's Freedom Movement, 113; anthropology studies, 34–35, 47, 49–50, 74; and anti-communism, 100; background of, 3–4; and CAA, 51, 52, 75, 87; cancer diagnosis, 111–12, 113–14; China visit (1949), 87–89; Clara Zetkin Medal award, 113; on colonialism/imperialism, 33, 48, 50–51, 84; death of, 114–15; FBI surveillance, 75, 87; and feminism, 7, 88–89, 101, 106; Germany visit (1963), 114; on interracial relationships, 19–20; and League of Coloured Peoples, 25, 33; marriage, 4, 5, 34; move to London, 13, 14; and Nardal, 19–20, 34; and National Council of American-Soviet Friendship, 100; political development of, 6–7; and Progressive Party, 87, 104; and racism, 32–33, 103–4, 112; and religion, 8; return to London (1958), 110; return to United States (1939), 67; and Sojourners for Truth and Justice, 104–5; sources for, 9; Soviet Union visit, 35–36; and Spanish Civil War, 39, 56–58; studies at University College London, 139n194; sub-Saharan Africa visit (1936), 46–52; sub-Saharan Africa visit (1946), 84–87; and United Nations, 68, 82, 100–104; visits to France, 33–34; and WASU, 33; and West Indies Federation, 105–6
Robeson, James, 25
Robeson, Paul, Jr. (Pauli): birth of, 14; and Soviet Union, 36; sub-Saharan Africa visit, 46–47, 48, 49, 50, 51
Robeson, Paul: anti-communist backlash against, 98–99; and CAA, 51, 52; depression, 112, 113–14; FBI surveillance, 75; and *Freedom*, 88; and League of Coloured Peoples, 25; marriage, 4, 5, 34; Marson on, 28; move to London (1925), 13, 14; Nardal on, 16; and racism, 32; and Eslanda Robeson's sub-Saharan Africa, 47, 48; Soviet Union visit, 35; and Spanish Civil War, 57
Robeson's visit (1936), 46–52
Roesad, Laili, 101
"The Role of Women in the Struggle for Peace and Development" (conference), 115
Roosevelt, Franklin D., 75, 104
Rwanda, 87

Said, Mohammed, 42
Sajous, Léo, 18
Salkey, Andrew, 116
Sandell, Marie, 29
Sanders of the River, 47
Satineau, Maurice, 15
Savage, Augusta, 15, 16
Save the Children, 53, 67
Scottsboro trial, 18, 25
Sekyi, Kobina, 34
Selassie, Haile, 37, 38, 43, 45, 46
Selvon, Sam, 71
Senghor, Léopold Sédar, 13, 17, 117

"700 Calendar Days" (Hunton), 39
Sharpeville massacre (South Africa), 93, 112
Sharpley-Whiting, T. Denean, 8, 77
Shepard, Clara, 16, 17, 18
Simone, Nina, 121
Sinha, Tarkenshwar, 101
Slate, Nico, 2
SLOTFOM (Service de liaison avec les originaires des territoires français d'outre-mer) (France), 18
Slowe, Lucy Diggs, 96
Sluga, Glenda, 82
Smith, Jessica, 100
Smith, Lillian, 75
Society of Composers, Authors and Music Publishers/Societé des auteurs, compositeurs, et éditeurs de musique, 94
Society of Peoples of African Origin (SPAO), 24
Le Soir colonial, 15, 19
Sojourners for Truth and Justice (STJ), 104–5, 121
Solanke, Ladipo, 24, 25
Soong Ching-ling (Madame Sun Yat-sen), 88–89, 102
Sorbonne, 12–13, 132n10
South Africa: apartheid, 93, 103, 112; and Ethiopian crisis, 37; and feminist internationalism, 105; Robeson's visit to (1936), 48–49
Southall Black Sisters, 121
Southern Christian Leadership Conference, 96
Soviet Union, 35–36, 100, 112, 139n205
Spanish Civil War, 39, 56–58
SPAO (Society of Peoples of African Origin), 24
Springer, Maida, 2, 70, 111
Staples, Peter, 97, 108
Stein, Gertrude, 14
STJ (Sojourners for Truth and Justice), 104–5, 121
Straw, William St. John, 85
sub-Saharan Africa: All-African Conference (1958), 110–11; feminist internationalism, 86; Robeson's visit (1936), 46–52; Robeson's visit (1946), 84–87; and World War II, 84
Sukarno, Ahmed, 103
Swanzy, Henry, 71

Tate, Merze, 96
Tell My Horse: Voodoo and Life in Haiti and Jamaica (Hurston), 46
Tendulkar, D. G., 33
Terrell, Mary Church, 1
Thaly, R. Cenac, 41
Thésée, Lucie, 74
Third World Women's Alliance (TWWA), 105, 121

Thomas, Stella, 25
Thompson, Dudley, 70
Till, Emmett, 92
Tobias, Channing, 51
"To Joe and Ben" (Marson), 45
Towards the Stars (Marson), 72
"To Wed or Not to Wed" (Marson), 5
travelling, 2, 6–7, 84–85, 120–21
Trenton Six, 105
Trinidad, 105–6
Tropic Reveries (Marson), 14
Tropiques, 74
Trouille, Pierre, 80
Tshombe, Moïse Kapenda, 87
Tuskegee Institute, 18
TWWA (Third World Women's Alliance), 105, 121

UFM (Union des femmes martiniquaises) (Martinique), 77
Uganda, 49–50
UNIA (Universal Negro Improvement Association), 3, 5, 33, 54
Union des femmes martiniquaises (UFM) (Martinique), 77
Union of Students of African Descent (USAD), 24
United Nations (UN): and Nardal, 68, 82–83; and Robeson, 68, 82, 100–104
United States: anti-communism, 92, 98–99, 100; black feminist organizations, 121; and Caribbean, 76; China policy, 87; civil rights movement, 92, 113–14; Executive Order 8802, 75; Marson's move to (1952), 90, 94; Robeson's return to (1939), 67; Scottsboro trial, 18, 25. *See also* African Americans; U.S. racism
Univers, bulletin catholique international, 55–56
Universal League for the Defense of the Black Race/Ligue universelle pour la défense de la race noire (LUDRN), 33
Universal Negro Improvement Association (UNIA), 3, 5, 33, 54
Universal Races Congress (1911), 13
USAD (Union of Students of African Descent), 24
U.S. racism: and Caribbean, 76; and colonialism/imperialism, 85; Marson's comparisons with Britain, 26, 32; Marson's postwar experience, 93, 94–96, 97; Robeson's comparisons to South Africa, 48, 49; and Sojourners for Truth and Justice, 104–5; and United Nations, 103–4

UTN (Negro Workers Union/Union des travailleurs nègres) (France), 41, 42

Van Kleek, Mary, 51
Véry, Anita, 43
Vialle, Jeanne, 86–87
Virtue, Vivian, 89, 116
vogue noire, 12
A Voice from the South (Cooper), 1, 10

Wallace, Henry, 104
Wallace, I. T. A., 42
Ward, Arnold, 42
Washington, Booker T., 18
Wasu, 24
Waters, Ethel, 12
Waters, Kristin, 8
Webster, Aimee, 52
"We Go to Spain" (Robeson), 56, 57
Wells-Barnett, Ida B., 1
West, Dorothy, 16, 34
West, Michael O., 14
West, Rebecca, 14
West African Students' Union (WASU), 24, 28, 33
West India Committee, 71
West Indian Gazette and Afro-Asian Caribbean News, 110
West Indies Federation (WIF), 70, 93, 97–98, 105–6, 107
White, Clarence Cameron, 34
White, Maude, 35
White, Walter, 33
white beauty standards, 23
Wickham, John, 71
WIDF (Women's International Democratic Federation), 87
WIF (West Indies Federation), 70, 93, 97–98, 105–6, 107
Wilder, Gary, 12, 17
Wilkins, Fanon Che, 14
Wilks, Jennifer M., 16, 20

Williams, Eric, 73, 96, 106
Williams, John Grenfall, 71, 90
"The Wolof Puppet" (Nardal), 21
Women Educators for Peace/Ligue internationale des méres et éducatrices pour la paix, 40
Women's Assembly/Rassemblement féminin (Martinique), 76, 83–84, 93–94. See also *La femme dans la cité*
Women's Association of the French Overseas-Metropole Union/Association des femmes de l'union française outre-mer-metropole, 86
Women's Civic and Social Union/Union féminine civique et sociale (France), 21–22, 55–56, 76, 83–84
Women's International Democratic Federation (WIDF), 87
Women's International League for Peace and Freedom, 29
women's organizations, Martinique, 76–78
Women's Social Service Club (WSSC), 30
working class. See class
World Committee against War and Fascism/Comité mondial contre la guerre et le fascisme, 42–43
World Committee of Women against War and Fascism/Comité mondial des femmes contre la guerre et le fascisme, 40
World War I, 12, 13, 40, 84
World War II: and African Americans, 75; Blitz, 72, 148n43; and British West Indian community, 68, 69–72; and Caribbean, 69, 72–73, 74; impact of onset, 67–68; and sub-Saharan Africa, 84
Wright, Ada, 25
Wright, Thomas, 70
WSSC (Women's Social Service Club), 30
Wu Yi-Fang, 82

Xuma, Alfred, 49, 51

Yerby, Cecila Kennedy, 34
Yergan, Max, 49, 51, 52

www.ingramcontent.com/pod-product-compliance
Lightning Source LLC
Chambersburg PA
CBHW030653230426
43665CB00011B/1074